THE GATES
WITCHCRAFT

Twelve Paths of Power, Trance & Gnosis

by Christopher Penczak

**COPPER
CAULDRON**
PUBLISHING

CREDITS

Writing: Christopher Penczak

Editing: Steve Kenson

Cover Design: Derek Yesman

Interior Art: Christopher Penczak (Fig. 35 by Derek O'Sullivan)

Interior Design & Publishing: Steve Kenson

For more information visit:

www.christopherpenczak.com

www.coppercauldronpublishing.com

ISBN 978-0-9827743-3-5, First Printing

Printed in the U.S.A.

Acknowledgements

Many people have helped advance my understanding of trance and altered consciousness. Some are personally known to me through direct contact and work, and others who have aided me simply by sharing their work in books, workshops, and events. I'd like to thank the following for their aid in this book: Steve Kenson, Adam Sartwell, and Ronald Penczak for their love and support; Laurie Cabot for the alpha trance technique; Stephanie Rutt for an understanding of eastern traditions; Apollon; Alaric Albertsson; Raven Grimassi; Doug and Joe for Otherworld Apothecary for inspiration and education in the plant world; Orion Foxwood for his advice on seeking the center; a very special thanks to Matthew Venus for his expert advice, instructions, tips, tricks and insights on mask-making and overall great conversation; Dale Pendall for his inspiring entheogenic mandala that inspired my own herbal mandala; and Belinda Gore and Felicitas Goodman for making sacred body posture so accessible to the modern practitioner.

OTHER BOOKS BY CHRISTOPHER PENCZAK

City Magick (Samuel Weiser, 2001)

Spirit Allies (Samuel Weiser, 2002)

The Inner Temple of Witchcraft (Llewellyn, 2002)

The Inner Temple of Witchcraft CD Companion (Llewellyn, 2002)

Gay Witchcraft (Samuel Weiser, 2003)

The Outer Temple of Witchcraft (Llewellyn, 2004)

The Outer Temple of Witchcraft CD Companion (Llewellyn, 2004)

The Witch's Shield (Llewellyn, 2004)

Magick of Reiki (Llewellyn, 2004)

Sons of the Goddess (Llewellyn, 2005)

The Temple of Shamanic Witchcraft (Llewellyn, 2005)

The Temple of Shamanic Witchcraft CD Companion (Llewellyn, 2005)

Instant Magick (Llewellyn, 2005)

The Mystic Foundation (Llewellyn, 2006)

Ascension Magick (Llewellyn, 2007)

The Temple of High Witchcraft (Llewellyn, 2007)

The Temple of High Witchcraft CD Companion (Llewellyn, 2007)

The Living Temple of Witchcraft Vol. I (Llewellyn, 2008)

The Living Temple of Witchcraft Vol. I CD Companion (Llewellyn, 2008)

The Living Temple of Witchcraft Vol. II (Llewellyn, 2009)

The Living Temple of Witchcraft Vol. II CD Companion (Llewellyn, 2009)

The Witch's Coin (Llewellyn, 2009)

The Three Rays of Witchcraft (Copper Cauldron Publishing, 2010)

The Plant Spirit Familiar (Copper Cauldron Publishing, 2011)

The Witch's Heart (Llewellyn, 2011)

TABLE OF CONTENTS

TABLE OF FIGURES

INTRODUCTION

There is a secret gate within you. There is a secret gate within me. There is a secrete gate within us all, deep within our souls, though few know how to open it. We lack the key. This gate is latched tight, and gives entry to worlds unimagined by most. It holds powers and blessings we dream of in our books, but is closed, for access to those powers and worlds are not always a blessing. They come with responsibility and need awareness. So with some intuitive power, we have barred the door in an effort to protect ourselves and others until the time is right.

When I began my journey in Witchcraft, I learned there was a secret gate in all of us. My teacher used the term the *nierika,* borrowed from the tribe of Huichol Indians in Mexico. Most people only pass through this gateway during sleep—to dream of otherworlds—or in death, to leave this world entirely. Only Witches, shamans, sorcerers, and seers know how to open this gate truly, while alive and conscious. We learn how to use the blessings of this gate, and travel to other worlds beyond ours, for wisdom and power. We hold the key. The key is a symbol of one of our most beloved Witchcraft goddesses, Hecate. She is the goddess who opens the way to the Mysteries.

The differences separating magickal practitioners such as Witches, from ordinary people, is that we actively seek the key, and undergo training to find it. Some of us are naturally talented. Children all know where the key is. It is only when we grow up we forget how to find both key and gate, and how to open it. Those who retain child-like awareness retain these skills and often become the naturally talented Witches. Some learn through their dreams, and remember how to open the gate when they wake. Some have memories of childhood guide them, or the memories of past lives where they actively used the gateway in their spiritual journey.

Modern Witchcraft teachings have established various keys to the gate, drawing upon older material and looking at global cultures for new clues. They are generally divided into eight main techniques, known as the Eightfold Path, the Eightfold Way, the Eight Ways of Raising Power, or the Eight Ways to the Center. Alex Sanders, in *The Alex Sanders Lectures,* called them the Eight Paths of Self-Realization. Though they number eight, they should not be confused with the eight spokes on our Wheel of the Year calendar, though correspondences can be made. Nor should they be confused with the eightfold path of Buddhism. In fact, eight is simply one division of the techniques. I believe there are at least twelve true keys to the gate, but I'm sure another perspective could give us more or less.

Though the teachings of this book, I hope to take you on a journey of exploration, to find the keys to open the gates of Witchcraft, so you in turn, can find your own blessings, power and wisdom and then guide others through their own gate. This book compiles some material found in a few of my other books, for parts of it are foundational techniques in the Craft, but it expands, adds and gives a greater context to this material in terms of opening the gates. This is a book of altering your consciousness, which is at the heart of magick. If you cannot change yourself, you cannot change the world. Inner change must precede outer world change. The first thing you can change in any situation is your mind, your consciousness. While there are a lot of instructions in this book, they are more suggestions than hard rules. Only you can find the keys that open the gates for you. If you don't explore with the material, you lose out on valuable spiritual experiences. If this is your very first book on the Craft, you probably want to put it down and seek out something more introductory, such as my *Inner Temple of Witchcraft* book. The audience for this book is those who have experience in magick, meditation and ritual, and are seeking different techniques to go deeper.

Many of us, even experienced practitioners, learn all about spells and rituals, but they can often feel empty and devoid of meaning, for we haven't learned to access the deep wells of power and wisdom in our own consciousness. Many of our teachings lack information on the eightfold, or perhaps twelvefold, paths to power, so we don't even know to look for the keys, to walk the path of personal gnosis, personal knowledge. *Gnosis,* coming from the Greek, refers to not book knowledge of facts and figures, but personal spiritual revelation that can only occur when one interfaces with the unseen, walking through the gates of power. Gnosis is the foundation of all mystery traditions. This book is for those with a basic foundation seeking to go deep within their spiritual practice, and for experienced practitioners looking for a new perspective on the arts they already perform. You must come with your own intentions. Only then can you apply the knowledge here for your betterment.

We will learn physical keys to change your consciousness and open the gates to deeper magick. When you know how to successfully do that, you have all you need for the mysteries to open before you. You will be able to open any spiritual doorway and perform any magick you choose.

CHAPTER ONE:
THE GATES

What exactly are "the gates of Witchcraft?" Quite simply, they are techniques to alter consciousness. By altering your consciousness, you have a greater perception of what Witches, magicians and metaphysical practitioners call energy, a subtle and intangible but nevertheless very real force. This psychic energy is known by many names in different cultures, from *prana* in India to *chi* in China. Witches don't have just one name for it; the cultures influencing an individual Witch often determine the name used, such as *pnumen, od, sekhem, nwyvre,* or *baraka*. In an altered state of consciousness, you can use this energy to aid your personal connection to the forces of the universe. With a greater connection, you can use the psychic energy not only from your own body, but your environment, the Earth, and the heavens themselves to fuel your intentions to perform a spell, or to send your awareness into different realms on a journey for wisdom, insight or power.

Humans are generally unaware of energy in day-to-day reality, and must train themselves to sense it. Even with rudimentary perceptions of energy in daily life, further techniques are usually needed to use the energy in any meaningful way. By opening the internal gate of consciousness, you can view a new reality, and if you choose to step through it, experience the worlds beyond the physical, existing wholly in the psychic realm.

THE NIERIKA

I was taught the gate is known as the nierika, the door people pass through in dreams and at death, unless they are Witches or sorcerers. Those who "know" have the keys that can open and close the gates at will, and pass whenever they desire. I believe this is the same as the "door that hath no key" referred to in the work of ceremonial magician and occultist Dion Fortune, in the poetic invocations found in her novel *Moon Magic*. It has no physical key. Magickal technique is the intangible key that opens the door.

Open the door, the door that hath no key,
the door of dreams whereby men come to thee.
Shepherd of goats, O answer thou me!

Often quoted today in Witchcraft circles as part of an invocation to the Witch's horned god, who in many traditions is the guardian of gateways and the opener of the door to the mysteries. Here she even alludes to its dream nature for most of us, though the magicians and priestesses of her novels can pass through this door at will. It is the Moon Gate of Ceremonial Magick. It is the Flaming Door of the faery faith traditions, between the living and the elder race beneath the land. It is the nierika of the sorcerers of Mexico.

If there was a teaching that specifically located the nierika in the body, I don't remember receiving it, though I do know I associate it with a specific part of the body. While many traditions talk about power centers, energy points, and chakras, I always felt a strange buzzing at the back of my skull when opening the gate. Traditions around the world see the skull as receptacle for spiritual power. Skulls are used in necromantic rites to commune with the spirits of the dead. Traditions of head hunting are found across the world, as to possess one's head is to possess their power. Sacred king traditions involve beheading the old king, bodily or in effigy. While we don't like to think about such things in the context of our modern spiritual search, the ancestors whose wisdom we draw up, the tribal people of the world, have had traditions of head—and scalp— hunting. While we like to paint them with the modern ideal of the "noble savage" it's important to know their cultures are foreign to our modern culture, along with their ethics, religion, and aesthetics. We draw on strands of their wisdom, but often do not see the whole picture. I was trained in a Celtic-influenced Witchcraft tradition, and one does not have to go far into Celtic history to find evidence of decapitation and head-hunting. Heads are vessels of power, and I believe they hold such power because of this gate.

Specifically I feel it where the top of the spine and the back of the skull meet. Here is the reptilian portion of the brain, most primal and survival-oriented. Known as the brain stem, here we also have access to our power. The keys to the nierika are very primal. It's as if they are hard-wired into our biology, buttons for the biological computer of our body. They are the birthright of every human being, encoded into our DNA and physical make up. We have simply forgotten them because our culture has changed so much. When we say that we use only ten percent of our brain's true capacity, (a controversial statement that is challenged by many in the scientific community,) I think this gateway represents the hidden, higher functions of the brain that lie dormant in most people. While consciously opening the gate is not going to grant you genius levels of brain power, those who regularly pass through the gate seem to be more creative, healthier, happier, and simply more engaged with life. Those involved in magick, meditation and shamanism are considered more inspired, more in touch with the divine source, when compared to other people.

A chiropractor once told me that that point where the spine and skull meet is one of the most important parts of the skeletal system. Adjusting it all affects the entire spine. Magickal practitioners who get it adjusted often see a great shifts in their ritual, psychic abilities, vision and magickal powers. Some esoteric traditions refer to it as the Alta Major chakra, Mouth of God (or Goddess) or Well of Dreams.

BRAINWAVES

The key to opening the gate within is inducing a shift in brainwaves. Different brainwave states generate different levels of consciousness. Generally by lowering the our brainwaves, we induce a state of consciousness more useful for magickal endeavors such as ritual, meditation and shamanic journey. Higher brainwave patterns also come with their own benefits, but it can be harder to induce higher brainwave states for longer periods of time. Even the more vigorous techniques on the eightfold path tend towards repetition and will lower the brainwaves, even if other body functions are heightened.

We all move in and out of altered states of consciousness throughout the day. To go from any one state of consciousness to another is natural. There is no great mystery to it. What the keys of Witchcraft do for us is allow us to pass through these states of consciousness at will, intentionally and fully aware. Most of the time we pass through them when our mind wanders, when we daydream and when we go to sleep or are in the process of waking up. To do magick, we must be fully aware in these altered states, and able to indicate our will, our desire, to make the magick work. Without that thread of awareness, our experiences become a dream-like jumble, with no cohesion. We train in the arts of altering consciousness to keep that awareness even under difficult and distracting circumstances. I learned a good Witch should be able to get into a trance on a crowded subway. Not that it was a good idea to get into a trance in a crowded subway, but the distraction of people, movement and noise should not stop you.

Beta	13-16 Hertz	Normal Waking Consciousness, Alert
Alpha	8-13 Hertz	Meditative, Relaxed, Day-Dream, Intuition, Accelerated Learning
Theta	4-8 Hertz	Deeper Meditation, Trance, Journey, Sleep
Delta	1-4 Hertz	Deep Sleep, Deep Trance, Coma

Fig. 1: Brain Wave Levels

While there are eight (or more) gates, or techniques, used to achieve an altered state of consciousness in the Witchcraft traditions, they can generally be divided into two basic types. Some are inhibitory techniques that suppress and quiet the body and mind to induce an altered state of consciousness. They are the restful, peaceful, and inward-focused methods. Attention is withdrawn from the outer world, and focused on the inner world. The physical senses are suppressed in favor of the inner senses to perceive the unseen.

The second type are exhibitory techniques. They excite, stimulate, and enliven body and mind to induce an altered state of consciousness. They are physical, sensory, and focus on the outer world or body, yet their result is a profound inner change of consciousness of ecstasy. Ecstasy is a difficult term. Many think of it as synonymous with sexual pleasure, but its true meaning is more akin to "free from flesh." It is an experience that sets you apart from the normal boundaries of your sense of self and, for most of us, that includes our body. It can be a sense of separation from the body, or a sense of consciousness including and expanding beyond the body.

Strangely, though they seem diametrically opposed, both sets of techniques take you to a similar level of consciousness and brainwave activity. I like to describe the inhibitory techniques as a slow and gradual descent into a meditative state, while exhibitory techniques are like a slingshot, propelling you around the bend of consciousness, getting you to that deep place of meditation by a different route.

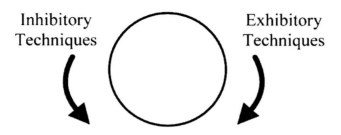

Fig. 2: Reaching Meditative Consciousness

Though not explicitly stated as inhibitory or exhibitory, the Gardnerian Book of Shadows, from the tradition of Witchcraft promoted by Gerald Gardner, outlines a variety of techniques in a section known as "The Eightfold Way." Arguably the root document of the modern Witchcraft movement, what I like to call the Witchcraft Renaissance, this is a section not often discussed in workshops and books. Even well-trained Gardnerian initiates I know receive direct experience in only few of the eight ways. There is depth here that can be explored by modern Witches of all traditions.

One of the greatest criticisms of Gardnerian Wicca and other forms of British Traditional initiatory lineages at the turn of the century has been emphasis on ceremonial magick techniques, tools, and style, rather than a nature-based Pagan tradition. The Eightfold Way, whether practiced by Gardner and his spiritual descendants in depth or not, gives us a view into much more Pagan, physical, and nature-based practices. Gardner claimed to be initiated into a traditional and hereditary coven in New Forrest, and took the fragmentary materials of the coven to compose his Book of Shadows, supplementing it with a variety of sources.

Upon reading this book you might think I'm a Gardnerian Witch. I am not, but I do find inspiration in the seeds he has planted that have grown in my own spiritual garden. I think its important to look to where we've been to know where we are going, for our ancestors, both blood and spiritual, are part of our foundation. I claim Gardner as a spiritual ancestor and I, along with all modern Witches, owe him a great debt for making the Craft so accessible to us today.

Some critics note the Eightfold Path bears a striking similarity in name to The Noble Eightfold Path of Buddhism, perhaps betraying Gardner's eastern influences upon his English craft, as he spent much time in the East, studying its culture and mysticism. But the techniques alone are probably the "witchiest" part of the Gardnerian Book of Shadows, in terms of old world Pagan magick. Public versions of the BOS date this section of the Eightfold way to 1953. The eight ways are outlined as such:

Eightfold Path or Ways to the Centre.
1. *Meditation or Concentration. This in practice means forming a mental image of what is desired, and forcing yourself to see that it is fulfilled, with the fierce belief and knowledge that it can and will be fulfilled, and that you will go on willing till you force it to be fulfilled. Called for short, "Intent"*
2. *Trance, projection of the Astral.*
3. *Rites, Chants, Spells, Runes, Charms, etc.*
4. *Incense, Drugs, Wine, etc., whatever is used to release the Spirit.*
5. *The Dance, and kindred practices.*
6. *Blood control (the Cords), Breath Control, and kindred practices.*
7. *The Scourge.*
8. *The Great Rite.*
These are all the ways. You may combine many of them into the one experiment, the more the better.

While the BOS states "these are all the ways" many modern practitioners see the original list of eight as jumbled. Intention is both listed as the first path and the first "essential" in a later list of Five Essentials for magick (See **Chapter Fourteen**). The list has been adapted in various ways since the days of Gerald Gardner. The particular list that I use is:

✦ **Meditation:** Focused Concentration, including visualization, focus on a fixed point, silent prayer, silent mantra or silent affirmations.
✦ **Breath:** Regulated, patterned breathing.
✦ **Sound:** Singing, chanting, audible prayer, audible ritual, drumming, chimes, and all forms of music.
✦ **Movement:** Dance, body postures, martial arts, aerobic exercise, spinning, shaking, and ritual gestures.
✦ **Isolation:** Separation from human society, often done in silence. Restriction of blood flow using cords and binding.

✦ **Intoxication:** Use of plant substances including alcohol, incense, oils, and entheogens.

✦ **Sex:** Sexual excitation alone, with a partner or with a group.

✦ **Pain:** Ritual scourging (whipping), piercing, branding, and tattooing

More ways can be added to it, such as hypnosis or modern technological techniques like biofeedback and subliminal patterns in music. The techniques of hypnosis can fall under pathworking and meditation and while techno-paganism and techno-shamanism has grown in recent years, electronic techniques can still fall under sound and music.

Upon more reflection and deeper experience, I've found that I like to add four more paths to the system of eight, making twelve in all. The remaining paths not fully expressed in the Gardnerian material are:

✦ **Land:** The place where you do magick has power. Ancient people knew the power of sacred sites and gathered at these places of power. Such places induce trance by shape, form and the natural flow of prana, be it a man made temple or church which were often built upon Pagan sacred sites, ancient temples and structures like Stonehenge, and even places with little obvious markers that can be located near you. Natural and crafted sacred geometry gathers energy and shifts brainwaves. Sacred sites are gateways of consciousness.

✦ **Time:** If place is sacred and trance inducing, time is as well. Certain times of day, month and year, both personally and globally, can be used to enter new states of consciousness. We have holy days to match our holy places, and our sacred calendars are built upon the observance of the tides of power through time. For Witches, we celebrate the flows of life and death with the Sun, the waxing and waning of the Moon and our personal cycles of life.

✦ **Ritual Clothing:** What we wear can be important in our rituals, indicating shifts in consciousness. Color, material, shape, and make can all influence the wearer. From ritual robes and jewelry to costumes and masks, how you, and others, perceive you, shifts your consciousness and gives you access to dormant parts of your own power, or builds links to those you emulate. Even the lack of any clothing whatsoever, being skyclad as the British Traditional Wicca groups call it, can induce trance by the virtue that most of us are not nudists in our daily life.

✦ **Dreams:** The path of dreams is a method of altered consciousness we all go through, even when we are not trained. Dreams are an opportunity for spirit contact, prophecy or simply working out your "stuff" by showing your conscious self something it doesn't know, but knowledge your unconscious self holds. The union of the two through the sharing of knowledge can create great magick and healing. The door is the "door of dreams."

The combining of the various paths is the spiraling path to the center of gnosis. As the paths to the "center" they bring us to the center of our self, of our being or consciousness, and from that center still point, all radiates outward to create our life and magick. By combining them, we can experience deeper states of awareness. Like the straight lines of a web reaching to the twelve directions, the spiraling thread leads us into the center. It must be supported by each spoke of the web, but holds the web together.

POWER

Power is a difficult word for many who walk a spiritual path. Our culture so often equates power as "power over" someone or something, conjuring ideas of abuse or control, rather than "power with" or even "power from within." So in an effort to be "spiritual" we reject power in favor of transcendence and detachment, as the ways of enlightenment. And for some paths, they are, but Witchcraft is a path of paradox. We hold the importance of both the material and the immaterial. We believe in both immanence and transcendence, releasing what doesn't serve and gathering power. Only when we are in our power and can partner with the power of our spiritual allies and nature, can we truly experience enlightenment, and then fulfill our own personal mission, our True Will, here in the world. We are in the material world not to escape it, but to create and transform, in partnership with nature.

The Eightfold Way is sometimes referred to as the Eight Paths to Power. While they are truly techniques for achieving a trance state experience gnosis, direct knowledge of spirit, they are also means of generating power to be contained by the magick circle. Some release more power, more life energy, prana, than others. That power can be used to cast spells, fueling the intention with the released energy. Most Witches generate energy for spellcraft. Yet power is also used to propel us through the gates of consciousness.

Simply opening the gates of consciousness is not enough. We must step through the gate, and sometimes the journey is hard. The proper implementation of power is essential for deeper states of trance. Many miss this crucial step in trance journeys because of their preconceived concepts of what meditation and trance should be, usually based on cultural models that are not oriented to the methods of Witchcraft. Many of these more passive concepts have become a part of Witchcraft today, eclipsing the older, more ecstatic forms of trance found in our traditions.

I was speaking with a friend, who based much of his own teachings on a beloved eclectic author of Wicca, and learned from this author's teaching to not put power behind your spells and rituals, but to simply be open and passive when doing meditation or other trance work, letting the information you need come to you without direction. My friend felt very called to work with the Fey, the underworld spirits of nature prevalent in Celtic lore known as the faery folk. Yet when he meditated, he couldn't connect with them. My friend was simply waiting for otherworldly allies to contact him when he was receptive. I told him he had to meet the Fey at least halfway. He needed to ritualize his meditation process, with clearer and focused intention, and possibly generate and direct enough power to make contact. We discussed the use of dance, drumming, and plant substances to both open the gate and give him a bit of a push through to visit with the spirits he sought, and with these more focused techniques for generating power to "meditate" he was able to have successful contact with the Fey.

Power is neither good nor bad. It simply is. Power can be directed toward any intention you have, be it a spell for some material event to occur, such as getting a new job, finding a new love, protecting yourself and healing, or it can be directed to seek the deepest mysteries of spirit and find enlightenment. From the Witch's perspective, power is necessary for all of these things.

THE SHADOW OF TRANCE

Magick is not always easy, and magick is not always safe, to paraphrase a magickal friend who often teaches ecstatic techniques. When you change, you run the risk of lasting change, of transformation, and inherent in such change is danger. While altering your consciousness through the course of the day is quite normal, ritualizing the experience with a specific intent to reach the deep places within your soul is not part of the normal experience for most of us. It requires risk. Teachers, traditions, and even books are like guides on the path, and responsible ones point out the dangers along it. You might still get stuck in the briars on the path, but at least you will know they are there to catch you. And you'll have knowledge on how to release yourself.

Each of the twelve paths of trance work has its own shadow to them. In magick, a shadow is not necessarily bad. In fact, shadow magick is quite good. It is a process of healing and transformation. Shadows are places where we rarely go. Shadows hide what we ignore and repress. They are unknown and offer both hidden treasure and danger, because we can more easily slip and fall on our path if we cannot metaphorically "see" where we are going. Yet many beautiful powers and insights grow in the dark if we are daring to explore.

The original eight paths, and the expanded twelve outlined previously, each have an extreme, an edge that skirts the outer darkness. Some are like traps, ultimately best avoided. Others are benign and represent the extreme end of the spectrum on that path. They can even be helpful. Some fall in between, giving us blessings, but detrimental if they are used too often. Some simply happen to us, as part of the process of life, and a wise one can take advantage of the situation for a greater experience of gnosis and move through the experience.

Path	Shadow
Meditation	Escapism
Breath	Breathlessness
Sound	Silence
Movement	Exhaustion
Isolation	Fear
Intoxication	Illness & Addiction
Sex	Obsession
Pain	Injury
Land	Fixedness
Time	Betweenness
Ritual Clothing	Vanity & Attachment
Dreams	Unconsciousness

We will explore the shadows of each of the paths in each chapter, to give you a greater understanding of the paths' edges, and how to walk them more safely.

GROUNDING

No matter what gate you enter through to find the center of personal gnosis, you must learn how to leave the center safely and effectively. To explore any of these gates, you should have a thorough understanding of and ability with grounding. Grounding is a basic, yet often overlooked, ability to anchor yourself in your body and your attention in the physical, consensual reality of day-to-day life. Some shamanic traditions call it Ordinary Consciousness or First Attention, yet many people go about their ordinary life very ungrounded.

You are ungrounded when you are focused on a meditative state or altered reality. Ungroundedness can be light, such as a momentary daydream or loss of your train of thought, or profound, in an extended vision or ritual. Being ungrounded is not a bad thing, when done purposely. We are purposely ungrounding ourselves to do magick, meditation, and psychic work. If we were fully grounded, we would not have access to those levels of reality and receive those experiences. But a good Witch knows how to return from those experiences, and ground the wisdom, power and healing she receives into physical reality. Otherwise, the experience is not helpful. If you return from a visionary state, and choose not to ground and integrate the energies, you usually won't remember the lessons or message received that were meant to be put into action. If you accepted healing energies on the journey, they do not unite with your body to affect physical changes in the long term.

Ungrounding can happen when we don't know how to come back from such experiences, or we have an excess of energy from the experience, which is overloading our physical form. In this case, we say we are "grounding" the energy, like a grounding wire or lightning rod harmless grounds excess and unwanted electricity.

Other times, shock and trauma, physical or emotional, can cause our spiritual energy to loose its tether to the physical form, causing us to be ungrounded and unable to process our experience in a healthy way. If you've ever experienced the kind of shock where you felt you were looking at it all from above, as if the events were happening to someone else, then you were out of your body and not in control of yourself completely. Prolonged periods of such a state invite spiritual soul sickness.

Many people are naturally less grounded than others. Some are naturally more flighty, distracted, unfocused or otherworldly. This is only bad when these traits prevent you from focusing on your intentions or manifesting your dreams and goals. There must be a balance. Some people find the world unpleasant, painful or unspiritual and don't like to be present, they prefer being ungrounded, yet are missing out in the experience of being incarnated in the physical world. If they did not need to learn how to embrace physicality, why are they here in the world?

Learning to ground is a life skill that should be taught to every child growing up. Energetic education is lacking in our society, but such knowledge is vital to the survival and success of every person on this planet. Sadly only those involved in esoteric pursuits learn these basic skills.

Here are some basic ideas regarding grounding:

Roots: A simple technique involves imagining your feet are like roots of a great tree and, with your exhale and intention, your feet and toes grow down deep into the earth as roots and ground you to the world. You are strong and solid like a tree. As you breathe, you are breathing up the dense, strong, grounded energy of the land, or the planet itself.

Anchor: Similar to the root technique, imagine dropping an anchor, like a ship dropping anchor, from the base of your spine, the perineum point between the anus and sex organs, deep into the earth. The chain from the imagined energetic anchor reaching to your perineum, grounds you. Like a weight, it prevents you from energetically "floating" away.

Earth Grounding: Particularly good after rituals where a large amount of energy has been raised and excess energy might be flowing through you, overloading you. Many people like the feeling initially, and feel high with the energy, not wanting to release the excess, but once they leave the ritual space and return to normal consciousness, the energy may make them ill, nauseous or delusional. Upon the conclusion of the ritual, or if guided by someone leading the ritual, direct the excess energy in you down into the Earth. It can be done by pointing your palms down toward the earth, directing it through the altar or through natural tools that help you connect to the earth (wands, walking sticks, staffs, swords), by getting on your hands and knees and pressing the energy down into the earth, or by getting on your hands and knees and pressing your third eye (brow) or crown down to the earth, and imagine releasing the excess energy through that point.

Stones: While all stones and crystals are heavy and dense by nature, certain minerals aid overall grounding, keeping your consciousness more present in the physical world: Generally dark stones, such as smoky quartz, black tourmaline, onyx, obsidian, jet, hematite, jasper, garnet and tiger's eye. Salt is also a grounding and protective mineral.

Plants: Not only stones but plant allies can aid in the grounding process. Carrying root herbs of non-trance inducing plants, such as comfrey, Solomon's seal, angelica, burdock, yellow dock or John the Conqueror. If carrying roots as a charm doesn't work for you, the modern usage of flower essences—dilute solutions of flowers soaked in water, preserved in a small amount of alcohol—can be powerful aids. A few drops are taken as needed. Essences of Potato, Queen Anne's lace (wild carrot), and Star of Bethlehem are great. A readily available commercial essence known as Rescue Remedy, a blend of five flowers used for trauma and shock, is also quite grounding and integrating.

Eating: One of the main reasons many Pagan traditions have feasting after a big celebration is to help ground the consciousness back in the body. By starting the digestive system, energy moves to the physical body, helping ground consciousness back into the world. While fasting is a path into an altered state, breaking that fast is a method out. In particular something with a bit of salt, or anything with citrus, particularly lemon, is good in bringing consciousness back to the waking world.

With a few grounding techniques to choose from, use the ones that work most effectively for you. If you have difficulty coming back from a particular experience, try a different grounding technique. A thorough knowledge of grounding and its importance is a vital aid in exploring all the gates of Witchcraft.

Chapter Two: The Secrets of Meditation

I'm a big believer that meditation is one of the major keys to any form of spiritual development, whether you're a Witch, Christian, Buddhist, or a follower of any other spiritual path. While I'm a big fan of ritual, I think it's important to learn how to quiet yourself and open your senses to the universe before doing a lot of other work. Meditation is one of the safest ways to do this, though it's not always the easiest. The reward for learning how to do it benefits not only your magickal life, but also every aspect of your day-to-day existence.

The biggest complaint I receive from new students who don't want to meditate is that it is difficult. That is true to a certain extent. Like any other skill, it can be difficult when you first start out. Think of anything you do well now. Did you do it well on the first try? Probably not. It takes time and patience to develop skill. Some people have an aptitude for it, like any other skill, and others have to start at square one and feel like they are struggling.

Part of the struggle comes from our definition of what "meditation" is, and our expectations on how to go about it. Many people who tell me they struggle with meditation because they have no idea what they are doing. The first thing I ask is, "What technique are you using?" and they look at me blankly. "Technique? I just sat there and tried to stop thinking of things. The more I tried, the more I kept thinking about things." That is not meditation. It's like getting into your car and wondering why you can't will the car forward with just intention. If you don't know how to turn the key in the ignition, you will never get anywhere. Intention is important, but knowledge is also necessary.

So first, what is meditation? Many people think it is simply having no thought, making your mind a blank while sitting in an uncomfortable crossed-legged position trying to look peaceful.

While that can be considered a form of meditation, it comes with a lot of preconceived ideas about what "no thought" is. Meditation really means to contemplate something, to focus your attention on it. Meditation is a type of focused concentration.

Many experiences can be a focus for meditation, and give you what we might call meditative consciousness, opening a gateway within. Various forms of exercise, crafts, and music can induce a meditative state. In fact, all the other gates in the following lessons lend themselves to a meditative state, and none of them require absolutely "no thought." The concept of no thought comes from a western misperception of eastern meditation techniques.

MEDITATION STYLES FROM THE EAST AND WEST

Just as the gates can be divided into inhibitory and exhibitory techniques, meditation can be divided into what we consider eastern and western techniques. While such divisions are a gross oversimplification, eastern techniques are the ones that generally seek to clear the mind of thought. The main goal of such techniques is to differentiate the thinker from the thoughts being generated. We come from a world where we often believe we are our thoughts. While we have the popular saying, "I think, therefore I am," by Rene Descartes, from a mystic's perspective, it is false. We are a divine being with the tool of the mind, but we are more than the mind. We are more than our thoughts, yet our thoughts can shape us. Are we in control of the mind, or is the mind in control of us? If you focus on something, and have reoccurring thoughts you try to banish, eventually you start to recognize that "you" are the being that is having the thought, but as you become more proficient at clearing your mind, you have a level of pure consciousness beyond thought, that is closer to the true self than your thoughts.

Eastern techniques don't simply tell you to have no thought, but give you something to focus upon. That focus helps build discipline and sharpen your mind and concentration. Improved ability to focus and concentrate occurs with a diligent meditative practice, spilling over into all areas of life, not just meditation. Such meditation also helps you slow down your reactive thought process. Rather than identify with thoughts and emotions and react to difficult situations in life, you learn to experience such thought and emotions and respond from a place of higher, or deeper, consciousness in a way that is difficult when you identify with your thoughts. When hit with the difficulties of life that induce anger, fear, sadness, despair, any of the "negative" emotions, you learn to respond to the reality of the situation, rather than your thoughts and emotional response. The same can be said with an overabundance of "good" emotions, wanting to trust someone too quickly or ignoring a problem or pain. You can still be optimistic, but you have a more neutral mind to perceive things as they are, rather than how you hope they will be, or fear they might.

Western forms of meditation are similar to eastern forms of mediation in terms of the level of consciousness you reach, and the benefits they give you. They differ in the fact of how they get you to that level. Rather than giving you the desire to have "no thought" these techniques give your mind something specific and somewhat creative to focus upon. Western techniques are more akin to what is now considered hypnosis or self-hypnosis techniques. They use guided countdowns, visualization techniques, and imagery to focus.

Western meditations are sometimes known as guided meditations when someone else, in person or via a recording, is suggesting imagery. The prescribed imagery activates the imagination, and the imagination is a bridge to cross over into other worlds. While I guide meditations, very few people experience things exactly as I say. The experience opens the gate to real spirit contact, and those individuals have an experience with the spirits, though many also comment on how they see things right before I say them. I guide the meditation as I experience it, and describe what I see, so we are making contact together. There is a natural pause between what I see, and how I'm able to cue the experience for an individual or group.

When done solitary with a pre-arranged set of correspondences, these meditations are typically called pathworkings. This name is most likely based upon Qabalistic visualizations. In ceremonial magick, the Tree of Life, the visual symbol of the Qabalah, is used as magickal device to organize concepts of rituals, ceremonies, states of consciousness, and the structure of the universe. Each state of consciousness is depicted as a circle or sphere, known as a *sephira*, and each sephira is connected to other sephiroth (plural form of sephira) via pathways. Each path is associated with a Hebrew letter, Major Arcana tarot card and a variety of other symbols, used to create a pathworking, an imagery-based meditation to change one level of consciousness into another.

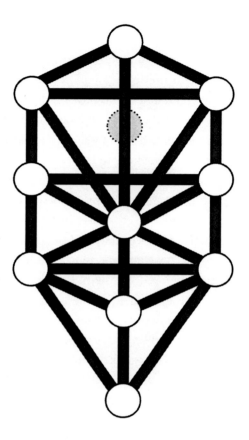

Fig. 3: Tree of Life

Such pathworking was born out of the more free-form shamanic traditions of trance and journey. Other paths you will learn about, such as the sound and rhythm of a drum, would induce visionary trance, creating an unguided visualization or pathworking. The quieter meditative techniques seek to do the same thing, but under different conditions.

The techniques of eastern and western meditation start to blur together in this modern age, where we have access to both philosophies. In the end, they are not that different, as they lead to the same place. Here is a list of potential meditative techniques to try for yourself, and see what is best for you:

Body Awareness

By focusing on your body and the sensations moving through your body, you can enter a meditative state. Most of us are grossly out of touch with our bodies. They hold tension and stress even when we are not aware of it. We learn to tune out the body. Getting back in touch with it is essential to magickal practice, for the body is the first temple of our work. Not only being aware of the body, but learning to relax the body, can be an excellent technique in itself, but also as a preliminary for other techniques. You must be able to get your body into a comfortable position for meditation if you are to be successful at it.

The two popular positions come from both eastern and western spiritual traditions. The western traditions use the Egyptian sitting pose, named as such because many Egyptian statues are carved in this position. You sit in a straight back chair, with feet flat on the floor and palms resting on your thighs.

Fig. 4: Egyptian Sitting Pose

The eastern traditions favor a cross-legged position on the floor, with wrists resting on knees, palms up. While one foot can be on the thigh (half lotus pose) or both feet on the thighs (full lotus pose) it is not necessary. A simple crossed-legged pose is known as "easy pose" in Kundalini Yoga. A variation good for inner journey meditation is to sit cross-legged and put your elbows on your knees and your face in your cupped hands, with the palms of the hands blocking out the light to your eyes, helping you focus on inner world experiences.

Fig. 5: Easy Pose

Body awareness works well with the gates of breath, sound, and dance. In fact it can be hard to separate body awareness from breath-work, showing how easily these paths support each other on the quest for magickal awareness.

Exercise: Relaxing the Entire Body

Body relaxation techniques can begin at the top of the head down or from the feet up. I've found that if you learned one way first, that, like many things, your first time leaves an imprint upon you and might be difficult to change the way you do it. I learned to start at the top down and find that most effective for my relaxation meditations. I reverse it, from the bottom up, for dream magick, and all exercises that don't require me to be completely conscious.

✦ Sit in a comfortable meditation position.
✦ Bring your awareness to the top of your head. Feel waves of relaxation flowing from your crown down throughout your body.

✦ Relax all the muscles in your head. Relax the scalp. Relax the forehead and around the eyes. Relax the cheeks and jaw. Relax the neck and throat. Relax the entire head. Feel waves of relaxation flow through the entire head and neck area.

✦ Relax your shoulders and arms. Relax the muscles in your shoulders, down through your upper arm and past the elbows. Relax your forearm, your wrists, your hands and fingers. Feel waves of relaxation flow from your head and neck down through your shoulders, arms and out your fingertips, sweeping away all that does not serve.

✦ Relax your chest and back as your breathe in and out. Feel waves of relaxation going down your spine.

✦ Relax your belly and your waist. Relax your lower back and buttocks. Feel waves of relaxation moving down your belly and lower back, sweeping away all tension.

✦ Relax your legs. Relax your thighs and knees. Relax your calves ands shins. Feel waves of relaxation sweeping through your legs, down through your ankles, feet and out your toes, taking away all that does not serve.

✦ Feel your entire body relax. Breath normally. Be aware of all sensations in your body. If there is any place of tension or holding, breathe into that place, imagining the breath sweeping way the tension and exhaling it out. Relax completely.

✦ Ground as necessary.

If you have difficulty with the slow and steady progression of relaxation, a quick means of relaxation is to tense the entire body, holding it for the count of three, and then let go completely, allowing total body relaxation to come over you. Repeat this holding and relaxing several times until you are entirely relaxed.

Silent Words

While song and chant more appropriately fall under the path of music, silent words are a simple meditative technique. A repeated word or phrase can be used as a focus for meditation. It can be as simple as one syllable, such as the eastern Om, or Aum, the sound of creation, or a complicated prayer. Your name, legal or magickal, foreign words, or even religious mantras from another language specifically designed and recorded for meditation can be used. Eastern mantras are said to each contain a frequency, and each one induces a specific level of consciousness. Those who partake in TM, or Transcendental Meditation, receive their own personal mantra they are not to share with others. Some receive mantras or words of power while in deep levels of consciousness. You can even simply count your pulse, breath, or ticks of a clock as a silent focus.

Affirmations are simple statements of the reality you wish to create in meditation. They are usually formed as "I am" statements, rather than as wishes or wants, for the mind creates the reality it hears. If your phrases is "I want health" your mind will create a stronger wanting of health, but not actual health. If you simply use "health" as your mantra, or "I am healthy," your mind will create the reality of health, rather than the want. What type of constructive change do you want to create in your life? Base your affirmation, or sets of affirmations, around those intentions.

Exercise: Silent Affirmation

Choose an affirmation or mantra comfortable for you and your beliefs. Though I love eastern mantras, I believe you shouldn't repeat anything over and over again unless you thoroughly understand its intention and meaning. For now, I prefer to stick with English. One of my favorite meditative phrases is the words *"Perfect Love and Perfect Trust."* They are two "keys" of Witchcraft and initiation in British Traditional Wicca and have highly influenced our modern Witchcraft movement. For this example, I suggest inhaling and silently thinking "Perfect Love" and exhale silently thinking "Perfect Trust."

Get into a comfortable meditation position. You can do the body relaxation if you desire. Inhale and exhale, repeating this phrase "Perfect Love, Perfect Trust." Let it be your focus and allow your consciousness to shift. If possible, set a timer to let you know how long you've been focused on your affirmation. If affirmation or mantra meditation is new to you, set a goal of five minutes. Then try to build up to fifteen, twenty, and then thirty minutes. At first, it may be difficult. Thoughts might seep in. Simply go back to the affirmation. Use it as your focus to return to a meditative state. This exercise builds up focus, concentration, and change your overall consciousness based upon whatever mantra you use. When done, ground as needed.

Starting at a Fixed Point

Literally focusing your attention on a single point brings your mind to single-minded focus. You can stare at any object in easy view of your meditative position, but often that object is a focus of power, devotion, or religion. Gazing at the statues of gods or saints is a way of inducing single-pointed trance. While there is a great theological difference between the Hindu at the statue of Ganesha and the Catholic at the statue of Mother Mary, in terms of magickal mechanism, they are using the same technique. Artwork can serve as a focus. Geometric designs serving a meditative focuses are known as mandalas, or yantras. Yantras are the visual form of mantras. Though Witchcraft doesn't have complex mandalas passed down through the generations as Eastern and Native traditions do, some primal symbols can serve to focus meditation.

Fig. 6: Symbols for Meditation

Spiral, Infinity Loop, Triquetra, Triple Spiral, Earth Cross, Pentacle, Hexagram

Many modern magickal practitioners choose a power object form their practice, such as a chalice or crystal ball, or focus on a candle flame or the shadows it cast. Candle flame meditations are a popular, basic exercise for budding Witches.

Exercise: Candle Meditation

✦ Light a candle and put it in a place easy to see before you. For this exercise, I've found taper candles easier than votives, jars, or pillars.

✦ Get into a comfortable meditative position. You can do the full body relaxation exercise if you desire.

✦ Focus your attention on the candle flame. You need not stare in a hard focus, straining your eyes, but a soft focus, looking at the light around the flame. Use the light of the flame as your focus, and let it induce your altered state.

✦ Snuff out the candle when done. In most forms of Witchcraft, spell candles are not blown out, but extinguished, so it is a good practice to get into the habit of doing.

✦ Ground as necessary.

Like the silent affirmation meditation, set a timer and build up your time.

If you don't like focusing on something as artificial as a candle, and have the space and time to do this work outdoors, you can fix your gaze on any number of natural objects and phenomenon. Two of the most powerful for inducing hypnotic trance are the Sun and Moon.

In *Aradia: Gospel of the Witches* by Charles G. Leland, a trance technique of watching the Noon day sunlight reflect off water, to induce trance and "conjure" or bless the salt for the sacred meal, is implied.

I do conjure thee, salt, lo! here at noon,
Exactly in the middle of a stream
I take my place and see the water round,
Likewise the sun, and think of nothing else
While here besides the water and the sun:
For all my soul is turned in truth to them;
I do indeed desire no other thought,
I yearn to learn the very truth of truths,
For I have suffered long with the desire
To know my future or my coming fate,
If good or evil will prevail in it.
Water and sun, be gracious unto me!

Though I never learned the Sun reflection as a method of trance, and never realized this passage referred to such a technique until author Raven Grimassi pointed it out in a lecture he gave on Aradia and Charles G. Leland, it did remind me of a technique I learned from my teacher, to gaze at the Moon's reflection, on a still pond, if available, or in the still water poured in a black cauldron. Such Moon gazing is usually a preface of psychic work such as divination, or using the water's surface as a gateway into the lunar worlds. Both Sun and Moon, as a source of light, can be very powerful in inducing trance. The candle flame or fire, is much like a substitution for the more primal sources of heavenly light.

The techniques of scrying are based upon this focused meditative attention. The classic archetype for scrying (also spelled skrying) is gazing at a crystal ball. Other methods include a black or silver mirror, a pool of inked water, fire, smoke, or the eyes of another. While most scry with the intention of seeking answers to questions or to "see" the future, it can be an effective method of trance induction on its own and useful for simple meditations.

While fixed gaze is usually suggested in occult literature, the new discipline of Neurolinguistic Programming (NLP), the study of language, communication, and alternative therapy, gives us information on how the eyes and their movement help us process information when communicating, and can give us clues to how we process information in meditation. Many yogic techniques have you stare upward, down at your nose, or towards a particular direction as a part of the technique, triggering themes in the meditative experience.

The standard eye movements mapped out in NLP are, as you are looking at them:

Upper Right – Visually Constructed – Image Fantasy

Middle Right – Auditory Constructed – Sounds, Words, "tape loops," imagining sounds

Lower Right – Kinesthetic – feelings, tactile and visceral

Middle – Visual Constructed/Remembered, Access to all sensory information, but usually visual.

Upper Left – Visual Remembered

Middle Left – Auditory Remembered

Lower Left – Aid Auditory Digital – Internal Dialogue

It's important to realize "standard" does not mean "universal," as this is usually based on the average right-handed person. Many are unusually cases, and might have to map out their own personal movements. The exploration of visual eye movement cues is still considered controversial, yet a basic understanding can help the occultist access particular kinds of information in meditation, be it memory retrieval or going deeper into inner visual workings. The eyes do not necessarily have to be fully open to trigger the inner communication signals of the movement.

Though not usually listed as part of the standard techniques, looking up toward the brow is also a trigger of visual information, stimulating the third eye energy center and, according to eastern tradition, opening the way for psychic information, not just memory or image construction.

You can experiment with eye positions if you are having difficulty with the countdown and visualization techniques in the following sections.

Countdown Technique

The countdown technique uses a silent count to induce trance. Usually the count starts at a higher number and goes backwards, diminishing in value. When the final number is reached, the guide, be it an another person, a recording, or the meditator acting as their own guide, will suggest that a meditative state has been induced. It is a hypnotic technique. We are familiar with numbers, so we use them, though any regular pattern or sequence can be used – colors, letters, shapes. Numbers are simply one of the more expedient and easy to remember patterns.

Though guides and recordings can be used, particularly to learn, an experienced meditator using the countdown technique must learn to be their own guide. By training part of the consciousness to act as coach and guide, you gain an invaluable ally. The part of the mind that likes to distract us with unwanted thoughts, worries, or humor—keeping us off track from the meditation—is now given a task. The ego voice wants you to pay attention to it. It wants to be taken seriously. When you give your focus to meditation, you are downgrading its importance, and it tries to distract you. It equates loss of attention with death, and it of course doesn't want to die. It doesn't want to go from being the most important voice in you to a level of non-existence. So it distracts you, so it cannot be destroyed. This comes in the form of an uprising of thoughts, worries, concerns, and distracting sensations. This is what makes meditation so difficult. You can dismiss this skeptical worrisome mind, but it can be more effective to make it work for you.

If you give it at task, something you are going to listen to, then it becomes more important, but works for you, rather than against you. By being your coach, it is responsible for bringing you into a meditative state, guiding you, keeping you focused and bringing you out again. You are harnessing the power of that voice for your purposes.

Repeat the instructions of the meditation, starting with the countdown, in your mind. By doing this, you are training the skeptical voice, much like we might train a parrot, through repetition, to remember a series of instructions. It will repeat these instructions to you automatically with practice, lulling you into a meditative state and bringing you out again. The structure of the meditation technique, particularly in this case, the count in and the count out, works for the skeptical mind, giving it a familiar, repetitive format to use.

Countdown techniques involve using the inner voice, silently counting, and some forms of countdown suggest visualizations, imagining the number in the mind's eye, adding visualization skills. It can be synchronized with breath and preceded by prayer and body relaxation. My own technique, found in *The Inner Temple of Witchcraft*, uses all of these. It uses two countdowns. The first, from twelve to one, is visualized in the mind's eye, described as an inner screen of the mind. The twelve count is for the masculine mind, for the twelve solar months of the year. It engages the more active part of the mind. Then, without any visualization, we silently count down from thirteen to one, for the thirteen lunar months of the year. It focuses the more intuitive part of the mind. After both counts, most people are in a meditative state, and able to do magick. To clearly come out of the meditative state, the steps to go down are repeated backwards, counting one to thirteen with no visualization, and then one to twelve, without visualization. Visualization is not necessary to come out of a trance state. The count down and count up help create an appropriate boundary, a doorway in and out of meditative state, and aids the grounding process upon return.

Exercise: Inner Temple Count Down

✦ Get into a comfortable meditative position. You can do the full body relaxation exercise if you desire.

✦ Close your eyes. Imagine a clear screen in your mind's eye, like a movie screen, television, or blackboard. On it, you can create anything.

✦ On the screen, drawn the number twelve. Hold your perception of it for a moment, then let it fade or erase it. Repeat this process with eleven, and continue down, counting until you reach one and let it fade.

✦ Tell yourself, "I am now in a meditative state, where everything I do is for the highest good, harming none."

✦ Release the screen of your mind, letting it fade. Silently count down from thirteen to one.

✦ Tell yourself, "I am now at my deepest level, where all things are possible."

✦ Relax at this deeper state of consciousness. If you have any meditative work to do, such as a visualization exercise, spellcraft or meditative journey, do it now.

✦ When your experience is complete, count up silently from one to thirteen. Pause a moment and then count up from one to twelve. Open your eyes.

✦ Bring both hands several inches above your head, palms down toward the crown. Sweep both hands down together from the crown, over the face, chest and then rotate the palms out by the belly and down towards the ground. This clears the energy field and aids in grounding.

✦ Ground as necessary.

My own technique is based upon what I learned from my own teacher, Laurie Cabot, and a technique found in the Cabot Tradition known as the Crystal Countdown. In her classic book *Power of the Witch,* she teaches the first countdown from seven to one, visualizing the numbers written in the seven colors of rainbow, starting with red. The second countdown is from ten to one, with no visualization. Other popular countdown techniques can be found in traditions such as *The Silva Mind Control Method* by Jose Silva and various books and tapes on hypnotherapy.

Visualizations

Visualization is the process of creating an inner reality to focus upon, rather than focusing upon the outer, physical reality. The energy of consciousness follows our intention, and directing our consciousness through inner visualization is a powerful method to direct our energy towards the goals and intentions we desire.

While it is generally called visualization, implying a focus on the visual sense, most "visualization" teachers will stress the importance of creating a full sensory inner reality. Visualization is simply the easiest sense to describe in our very visually-oriented society. The best "visualizations" have sound, smell, touch and taste when appropriate. They are not actively engaging those senses, but their inner psychic equivalents. You can "see" by imagining something when your eyes are closed. You can also "hear" with the inner ear, "smell" with an inner nose, "touch" with an inner hand, and "taste" with an inner tongue.

For some, one or more of these senses will be stronger than the experience of inner vision. Those new to visualization often get hung up on the "visual" part, which is to be expected. Many successful Witches and magicians have poor visualization skills. They have little psychic seeing skill, known as clairvoyance, or any of the other popular psychic senses, such as clairaudience, or psychic hearing. But they are good with clairsentience, a psychic knowing that is not sense oriented. This skill can grow through being secure in your intentions when visualizing.

When instructed to visualize a tree, even if you do not clearly "see" the tree with your inner mind, know the tree is there. Be firm in your inner psychic knowledge, rather than visualization. Many people expect their visualizations to be crisp, clear and solid. While that is a goal, it does not mean you are prohibited from doing magick if your visualizations are not that clear. Seeing, in the psychic sense, is not always seeing, in the visual sense. The term seeing could just as easily be, and perhaps more accurately be called sensing, but the term "seeing" is popular occult parlance. As you gain in experience, you will be able to verify psychic phenomenon you did not see, but perceived. As the years have gone by and I've taught many psychic development classes, I've learned to replace the popular "see" with "perceive," as we each perceive the inner world differently. When you are urged to visualize something, you are really being urged to perceive it, in whatever manner is appropriate and successful for you. It doesn't matter if your visualizations are the same as others, but that your visualization experiences work for you. Everyone is unique.

Simple visualization exercises start with recreating an object you have studied in the physical world within your imagination. Any object you used in the fixed point exercises can serve as an aid. Simply close your eyes and try to recreate that object in your mind. Once you can hold your perception of it from the angle you were viewing, try to move it in your mind. Look at it from a new angle – above, below or behind. Can you still hold your perception?

Once you have greater mastery over physical objects you have seen in the world, you can move onto creating new objects, never seen before. For some this is more difficult, for others its is more freeing. You don't have to conform to a predetermined reality, but shape it however you want. It takes intention and concentration.

The next step is to create "scenes" for yourself. If you want to create something in your life, the technique of creative visualization tells us to imagine yourself in that setting, as if your desire is already a reality. How would it look? How would it feel? Engage all your senses and perceptions. Some forms of creative visualization are symbolic. If you are unhealthy, imagine a golden light entering the place of illness and pain, absorbing it and removing it, granting you health. Other forms of creative visualization are more literal. If you are sick, imagine the virus or bacteria being killed off by your white blood cells. Both techniques work. They just depend on your level of literal knowledge, and what personally resonates with you.

A more advanced technique, yet fairly easy for most people, is to create a "happy place" for the self. In meditation you can return to this place of healing and rest. It rejuvenates you and centers you. Even in the midst of the chaos of your life, without a vacation or day off in sight, you can still retreat to a sacred space through a short meditation. The happy place can be a place in nature, a place you have visited before, or a brand new, uniquely created place you have devised. Our own creativity is the only limit we have when creating these psychic places. In my Witchcraft teachings, we call this place the personal Inner Temple. Other traditions call it the Soul Shrine, Inner Keep, or Interior Castle. It doesn't matter what you call it, as long as you go to it regularly and use it to center, heal, and find peace.

Exercise: Visiting the Inner Temple

✦ Perform the first half of the Inner Temple Count Down meditation, getting into a meditative state.

✦ Imagine a tree on the screen of your mind. This is the largest tree you have ever seen, what shamans call the World Tree. Its branches reach to the heavens, to the stars. Its roots reach deep into the Earth, to the realms below. The trunk is in the world of space and time.

✦ Step through the screen of your mind as if it were a veil or screen, or open it like a window or door and step through.

✦ Stand before the great tree and touch the bark. Feel the bark. Hear the wind through the branches. Feel the wind. Smell the good earth turned up by the big roots.

✦ Look around the giant roots for a cavern, an opening that leads to the otherworld within. There may be many openings, but only one feels "right" to you, to your inner sacred space, your Inner Temple.

✦ Enter that opening and follow the tunnel down into the darkness. The tunnel winds and spins, but at the end, you see a light. Enter the light and come into your Inner Temple.

✦ Look around at your inner sacred space. What do you perceive? This place reflects your inner self. Explore and learn about it, and in so doing learn about yourself.

✦ Rest, relax, and rejuvenate in this place. You might find doorways leading to other realms, pools of healing water or libraries filled with mysteries. Each Inner Temple is unique and different.

✦ When your experience is done, return through the tunnel and come back out through the tree roots. Step back through the veil and integrate your awareness back with your bodily senses.

✦ Perform the second half of the Inner Temple Count Down meditation, counting up out of a meditative state.

ASTRAL TRAVEL

In the original Gardnerian Eight Ways of Power, meditation is summed up simply as intent, being a form of concentration or focus, often visualized, and it is listed separate and distinct from Trance, Astral Travel, and Rising on the Planes. But don't the various meditation techniques induce trance? Doesn't focus and concentration give rise to astral travel if that is the intent? To me, these two paths seem entwined. I find little difference between guided pathworkings and astral travel. They use many of the same psychic "muscles," yet their intention or result might be different.

When mystics refer to the astral body and astral travel, there is always some confusion, as different traditions define these terms in their own way. In the most original meaning, the world "astral" refers to the stars – *astra* in Latin. So the astral body is the starry body and the astral plane is the starry world. The starry connotation has fallen out of use amongst most modern practitioners and it has instead simply been used synonymously for the spirit body and the spirit world. Those who perform astral travel are able to project their spirit body out of the physical, and into the spirit world.

Many systems of occult knowledge divide the non-physical world into layers, and divide the non-physical self into many spiritual bodies or sheaths. Rather than look at a simple cosmology and spiritual anatomy of two levels of existence, physical and non-physical, the simple body and soul model, occultist describe a complex system of levels, each describing a different level of awareness. One of these levels is described as the astral, and has different properties than the others.

I teach a system of seven levels and seven bodies, similar to many older occult traditions, but renamed in a manner more easily understood by the modern practitioner.

Physical	The physical world and body. That which can be measured by science.
Etheric	The energetic template for all things physical. Anchored to the physical.
Astral	The image or pattern behind the energetic template. Can be separated or extended from the physical. All things physical have an astral counterpart, but not all things astral have a physical counterpart.
Emotional	The emotional energy of creation that can fuel and sustain physical creation. The emotions within a physical being.
Mental	The mental energy behind creation. The place of concepts and ideas.
Psychic	The psychic energy of creation, the inspiration and vision that precedes the concept of the mental plane.
Divine	The divine energy of creation, beyond shape and form. Pure spirit.

As this list describes the seven levels of existence, we each have a "body" or "sheath" on each level of existence. Each one surrounds and interpenetrates the other, moving from human form to a more egg or sphere shape much larger than our physical body. At the core of this energy we have our physical body, supported by an etheric body, the energetic template. It is what some scientists are referring to as a morphogenic or morphogenetic field.

The astral body is your self-image. It can be referred to as the ego or the personal self. While the etheric body is what is, the astral body is what you feel and believe. When you do visualization exercises on yourself, and for your health, you are influencing the astral body, which in turn is influencing the etheric body, and then the physical body. Your astral body can be the source of your magickal persona, as well as contain images about yourself that are not true, but are what you believe. If you have ever lost a significant amount of weight, but could not change your self-image and looked in the mirror and still saw the "fat" person, you were looking more at yourself in the astral than the physical. Most people who cannot change their astral image easily regain the weight, where those who do change the astral image keep it off.

Where you feel your emotions is the emotional body. Sometimes the astral is referred to as the lower emotional plane or lower astral plane and the emotional plane is the higher emotional plane, or the higher astral plane. Our capacity for love and compassion is found at this level. Our emotional body is the container for our emotions. In some traditions of magick, it is described as our chalice or Holy Grail, for like a cup it contains our emotions, esoterically described as the element of water.

The upper three planes and bodies are more abstract. Our mind is the mental body. It contains our concepts, ideas, memories, and patterns of thought. It contains language and words. The psychic body works entirely in intuition and images, beyond words and language. Our flashes of inspiration and knowing come to us from the psychic body. The divine body is what we might think of as the true self, the soul, or Higher Self. It is the part of us beyond all space and time, infinite and vast.

While some would refer to just the etheric and astral bodies as the aura, the aura is truly all the layers of the subtle bodies looked at as a whole. The aura is both the electromagnetic energy of the body that science is learning to measure, and the more subtle forms of consciousness that might never be mapped by science.

It's important to understand the various levels of consciousness when approaching astral travel. Many aspiring practitioners come from a simple body/soul concept of consciousness, and feel if they are projecting their "soul" outside of their body, then their body will be empty and vulnerable to attack or other harm. It would be an empty shell. Some teachings reinforce this idea, and many movies, television shows, and books do as well. If you understand that you have many levels, you realize the projection of one does not leave you empty. There is always some form of consciousness maintaining your body. You also realize that your conscious awareness can be split, and you can have a fully successful projection experience while still being slightly aware of your physical body and physical surroundings. In essence, you have psychically "bi-located" in two places at once. You are extending a part of yourself to another location or dimension of consciousness.

I actually don't even like to use the term "astral travel" when it's not necessary. It comes with a lot of baggage. Due to popular images and teaching on the astral, people believe it must be like an N.D.E., a Near Death Experience. People under life-threatening illness and injury have reported leaving their body completely and experiencing a tunnel of light to another world. While this has become a universal phenomenon that matches with many magickal and shamanic practices, all astral travel is not so grand and intense. In fact, when you understand the concept of the many layers of consciousness, you realize the various bodies, our souls, are not in the body, but the body is in the souls. The body is the densest manifestation of our consciousness, yet our true self stretches beyond the confines of the body. Unlike the image given in popular mainstream

Christian teachings, it is not trapped in the body awaiting to be freed. It is always "free" and operating on many levels at once. You can simply switch your attention to a different level.

The energy body does not really "leave" the physical body, but its nature is like elastic, and it stretches, going out where you direct it. You can project the astral, emotional, mental and psychic bodies in various combinations, and each yields different results. Some practitioners are more prone to project one than another. If you pick up feelings from your travels, you might be projecting more of the emotional body. If you are simply "seeing" a location but not really feeling present, you might be projecting the mental or psychic bodies. Such an experience is now labeled Remove Viewing, and can refer to both Mental Projection and Astral Projection. If you feel present, and have a multitude of sensory stimulation, you might be projecting the astral body, and feeling like you are "really" there. Depending on what kind of experience you want, and why you are doing it, one body might be better than another. Most people fixate on the astral, desiring a N.D.E. style of experience, and ignore the blessing and gifts of the other bodies. The astral is the body most referred to in occult literature.

The astral body is known as the "double" because it mimics our physical form, though it can appear different than our physical form. Some reports indicate it can embody our grandest magickal self image, switch genders, or assume the form of an animal. While most of us think of astral travel as a refined psychic skill, it is the same mechanism used in pathworking, shamanic journey, and the variety of other paths described in this book. In fact, the Witchcraft practices of astral travel were much more shamanic in nature.

Modern Witches believe the broom, besides being a tool to ritually cleanse a space, was used as a focus for shamanic or astral flight. Old woodcuttings show Witches riding their brooms, though unlike the popular images of Halloween decoration, the bristles are in the front, or instead, a forked staff, known as a stang, is used with its fork in the front. The broom is a metaphor for the universe, for what shamans refer to as the World Tree. The bristles are the branches reaches for the heavens, the stick is the trunk, and it's "planted" into the ground, where the underworld "roots" are hidden. The Witch would sit on the ground, straddle it and imagine the broom as the "steed" taking flight to other worlds, resulting in the image found in the woodcuts. The physical broom becomes a focus for the spiritual flight to come. I was first exposed to this practice through a workshop by author Raven Grimassi and later exposed to those descending from British traditions of a non-Wiccan variety who used similar techniques. I have since practiced with it using staves and broomsticks, with powerful results. Both the tool and the position seem to enhance the astral travel I experience.

Traditionally broomsticks are made from three specific woods. Also known as a besom, the handle is ash, the twigs making up the bristles are birch and the binding around the two is made from willow. Though that is the most popular alignment, I've also seen besoms made from other woods, including the flowering scotch broom plant itself as twigs. Make or obtain a broomstick to try this version of astral travel.

Exercise: *Astral Travel with Witch's Broom*

✦ Ideally work outside, and "plant" your broomstick handle in the ground, with the bristles reaching upward.

✦ In the north, start a small fire. For our purposes, a candle, oil lamp, or small cauldron fire will do. To make a cauldron fire, fill the small iron cauldron with a higher proof alcohol, even rubbing alcohol or a cologne such as Florida Water, and set it on fire with a match, letting the blue flames dance above the liquid. The north is the direction of the North Star Road, a spirit path that makes journeying easier.

✦ If you are concerned about the spiritual safety of your physical body, you can create a circle. If you are versed in ritual circle magick, do this exercise in a Witch's circle (see **Chapter Fourteen**). If you are looking for something more primal, create a boundary around your space, either marking in the dirt a circle with a staff, wand, blade or the broom handle itself before planting it, or mark a boundary in stones, one for each of the four direction and the four points between. Build the circle with the intention of protection, protecting you and your body from all harm while you are in it.

✦ Sit cross-legged around the broom handle, holding the broom for support, and face the fire. Stare at the fire and use it as a focus for your meditation.

✦ Hold an intention about where you want to go. Where do you want to visit? Though the astral plane encompasses both the physical world and spiritual realms, start by picking a physical location in the world.

✦ Close your eyes, and imagine the broom, and yourself, getting lighter and lighter, until you rise up and can look down below at the fire and your body below. Take a moment to look at your astral self, on the broom. How do you appear?

✦ Fix your intent on your location, and imagine "flying" on the broom to that location. You need not know how to get there through the geography, your intention to visit it will be enough to intuitively take you. The journey might be scenic, with the ability to perceive the space between, or a blur, where you are moving through a tunnel of light, a spirit road, and arrive with no information about places in between.

✦ Explore your chosen target destination. What do you perceive? The information might be visual, but it might not. All the psychic senses can be at work through such projection exercises. You could see, hear, feel, smell, taste, and even just "know." One psychic sense may be more dominant than the others.

✦ When done, return back to the path from where you came. Reverse your travel, and return to the space of the fire, broom and body. Using your will, integrate your consciousness, your astral self-image, with your body's awareness. Do any further grounding that is necessary.

Even though you perceived it as a "separation" you were really just extending from the body, and never truly "gone." You might have still retained awareness of the fire, broom, and body, and that's perfectly fine.

If you cannot use a broom for this exercise, it can be successfully done in a simple meditative position, cross-legged, in a chair or, assuming you will not fall asleep, laying down. Rather than travel on the broom, you will feel as if you are flying on your own, much like a modern super hero. If you must, you can do it indoors, and simply hold the broom to the floor. As you progress in this book, you might find adding other techniques to this exercise, such as drumming, a preceding dance, fasting, or plant allies via a flying ointment will facilitate the experience even more.

Rising on the Planes

The concept of Rising on the Planes means to have your consciousness "ascend" through the various levels described. Each level is said to contain an infinite amount of subdivision. In the seven plane systems, each plane has seven more sub-divisions, making forty-nine planes. Each of those planes has seven more subdivisions, and so on. Rising on the planes moves your consciousness further and further away from the physical and human experience, to understand and experience the more subtle aspects of creation. Though we use the term "rise" these energies are really in a direction we cannot point to. "Up" is not necessarily the direction of spirituality, as many Pagan myths describe the blessings of the underworld below, and the otherworld existing side by side. Rise is just a terminology for the sensation that occurs, and a reference to the starry nature of the astral body.

Exercise: Rising on the Planes

This exercise can be done with or without the broom. I first learned it without the broom, simply sitting in a cross legged meditative position, so that is the position I still find most conducive. Like the previous Astral Travel exercise, you can construct a circle of protection

Use one of the previous techniques to enter a meditative state, such as the Candle Meditation or the Inner Temple Countdown. Once you are in a meditative state, with eyes closed, imagine rising up from your physical awareness. Much like the previous exercise, feel yourself getting lighter and lighter, more refined, like a mist that rises up.

Rather than moving along the horizontal axis, to go someplace else in the physical world, continue to rise on the vertical axis of reality. Take notice of what you perceive. Like the previous experience, your information can be visual, from other senses, or simply a sense of psychic knowing.

Continue to rise and notice all that you perceive. You might notice "shifts" between planes, where things are disrupted and change dramatically. You might experience them as the seven planes of consciousness outlined above, or find they correspond to some other system.

Entities of this spirit world might attempt to contact you. For now, don't get too attached to any one plane or entity, but simply observe. As you grow in experience, you can interact with the entities and explore specific planes of consciousness.

The rise can truly be infinite, so when you are done and feel the experience is as complete as you can make it today, will yourself down back to the physical plane. You might perceive yourself dropping an "anchor" or other grounding roots and weighing yourself down to reach the physical.

Integrate your projected consciousness back with your physical consciousness. Do any further grounding that is necessary.

It's easy to feel "lost" when rising on the planes. Know that your will to return is all you need. I had a teacher who once suggested using the command "return return return" whenever you were ready to come back, and you would easily be able to return to waking consciousness. I think it can be a good idea to have a timer set, or a piece of music of a pre-determined length, to remind you to come back when its done.

ESCAPISM

While many think there can never bee too much of a good thing, (and meditation is a good thing,) to a Witch, that's simply untrue. Too much of anything causes imbalance, including meditation. Too much meditation becomes escapism from the material world, where you are urged to put your meditative insights into practical use. What good are all the meditation practices, if you cannot apply them to a better life and a better world? Escapist meditation becomes just as toxic as too much television or other media, or too much of any substance that numbs the senses, such as indiscriminate uses of inebriants.

While sometimes its fun to simply bliss out in a meditation, and have no recall of the experience, too much of such practices defeats the point of Western meditation, to open the gate to deeper levels of spiritual awareness, and, like the shaman, retrieve it not only for your practice, but return with something of value to your community. At times we go so deep we do not remember our experiences well, but training and practice helps us remember more and more. Such ability and discipline should be our goal.

Such "bliss" sessions balance the simple sitting experiences, where we feel we cannot escape our thoughts, feelings, and psychic baggage, but to dwell too long on either practice is a mistake. The purpose of the meditation practices here is to learn to easily and reliably open the psychic gate to inner power.

To not be seduced by the allure of escapism, maintain a disciplined practice. Set regular times, and use a timer or timed music to limit the time in meditation. Don't practice for more than an hour per session. You can find that with discipline, you can have a very lucid experience in a much shorter time, and learn to recall everything. Write down everything from your meditation immediately afterwards, even if all you can write is "I don't remember." Get into the habit and eventually you will remember more and more.

If you find yourself escaping too much, vary your technique. Try other methods of meditation until you find the ones that work best for you.

Most importantly, hold a clear intention for your meditation session, even if the intention is simply, "I will meditate easily, clearly and remember all that I experience."

Aids for Meditation

The following tips can be helpful for any of the techniques of meditation

Atmosphere: If the mood in the area is conducive to meditation, then you will have a much easier time meditating. Decorate the area in soothing colors. Use objects and items inspiring to meditation. Light candles. Play soothing music (see **Chapter Four**). Do whatever you need to do to inspire a meditative state.

Incense: Incense can be conducive to a meditative state (see **Chapter Seven**). The easiest and most benign to induce meditation is sandalwood, though frankincense is also very helpful.

Crystals: Holding a stone that helps induce a meditative state is a powerful aid. Clear quartz, either as a point or a polished stone, is an excellent ally in meditation. Quartz amplifies whatever intention you put into it. If you are focused on meditation and tranquility, it will aid those intentions by amplifying them. Other meditative stones include aragonite to keep yourself focused, lapis lazuli as a general meditative stone, amethyst for peace and tranquility and aquamarine for expanding consciousness.

Flower Essences: A few drops of flower essences can be helpful for meditation. Each flower has its own use, it's own signature, useful for different types of meditation. For general meditation, horse chestnut, lavender, lilac, aconite, bloodroot, lotus, mugwort, and St. John's wort are all helpful.

CHAPTER THREE:
THE BREATH OF THE GODS

Breath is the kiss of the gods upon our lips. Breath is life, and life is breath. Without it, we would not be alive. Many magickal cultures have linked words for life force or vital energy with the word for breath. Both are invisible. Both are intangible. Both are divine, and essential to our being, whether we see them or not, or whether we think about them or not.

In China, the term *chi,* also *ch'i* or *qi,* is associated with both the air and breath, and with vital life force. Traditions of directing and manipulating chi are at the core of their indigenous health practices and martial arts, as demonstrated in the arts of Tai-Chi. The Japanese form of the word is *ki,* found in the modern tradition of Japanese healing known as Reiki. *Pnuema* is Greek for breath, and has come to refer to invisible spiritual presence, the universal substance permeating the universe and, in later Christian times, for the Holy Spirit. The Latin *spiritus* means both breath and spirit. In Hebrew mysticism, the word *ruach,* meaning wind, breath, or air, is also used to denote vital life force within an individual. *Athem* is a term used in Anglo-Saxon magick to denote vial life force found in the breath, and is the portion of the "soul" that interconnects all the other parts.

The term *awen* is a Welsh word used in some Celtic spiritual systems in a manner similar to chi, ki or pnuema. Awen usually refers to the poetic inspiration of bards and druids. It possibly derives from root words meaning "to blow" or "breeze" so it is described as the breath or wind of inspiration, passion from the gods to the bard; granting genius, ideas and poetic eloquence. Though it might seem strange to some of us, the concept of poetic talent and spiritual ability is often equated in Celtic literature. To the Celts, the poet and bard was cut from the same cloth as the magickal practitioner, for words have magickal power.

Probably the most well known in our modern mystical revival is the word *prana* from the Hindu tradition. It is another world associated with both life force and air. Prana is sometimes misunderstood to be literal air, the gases of our atmosphere, or at least oxygen, but this is an oversimplification. The life force is carried with, and resides in, the physical air, but it is not the same as the physical air. Prana is a subtle and unseen force that flows with air, but also flows with water and light, resides in stone, plants, and animals. People require prana to live, and we absorb various forms of prana through breath, through sunlight and moon light, and through the foods we eat. Breath is simply one gateway into the realm of prana, and can stimulate and alter its flow within the body.

The Hindu study of prana has lead to the practices of *pranayama*, specific breathing exercises designed to heal and transform. While many of these exercises are simple and safe, uneducated use of pranayama can result in unbalancing the body, just as uneducated use of exercise equipment can injure the body.

The Hindu traditions have it right. Altering your breathing patterns, breathing with intention, is one of the fastest ways to alter your consciousness and open the gate to the world of energy. It physiologically alters the flow of oxygen to your brain, inducing altered states. The breathing practices can be inhibitory and relaxing, or exhibitory and revitalizing but, more importantly, it alters the flow of energy through your subtle bodies.

Witches and magicians have a magickal axiom: "As above, so below. As within, so without." Also known as the Principle of Correspondence in Hermetic lore, it tells us all things are related and affect each other. You can understand or change one thing by affecting it on a different scale. In this case, you can change the intangible and invisible world of energy and consciousness, which is difficult to "see" or measure, by affecting the physical body. We can more easily control and affect the physical body, and our degree of control over our actions can open the gate to greater awareness.

Mystical traditions all over the globe have their own forms of pranayama, though they don't all use that name. Modern Witches, reconstructing our traditions and practices, have borrowed from a number of sources, particularly yoga, Sufism, Rosicrucianism, hypnotism, and strangely Hawaiian practices to find our own ways. Many practices of regulated breathing, just like drumming or focused gaze, are universal to the human condition. Many traditions figure out how to use them. Others are more culturally specific. Even if we do not use breath as a primary method to induce trance, breath affects everything we do. We are (hopefully) breathing when we are performing any other technique, so the breath influences all our experiences.

THE COMPLETE BREATH

If breath is connected to life force, you'd be surprised how many people are running around not breathing correctly. Yes, there are correct ways, or at least more healthy ways, to breathe. Most people get into the habit of restricting that breath. We hold tension in our bodies, and one of the easiest ways to hold tension, and to release it, is through the breath.

Have you ever noticed yourself holding your breath when you don't want to feel something? When we anticipate bad news, pain, or shock, we suspend the breath. For those of us feeling tension, stress, or generally not wanting to deal with aspects of our life, we hold our breath. Our breathing patterns then become more and more shallow. Not breathing fully prevents the life force from circulating fully in our bodies, and results in us not being fully present and grounded in our body and in our life. A little bit of our consciousness stands outside of our bodies, to not be harmed. While it can be an effective temporary defense mechanism, it becomes detrimental when the condition is our long term state of being.

My favorite yoga teacher, Stephanie, taught a simple key to meditation with breath. "Where the breath goes, the mind goes. Where the mind goes, the breath goes." If you are tense, fearful, stressed or angry, your breathing will reflect that, and affect your body. Likewise if you are happy, joyful, relaxed and open, your breathing will reflect that, and affect your body. While it's easy to say stop being stressed, or angry, or just be happy, it's much harder to do it on command. We think and feel whatever we are thinking and feeling, and through sheer will alone, most people cannot change what they think and feel. But we can change our breath and thereby change our mood.

By making a physiological change, we can change how our body responds, and that in turn, affect our mood, thoughts and overall health. It is another example of "as above, so below," used not only to alter consciousness and induce trance, but also to change our unhealthy thoughts and feelings. It doesn't banish them, or make them disappear, but through breath we process them rather than holding onto them. Breathing fully and properly gently rocks the sacrum and occipital bones to stimulate the movement of cerebrospinal fluid up and down the spine, thereby stimulating the energy centers associated with the spine, as well as nourishing the overall nervous system.

Through full, regulated breathing exercises we relearn breathing patterns and set a new default state of our breath and energy. It does take time and practice, because you have to retrain your body. Our breathing is fairly unconscious. We didn't set about to learn restricted breathing. It arose out of our thoughts and feelings, and affected our breathing in ways we did not notice. We now have to become conscious of our breathing, and relearn patterns until they are second nature for us once again. It's easy to slip back into old bad habits.

Checking on our breathing pattern—how full, deep and relaxed our breath is during times of stress—becomes a pivotal practice of meditative mindfulness. Also taking up practices that naturally induce full breathing but are not specific breathing exercises can be quite helpful. Cardiovascular exercise, weight training, yoga, martial arts, dancing, and even simple walking are forms of exercise that help re-pattern our breathing.

Our lungs are actually separated into three parts, and with a simple exercise, you can learn if you are breathing fully from all three parts. The lower part of the lung, closest to the belly, is known as the abdominal lung. It is just above the diaphragm, the primary muscle of breath. The middle part of the lung is the thoracic lung, parallel with the sternum area. The upper part of the lung is called the clavicular lung. It is closest to your shoulders, specifically close to your clavicle bones. A full breath consists of using all three parts of the lung.

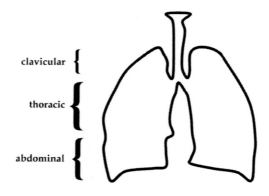

Fig. 7: Parts of the Lung

Exercise: Breath Evaluation

Lay down on your back on a comfortable surface. If you need a pillow for your head, or beneath your knees, please use one to be comfortable. Place one hand on your abdomen, beneath the ribs, and another at your sternum. Breathe normally. (Now that you are paying attention to your breath, you will have a tendency to breathe deeper than your normal breath. That's okay. Just try to breathe normally.) Do your hands rise up as you breath? If so, which one rises first? When you exhale, which one falls first? Most people, tend towards shallow breathing, will not feel much movement on both hands. Move the hand on your abdomen to your upper chest, above the sternum and closer to, but not on, the throat. You now have one hand on the sternum and one hand above in the clavicular region. Breathe again. Do your hands move up and down? Again, which one moves first and which one falls first?

Ideally to take a full and complete breath, all three areas of the lung have to be active. Did you notice any one or two were more active, or less active? That tells you were your breathing is shallow. Some people take deeper breaths, but never fill the clavicular part of the lung. Others breathe more from the upper lung, and do not move the diaphragm much. All three segments of the lung are needed for healthy breathing. Without them, you are not using your full capacity for breathing. It's like thinking you've filled up your gas tank, but you only fill up two-thirds, and wonder why you are running out of energy.

Exercise: The Complete Breath

Lay down again on the floor or other flat surface. Place your hands as you did in the previous exercises, with one on the abdomen and the other on the chest. If possible, breathe through your nose, and breathe deeply. Imagine your lungs are like balloons. To fill a balloon, the bottom of the balloon inflates first. Imagine the body of the lung filling with air, and the diaphragm will naturally move, massaging the organs in the abdomen and raising that hand. Then the middle of the lung balloon fills, lifting up the thoracic area, and the hand resting there. Lastly, imagine the top of the lung balloon filling up, filling up the clavicular area. Pause for only a moment, and then exhale in a slow, controlled manner. Like a balloon deflating, the top part deflates first. Feel the air from the clavicular area release, then the thoracic, lowing the hand on the mid-chest. Then release the air in the abdominal area, lowering the hand on your belly. Pause for a moment and repeat. Do several breaths and then move your abdominal hand to the clavicular area, to make sure you are filling that area too. Feel your clavicular hand raise on the end of the inhale, and lower at the start of exhale. The pattern, for easy reference is: Inhale abdominal, thoracic, clavicular. Exhale clavicular, thoracic, abdominal.

After short time of breathing the complete breath, how do you feel? You might feel lightheaded, particularly if you are not used to taking in that much air. You might feel energized. You might even feel relaxed and sleepy, as you have been releasing a lot of stress and tension held in the chest. Full and complete breathing, also known as "wave breathing" as it forms a wave pattern in and out of the lungs, is the cornerstone of all other breath exercises, and its regular use aids not only your overall health, but your magick. If breath is life and life is breath, you must have life force to do magick.

The following techniques are ones I've learned and found helpful in both my own Witchcraft training, and in explorations of other traditions. Some of these techniques are inhibitory and relaxing, while others are more exhibitory. Like any exercise technique, all should be used with caution. Just because it's breathing doesn't mean it won't have an immediate effect on your body. If you have never done breathing exercises before, start slowly and build up your stamina. If you have any respiratory issues, talk to your health care provider before attempting these exercises.

REGULATED BREATHING

Regulated breathing is one of the simplest breathing techniques, and variations exist in many different traditions. It is simply a controlled, measured breath, regulated by a rhythmic count. The count keeps the breathing even and controlled. Most techniques of regulated breathing involve slow inhalation, to gather up energy, and then holding the breath in for a period of time, to build up and circulate energy in the body. The slow exhale is to release unwanted energies and sometimes includes holding the breath out for a period of time. Holding no breath increases your capacity to be able to hold energy, and in Kundalini Yoga, it is said to stimulate your connection to your divine source.

The Eight-Four-Eight Breath

The 8-4-8 breath releases tension, increases lung capacity and relaxes your entire body and consciousness. Breathing through the nose is said to activate the energy flowing through *ida* and *pingala*, the two energy channels, or *nadis*, in Hindu metaphysics said to flow like entwined serpents up the spine and pass through the nose. The 8-4-8 Breath can be varied by adding the path of movement to breathing, transforming it into walking breath. Walk in a circle, say around your block, following the pattern.

Exercise: The 8-4-8 Breath

Inhale through the nose to the count of eight, holding the breath to the count of four, exhaling through the nose to the count of eight and holding out the breath to the count of four. Repeat the pattern at least four times.

As your control and lung capacity expand, you might find the count too short. You can either slow down the rhythm of your count, or you can increase its length, but if you increase the number of beats to each section, make sure you maintain the ratio of 2:1:2. If you increase the inhale to the count of ten, then alter the exercise to the 10-5-10 breath.

A variation of this breath, known as the "Little Death" in eastern practices, uses the count of seven. Inhale for seven beats. Hold for seven beats. Exhale smoothly for seven beats. Hold out for seven beats. The patterns is repeated for a total of seven times.

The Ha Prayer

The Ha Prayer is a form of breath magick I was first exposed to through the Feri Tradition of Witchcraft. Often know as the Anderson Feri Tradition, for founders Victor and Cora Anderson, it draws upon a variety of cultures and traditions, including those of Hawaii. According to the Feri, "Ha" means both "four" and "breath" in Hawaiian, and this prayer uses both the count of four and the breath as its vehicle. It works with the fourfold nature of humanity, described by some as the three selves or souls – the Higher Self, Middle Self, Lower Self, and the body, or the four elements as embodying the flesh, emotions, mind, and soul. Since learning it, I've used it more often than the 8-4-8 Breath, simply because it has a more magickal and spiritual intent behind it.

The Ha Prayer builds energy, called *mana* in Hawaiian, and sends it to what is generally referred to as the Higher Self, though the various lines of Feri have different names for it, including Godself, Sacred Dove, and Holy Daimon. Feri Tradition lineages have individual names for the three souls or three selves, but here I will simply call them the Higher Self, Middle Self, and Lower Self. The Higher Self is your divine self or soul. Your Middle Self is your personal self, your ego and personality, while the Lower Self is your animalistic and instinctual self. It is sometime seen as an animal or child.

The energy can be sent for one of two purposes: First, a prayer for something specific, and often tangible. This form of prayer is much like a spell in other forms of Witchcraft. You are asking not another god, but your own personal Godself, for whatever it is you desire, and making an offering of life energy to it. The Higher Self returns the energy to you, transforming the mana into what is known as *mana-loa*, a higher and more refined form of energy, manifesting your intention. Or the Ha Prayer is a prayer to gain a closer and stronger connection with your own Higher Self, to more fully embody it, with no other specific intention or outcome.

Both are acts of magick. Some would divide these two styles as thaumaturgy and theurgy, or low magick and high magick. Thaumaturgy is usually operative magick, a ritual to get what you desire, while theurgy is god magick, to attune with the divine and higher purpose. Yet in this case, they are both theurgy, for you are first attuning to your own Higher Self before doing anything, making all actions in divine alignment with the Higher Self.

Exercise: The Ha Prayer

To perform the Ha Prayer, sit or stand in a comfortable manner, with your spine straight. Inhale through the nose to the count of four. Hold to the count of four. Exhale through the nose to the count of four. Hold out to the count of four. Repeat for a total of four cycles. Inhale deeply, tilt the head back as if looking to the heavens and exhale through the mouth, sending the mana to the Higher Self. In some views, it is really the Lower Self carrying the energy to the Higher Self. You might feel a rising of energy as you do this, particularly sexual energy, as that is also life force and mana. Return your head to a normal position. Then a refined, sometimes cooling energy will descend down through your crown and spine and even down to your feet, connecting you to the Higher Self and aligning your entire consciousness, your Middle and Lower Selves, with your divinity

While the breath is the true prayer and offering, a verse is often recited at the end, silently or out loud, as a reminder of the purpose of the prayer. Written by Victor Anderson, the poetry is:

Who is this flower above me,
And what is the work of this god?
I would know myself in all my parts.

For those looking for a detailed exploration on the Three Soul Cosmology, I suggest my book, *The Temple of Shamanic Witchcraft*. For those looking for more information specifically on the Feri Tradition and its view of the Three Souls and Ha Prayer, I highly recommend T. Thorn Coyle's *Evolutionary Witchcraft*. As I am not a Feri initiate myself, but do love many of their techniques, my understanding and experience of the Ha Prayer is simply my own, and those seeking an understanding from an initiate of Feri would do well to start with Thorn's book.

The regulated breathing of both the Eight-Four-Eight Breath and the Ha Prayer can be used to induce trance, as a preparatory ritual before entering trance for meditative journey or ritual work. They can also be adapted and done in group settings, to synchronize everyone's energy and intention as a group. When you breathe together, your group consciousness forms. The only difficulty is finding a pace of the breath that works for everybody, as those with different body types have different lung capacities.

Serpent Breathing

Often the imitation of animals considered to be magickally powerful is a method to induce trance. One popular animalistic breathing technique is to imitate the hissing of the serpent. While similar concepts are found in eastern yogic traditions venerating the serpent of life force, of Kundalini, the Serpent Breath technique has been popularized in magickal communities through the work of Traditional Witchcraft author Robin Artisson.

Exercise: Serpent Breath

One takes a deep breath and releases it slowly through the clenched teeth for a prescribed number of times, say ten, or throughout the vision trance. It can be helpful to rhythmically sway while doing so. The breath builds up power, and the noise also helps induce trance, along with connecting to the serpentine life force of the sorcerer.

HEALING BREATHS

Simple breathing exercises are said to fill the body with vital energy and bring healing, similar to the many hands-on healing techniques that provide energy for the body to do its own healing, rather than manipulating tissues or focusing on specific intent. Any of the breathing exercises above are healing, though some breathing exercises are considered healing in specific ways.

While these breaths are not necessarily going to induce a long term trance state as the meditation techniques from the previous chapter do, they prepare you for further ritual and energy work.

Positive and Negative Breathing

Positive and Negative Breathing is also known as Polarity Breathing. Contrary to the name, it is not "good" and "bad" breathing. It refers to the flow of energy in the body, often referred to as our polarity, our personal balance of the two opposing, yet complimentary, charges in the body. Popularized in modern Polarity Therapy, the concept can be found in most traditions looking at energy as positive/negative, male/female, or projective/receptive. In Chinese medicine such polarity is described as yang and yin. In Hindu literature it is named for the deities Shiva and Shakti. Witches use these energies, and simply see them as God and Goddess. I learned these techniques in the Cabot Tradition of Witchcraft during my initial training, though they originate from Rosicrucian teachings found in *Wisdom of the Mystic Masters* by Joseph J. Weed.

Polarity breathing is used to correct imbalances to the energy system. You need to know what the imbalance is to decide which breath to do. Positive Breathing is used to counterbalance "a negative condition." You use it when you are feeling down and out, depressed and unhappy. It returns our sense of optimism. Though you can repeat the technique, ideally you should wait at least two hours between healing sessions when working on chronic conditions.

Exercise: Positive Breathing

Sit in a chair comfortably, with your hands in your lap and your feet squarely on the floor. Do not let your feet touch. You can be in shoes, socks, or barefoot, as long as your feet are apart.

Place the index finger, middle finger, and thumb and touch the matching index finger, middle finger and thumb on the other hand, forming a triangle. It can be held in your lap, or slightly above it.

Close your eyes. Take a deep breath, ideally through the nose, and hold it for a count of seven seconds. Exhale. Repeat six more times for a total of seven. Release your hand position and breathe normally. Let your energy naturally return to balance.

Negative breathing counteracts an "overly positive" situation. It should be used if you have too much energy, if you are frantic or manic or nervous. It diffuses the excess energy. It is also very powerful in the early stages of catching a cold or the flu. It reportedly removes the germs that cause colds. I've had great success in warding of colds if I remember to do this breath when I first feel sick. The trick is being grounded enough in your body and aware of it to know when you need to do Negative Breathing.

Exercise: Negative Breathing

Sit in a chair comfortably, with your hands in your lap and your feet squarely on the floor. In this exercise, make sure your feet are touching, side by side.

Hold your hands out in front of your body at the level of your chest. Bring your thumb tips to touch each other, and all finger tips to touch the corresponding finger tips. The index fingers will be touching. The middle fingers will be touching, and so forth.

Close your eyes. Take a deep breath and exhale slowly. When your lungs are empty, hold your breath out for seven seconds. Continue to hold the hand position. At the end of the count of seven, relax your breath but maintain the hand position. Take five or six normal and relaxed breaths. Let your breath return to normal.

Six more times, for a total of seven, repeat the deep breath and slow exhale, holding out for seven second and then taking normal breaths. When done the seventh cycle, relax your hands and your breath. Put the entire exercise out of your mind and let your energy return to balance.

Sufi Elemental Breathing

Another technique borrowed from a different tradition, but one that works quite well with modern Witchcraft, is the Sufi practice of elemental breathing. Having basically the same system of elements – earth, water, fire, air, and a fifth element of ether or spirit, the practice can be adopted by Witches seeking to deepen their connection to elemental energies through breathwork.

Through a simple pattern of breathing, you can activate and attune to the five elements already present within you. The breathing exercises can be augmented with visualization of colors, focusing on the energy centers of the body and the intention of feeling certain suggestions, as well as using hand postures known as *mudras*. But it is the breath patterns themselves that do the work. The other parts simply enhance the experience.

Exercise: Elemental Breathing

Start by sitting or standing in a comfortable position, with a straight spine. Each element has a pattern of breaths through the nose and/or mouth. Breath a full deep breath in each element, using the pattern of inhale and exhale given. Each element should be done for at least five breaths before moving on to the next. The optional visualizations of colors and placement in the body is also given in the chart, but first focus on the breath itself, and how that breath alters your energy, your awareness, and your overall balance.

Element	Breathing Pattern	Color	Feeling	Body
Earth	In Nose/Out Nose	Yellow, Green	Magnetic, Grounded	Root, Bones
Water	In Nose/Out Mouth	Green, Blue	Cool, Fluid, Clean	Belly, Blood
Fire	In Mouth/Out Nose	Red	Hot, Energized	Solar Plexus, Stomach, Heart
Air	In Mouth/Out Mouth	Blue, Yellow	Lightness, Expansive	Throat, Lungs
Spirit	In Nose/Out Nose	White	Connection	Head, Crown

While five breaths is the minimum for each element, you can spend far longer on each if you desire. Just make sure you go through the pattern fully, completing each element. It can be helpful to have timed music with a regular soft beat, or a metronome or wind up clock with an audible tick to keep a regular and even pace, or you can count the breaths, like the 8-4-8 Breath or Ha

Prayer. I've combined the pattern of the Ha Prayer with the Sufic Breaths, and found it quite powerful.

BREATH AND ENERGY

If breath is the medium through which life force flows, and a way in which we can receive it, then breathing is a technique for raising our own energy. One analogy my friend Apollon uses for the spiritual seeker is that we are light and fire because we are really "on fire." The oxidation process is like a slow burn, and breath is the method through which we transform ourselves. The oxygen of breath, along with the prana it contains, is what fuels our transformation. Some specific breathing exercises literally give us more energy for our magickal practices and spiritual journey.

Breath of Fire

Breath of Fire is an energizing breath found in the Kundalini Yoga tradition, taught by the late Yogi Bhajan of the Sikh Tradition. Breath of Fire is a rapid, shallow breath that energizes the body with prana. Practitioners claim that Breath of Fire does in two minutes what an hour of normal breathing does for the body, in terms of raising the metabolism, burning calories, and detoxifying the body. It is used on its own, or with specific yogic exercises to transform the body and consciousness. Though it is a staple of Kundalini Yoga, I've found it an excellent exercise in all forms of energy work and magick, as well as an exercise in "mundane" life. I've done it to energize myself during the work day, before a class, at the gym, and even in the car.

Exercise: Breath of Fire

Sit in a comfortable position with your spine straight. In Kundalini Yoga, you are usually sitting in easy pose, a simple cross-legged position on the floor. If that is uncomfortable for you, you can sit down in a chair, and once you are familiar with the breath, you will find you can easily do it sitting, standing, and doing other activities.

Breathe in and out equally with a quick, rapid breath. The pace should range from 120 beats to upwards of 200 beats per minute. A musical metronome can be used to help find a comfortable pace. The Breath of Fire is powered by the diaphragm near the Solar Plexus, but the belly stays relatively still, as the breath is shallow. You are not taking the Complete Three Part Breath as described above. You might feel as if you are hyperventilating, but the breath is controlled, and you can stop at any time.

In Kundalini Yoga, an internal silent mantra is used to mentally focus the practitioner on the breath. The mantra is *Sat Nam*, meaning True Name, and it's a call to your Higher Self, not your personal, ego self. As you inhale, think Sat, while on the exhale think Nam, created a rapid internal dialogue of "sat nam sat nam sat nam sat nam…" as you do the Breath of Fire.

Perform the breathing exercise for approximately two minutes, learning to build up to longer intervals with practice.

The breath is often ended with an exercise known as the root lock, or *mulbandh*, though it is not mandatory to benefit from the Breath of Fire. This physical contraction locks the energy generated by the breath and allows it to circulate in the body for healing and purification. To perform the root lock, contract the rectum and sex organs and squeeze the naval point back to the spine as you inhale. Hold the breath for 2-5 seconds and then exhale fully. The inhaled moments will circulate the prana within your body.

Return to a normal breathing pattern. Relax your body and rest the mind.

Pranic Breathing

While all breathing and particularly all breathing exercises, could be considered "pranic," pranic breathing refers to a specialized breath used in the tradition of Pranic Healing. The breath draws upon the life force of the environment around you, and processes it through the body, for self-healing, or the healing of others. It prevents you from depleting your own personal energy when doing healing work.

Intention is the key to pranic breathing, as your intention directs the prana. Visualization is often stressed in instructions on pranic breathing, telling you to visualize yourself connecting to the source of prana, using the earth, the sky, the sun, and stars as sources, and imagine it drawing through your body, particularly your spine. While visualization is effective, your own experience might be more sensory, or even something akin to an auditory hum or buzz.

Exercise: Pranic Breathing

While sitting or standing, get into a comfortable position. Imagine your body like a tree, where the base of your spine grows roots, perhaps down through your legs and feet, that dig deep into the earth. As you inhale, imagine drawing up the prana from the land. You might imagine it as a green or blue energy traveling up your legs and into your body, into your belly specifically, or you might feel a warmth or tingle as the energy travels. Move the energy upward with each breath. Take notice of the energy. How does it feel? Program the energy with your healing intention, saying silently, "This energy heals me and balances me in all ways." Continue for a few minutes, until you feel the energy circulate within you and expand throughout your limbs. You might even feel it radiate out from your pores and fill the space around you.

Bring your attention to the sky. Imagine your crown reaching up and growing branches, like a great tree, to touch the sky and head toward the Sun, Moon, and stars. As you inhale, imagine drawing down the prana of the sky. Move the energy with your breath down through the branches and into your crown. Feel the energy descend into your body. Again, you can visualize it, perhaps as a blue or white light, or simply feel a sensation of warmth or a tingle as it descends. Feel it fill your body with each breath. Try to notice the energy's quality. How does it feel to you, in particular in comparison to the earth prana? Program the sky prana with healing intention as you did the earth prana. Continue until you feel the energy circulate, mingling with the earth energy and moving around your body.

For the next step, try drawing on prana from above and below simultaneously, if this hasn't happened naturally already. Feel the energy from below and above mingle and mix in the heart with each breath, and circulate through the body with your healing intention.

Using your intention, direct the energy from the heart to any place in your body in need of extra healing energy, or imagine it like a star in your heart, expanding and radiating out to your entire body, and around your body, filling the energy field known as the aura around you. Fill your body and aura with this healing prana.

You don't have to specifically end this exercise. It will continue naturally for a while, even when you turn your attention to other matters. If you feel an excess of prana and are ungrounded, use grounding techniques such as negative breathing or your roots, to bring your energy back to a normal energy.

If you are involved in healing work, you can direct the flow of prana through your hands, through a magick wand or through a crystal, and use it to aid other people, animals, plants, and the environment.

Pore Breathing

Pore breathing is a traditional technique taught in some forms of occultism that has been forgotten by a lot of more recent traditions. There are quite a few variations on the techniques and ideas found in pore breathing, but basically it's much like an extension of pranic breathing. While basic pranic breathing looks at the top and bottom of the energy column, the crown and base of the spine, as additional "mouths" to the pranic system, capable of taking in and expelling energy, pore breathing looks at all the pores of your skin as additional points where we can absorb or release energy.

Pore breathing usually focuses the energy as a particular intention. Rather than simply looking at prana from the earth or sky, a specific type of energy is intended, often aligned with an abstract principle such as "love" or "healing," or the energy is specific to a location, such as the energy at a special site in nature.

Color can be used as a focus for poor breathing, as you visualize a particular color with magickal qualities, and envision you are breathing it in through your pores, letting it affect every cell of your being.

Color	Magickal Qualities
Red	Energy, passion, warmth, warrior, protection, drive, leadership, aggression
Orange	Healing, instinct, intuition, communication, energy, vitality
Yellow	Uplifting, clearing, focusing, energizing, awakening
Green	Healing, growth, renewal, fertility, love, harmony, relationship
Blue	Peace, clarity, hope, communication, intellect, memory
Indigo	Tranquility, wisdom, prosperity, spirituality
Violet	Transformation, magick, healing, alchemy, change, clearing
Black	Grounding, invisibility, feminine, rest, earth
White	Energizing, protecting, masculine, activity, sky
Silver	Feminine, goddess, emotional, healing, intuitive, family, psychic, fertility
Gold	Masculine, god, intellectual, inspiring, dynamic, successful, intelligent

You can also focus on the energy of a particular element. While it helps to have that element around you physically, elemental energy really refers to a quality of energy, not the literal tangible substance. Elemental water refers to a quality of energy, being emotional in nature. Being around water, H_2O, helps us understand and experience that quality, but the quality can be evoked without the physical presence of H_2O.

Element	Realm	Areas of Life	Highest Quality	Colors
Earth	Physical	Money, Home, Security	Law, Sovereignty	Green, Black, Brown
Water	Emotional	Relationships, Family	Love, Healing	Blue, Green
Air	Mental	Communication	Life, Truth	Blue, Yellow
Fire	Energetic	Passion, Identity	Light, Will	Red, Orange
Akasha	Spirit	Mysticism, Religion	Spirituality	White, Black

Pore breathing is done like regular deep breathing. You exhale anything that blocks the quality or power you are trying to instill, and inhale the energy of the quality itself. You continue to inhale the energy until you are "full" and then let the energy take its effect. You can build up a charge prior to doing spell work or vision work, and use that energy to propel your intention. It can also be used for healing work. If the energy is too much, you can always breathe the energy out again, emptying yourself, rather than "metabolizing" it.

Exercise: Pore Breathing

Sit or stand in a comfortable position. Ideally you should have as little contact with objects as possible, like keeping your back from touching a chair back, in an effort to keep as much of your pores free as possible. If you need back support, then please take it. By this theory you should also expose as much of your skin as possible, but I've found the energy can flow through clothing (and through chairs for that matter).

Decide upon what type of energy you wish to focus. Will it be a quality? What kind of quality do you wish to fill yourself with? What would be appropriate for your magic? Will it be a color, an element or something else? Imagine yourself surrounded by that energy and you will be surrounded by it.

Focus on your intention and breathe. Imagine all your pores like tiny mouths, also breathing as you breathe. Each one is inhaling then exhaling.

Exhale whatever blocks you from that energy. Release not only through your breath, but also through your pores.

Each breath draws in more energy, building up a "charge" of energy based upon your intention. Each breath exhales unwanted energies, releasing all impurities from that charge. Feel the energy draw deep inside you, through your flesh and blood, down to your very bones.

Continue this breathing, building the energy up until you've reached maximum capacity. You can imagine circulating the energy through the body, release the energy toward a specific goal with your hands or breath, or direct it towards your Higher Self, as you did in the Ha Prayer. You can also ground any excess as you would normally ground excess energy.

Pore breathing is very effective, so much so that many practitioners do not teach it because they feel it is too powerful and too dangerous for beginning students. While it can be dangerous, like any form of magick, you need to exercise care in any practical energy application. Like any form of energy work, there is a possibility you can overload your system. But if you follow these instructions and ground excess energy if you have any discomfort, you should remain safe and healthy.

TRANSFERRING ENERGY WITH BREATH

Many of the exercise in this chapter have suggested directing the energy of your breath in spell work, healing, or visionary experience. How exactly is that done? Each practitioner has their own methods but like the pranic breathing itself, it is best done with clear intention.

The energy contained in the body can be directed through the body, and expelled in an number of ways.

Hands: Most common is to direct the energy through the hands. The energy points in the palms and fingertips can direct energy. Simply by directing your arms and hands towards the goal, the energy can be released. In traditional Wiccan Cones of Power, a spell can be performed and then culminated with the Witch or group of Witches directing energy up in a cone formation from the center of the circle to the heavens, to manifest the intention of the working. The cone of energy can also be directed towards an object, a talisman to be consecrated. One can usually speak the intention behind the consecration out loud, or simply think about it silently as the object is being blessed with energy. This process is also known as hallowing, charging, and imbuing. Generally the ritual tool is cleansed of unwanted energies using sacred smoke, salt, water, sunlight, or ritualized intention before being consecrated.

Tools: The hands can be holding a working tool used to direct energy, or to become the new container for the energy. An object can be consecrated if the charge of built energy, with intention, is directed into the object. It can also be focused through a tool, such as a crystal point, wand, or athame, and then directed outward to a person, to another object, or toward the intention of a spell.

Chakras: Energy can be directed outward from not only the energy points within the hands, but also the seven main energy points in the human body, known as chakras. The chakras run from the base of the spine to the top of the head, and are used, consciously or unconsciously, in our pranic breathing work. Generally energy is directed out from the third eye at the brow, the heart center at the sternum, or the solar plexus, just beneath the diaphragm.

Fig. 8: Chakras

Odic Breath: In the mid nineteenth century, Baron Carl von Reichenbach coined the term "Odic Force" (also known a *Od, Odyle, Odes, Odylic, Odyllic,* or *Odems* among others) for the vital life force. Reichenbach drew its name from the Norse god Odin. Though similar in concept to prana, he related it more strongly to the electromagnetic fields of a living organism, and worked in positive and negative expressions rather then being the vital life force of the breath. It was associated with similar research in hypnotism and spiritualism and later adopted into occultism, ceremonial magick, and Witchcraft, with stronger correlations to prana and breath. It was popularized in modern Witchcraft under the name Odic Breath by Raven Grimassi. Odic force today is seen as the power that builds up within the body through breathwork and a mental-emotional response triggered through ritual, visualization or will, building up in the blood and transferred, through breath. The energy carries a "charge similar to the previous polarity breathing, and the charge is described as magnetic or electric. In terms of magickal occultism, electric and magnetic describe forces similar in function and quality to the scientific concepts of electricity and magnetism, but not literally the same thing. The type of breath can determine the charge, and the response one gets. A warm breath from a slow and deep exhale releases an energy electrical in nature. Upon another person, it results in the magnetic response within the aura. Magnetic responses draw and attract power. It can enhance meditation, but used in terms of long term healing to open a person to other magickal techniques, used in invocation rituals, initiations, and sexual workings. A cool breath, from a shallow and short puff of air releases a magnetic energy, creating an electric response in another's aura. Electrical responses vitalize the body and can be used to heal by increasing the immune system and natural healing abilities. It is used in Reiki initiations. It can be a "shock," snapping people out of trance, waking them up, or causing an annoyance. Is can disconnect a magickal circuit. These opposite responses are only caused on living beings. If you were to breathe an electrical breath on an inanimate object, it remains an electrical breath and infuses it with vitality. The only exception is breathing upon a properly consecrated tool, which will often behave like a living being, manifesting the opposite response.

Eyes: Just like the chakras, the eyes too can direct the energy built in the body. While it can be used for any manner of magick as long as you hold your intent clearly, it is most often used benignly for fascination and malignly for the curse of the "evil eye." Fascination is a form of mesmerism or glamour, entrancing the recipient. It can be helpful to hold the attention of another, or to induce hypnotic trance for healing or magickal training in a student or client. The evil eye is a curse to disrupt the energy of the target, causing misfortune. Energy is transferred from the eye as if you were "breathing" out of the eye, but holding your physical breath. Imagine an energetic vapor, infused with your intention, being sent to your target.

Pores: Just as the pores can be used to take in energy, they can also be used to release energy. Rather than directing a "blast" of energy like in the other methods, releasing energy through the pores creates a diffuse "cloud" of energy around you, and can be used along with the breath to change the energy of your aura, the field of energy around you, quite quickly. With a few breaths you can build up a charge of energy, program your intention, and then release it into the energy field to change your aura, affecting both how you feel, and how other people perceive you.

In the classic version of the Eight Ways to the Center, blood control, through the use of binding cords, is included with breath control. While they both share the nature of control and blood movement, I find the two practices very different. Even though the use of cords is not particularly painful, the restrictive and more disciplinary gnosis traditions will be further explored on the Path of Isolation in **Chapter Six**.

BREATHLESSNESS

The shadow of breathwork is one of the most fearful shadows of all the paths – breathlessness. While restricting the flow of oxygen to the brain is indeed trance provoking, it usually manifests a state of consciousness not particularly conducive to magickal work because your body reacts as if it is dying. While some forms of breath restriction are practiced on the path of isolation, I strongly suggest not seeking out this paths of gnosis.

It is the shadow to breathwork because, at rare times with more vigorous breathing exercises, we can feel as if we are suffocating or hyperventilating. Hyperventilation is excessively rapid or deep breathing that results in lowering the carbon dioxide levels in the body much more than usual, and can cause lightheadedness, dizziness, tingling in the extremities, headache, chest pains and fainting. Some find it brings an adrenalin rush or moment of clarity, and try to induce this state, though for most experiences hyperventilation or related breath problems, it is generally a frightening and unpleasant state, and can be induced by, or then induce, anxiety and panic. Though you are not deprived of oxygen, it does create a feeling of breathlessness. The classic "cure" for it is to breath into a paper bag, increasing the carbon dioxide levels, or to simply breathe through pursed lips, or close your mouth and one nostril, and breathe through the remaining nostril.

AIDS FOR BREATHWORK

The following can aid your exploration of breathwork:

Herbal Teas: Teas made from respiratory herbs, such as lobelia inflata, coltsfoot, mullein, horehound, elecampane, hyssop, thyme, licorice, plantain, and sage can greatly improve and heal the respiratory system, encouraging deeper and clearer breaths with less discomfort. Such teas can be taken as a tonic, with one to three cups a day for a few months to increase respiratory health. Consult a qualified herbalist to find a blend best for your own respiratory needs.

Herbal Tinctures: Herbal tinctures, formulas made in alcohol rather than water, can have a more immediate effect than an herbal tea, and many of the same respiratory herbs, in tincture form, have great benefit to the respiratory system. I have particularly found lobelia inflata tincture, just a drop or two, to aid when the lungs are congested and respiratory pathways are clogged. Larger dose of lobelia can result in vomiting. Like herbal teas, consult a qualified herbalist to suit your personal needs and condition.

Incense: While incense is generally discouraged if you are having any breathing difficulties, some herbs, when burned, promote respiratory health. Notably are coltsfoot and white sage. Use sparingly at first until you find how your own body and lungs react to them.

Essential Oil: Several essential oils are known to clear the respiratory passages when sniffed, including eucalyptus, cajeput, cedarwood, galbanum, helichrysum, sweet marjoram, and ravensara. Such oils are potent chemicals and should not be used without education or supervision, as many essential oils are considered dangerous to pregnant women, and toxic or caustic to the skin when not diluted properly.

Stones: The following stones have been used by crystal healers to aid with the health and well being of the respiratory system, or to specifically heal respiratory conditions such as asthma, bronchitis, emphysema, and pneumonia: Amethyst, Apopholite, Aventurine, Iolite, Pyrite, Lapis Lazuli, Rhodocrosite, Rhodonite and Turquoise. They can be held during breathing exercises to enhance the experience.

Grounding: While breathwork can energize and induce trance, a simple awareness of the breath in the body can return your attention to the physical world and consensus reality.

CHAPTER FOUR:
THE MYSTERY OF MUSIC

Music is a mystery. In every culture and in every time, music has arisen. It appears to be something that is needed in human consciousness. While we can think of it as a luxury, I believe music is a necessity, otherwise, why would it be such a dominant factor in human culture? Humans need music. It is one of the ways we consciously, and unconsciously, touch other realms of consciousness and expand our awareness.

I believe the first songs were spiritual. They were inspired by the shamans and seers visiting the otherworld. Their beats became their shamanic steeds to ride into the realm of spirit. Their words detailed their experiences with the gods and ancestors, creating the first myth cycles. They became the anthems to inspire the hunt and the harvest.

Since then, music has evolved in a variety of ways. We still have religious music, and in many ways organized religion has been the impetus of much of our music history. Religious institutions have been the patrons of great musical innovation. Music solely for entertainment, or for artistic expression, has diverged from the religious tract. Most popular music today is secular. Music has continued to influence our society, as a focus for gathering, social groups, and religion still. The power of music lends itself to the mysteries of magick as well.

Purposely or unconsciously, music sets a mood. Music alters our awareness. We respond differently when different types of music play, even when we don't think we are listening to it. Background music has an effect. Our society subliminally uses it for specific effects. Music in doctors' waiting rooms, elevators, department stores, bars, and restaurants alters your perception, granting patience, or inducing you to shop, eat, drink, or dance. When you are specifically focusing on the music, such as listening to an album, going to a show, or performing your self, the effect is even more pronounced. The music direct interacts even more profoundly with our consciousness and our physiology because our attention is directed towards it.

Music can be used in the same way in ritual, to induce altered states. Mood music sets the tone of the ritual, and fills in the silences where the mind of a novice could easily be distracted with outside sounds, or inner thoughts. When music is moved from the background to a major component of the ritual, then its power is even more potent. Rituals involving drumming, chanting and singing are particularly powerful, for they give the participants a directed focus, an exhibitory task to induce new states of awareness. They raise a tremendous amount of energy and become a common element to focus a larger group and coalesce a group consciousness. They are particularly great for public rituals with participants of various levels of experience and training.

Music can temporarily short-circuit the rational mind. Flooding the senses, you have no time or space within your consciousness to question the experience, formulate doubts, or intellectually analyze. All of that is helpful after the experience, but too much analysis during the experience can inhibit it. For people who are very rational, logical, or simply skeptical about magickal reality, exhibitory techniques, or other long and involved sensory or detailed oriented practices, are best to induce trance. I know by my very nature I'm a skeptic and I like to analyze. Magickal training helps you put that part of yourself aside until the appropriate time, like using the right tool for the right job. Music can help us access the appropriate internal tool.

INSTRUMENTAL MUSIC

Instrumental music, with sounds created from a tool, is an excellent aid to ritual. Instrumentation leads to a variety of timbres and qualities of sound, mixed with the tones of melody, rhythm and volume, to create a magickal mood, and move the mood along through changes in the music. A ritual can start mellow and meditative with the quiet sounds of chimes, harp, or woodwinds, and build to the furious force of a full symphony, bringing the ritual listeners into the depths of the otherworld to face their greatest fears. Then the music can lead you out once again.

Recorded Music

We live in a blessed age in terms of our choices for ritual music, and our methods for delivering it. While we always have the option of live music, we don't always have access to musicians who are also interested in the rituals of Paganism. We can love music in our rituals, but be a solitary practitioner. Having a harp player in your bedroom on the full Moon would be rather strange. Though I know many solitaries who have enhanced their ritual experience through the use of music. They used recorded music. Usually the music is for background mood, but it's interesting to watch how often the background can dominate the theme and temperament of the ritual.

Today we have a wide range of recorded music delivery systems. We have antiquated vinyl records, and even now cassettes are a thing of the past, as well as digital music through compact discs and MP3 files. Portable players, laptop computers, and MP3 players such as iPods all make our music available at the touch of a button. Electronic media allows you to create play list and even time your ritual to the music you are using, or easily "rewind" to the start of a track or "skip" to the end if you need to do so to change the mood of your ritual.

Where your ritual takes place, who is with you, (if anyone), and what kind of ritual magick you will be doing, can determine both your selection of music and your delivery system. Your ritual space might be equipped with a sound system these days. I was taught that when you perform circle magick, meaning you are casting a circle to contain the energy, you were ideally to have no wire crossing in or out of the circle. The wire would disrupt the flow of energy and leave a "hole" in the container. So either your music was on a portable device inside the circle, battery operated, or outside of the circle and untouched after the ritual began, if plugged into the wall. Though there are ways around this, and many Witches disagree as to how important this "rule" is, I've always tried to follow it and found my magick circle rituals to be better when I didn't have a wire crossing the circle. Now I use a battery-operated iPod speaker mount. You can find that electricity operates rather funny in a magick circle, much like temperature. Batteries can lose their charge easily, or seemingly never get drained in the circle. Tracks will mysteriously skip, yet often land on the perfect bit of music for that part of the ritual.

Here are some ideas of musical selections and genres to inspire your own ritual music. Some are strictly instrumental, while others include vocals, but for the purposes of this chapter, we are dividing music for ritual between the music you play and the music you sing yourself. So the music player is being seen, in a sense, as an instrument or tool.

Gregorian Chant: Perhaps it's the lapsed Catholic in me, but I find something dark and witchy about old medieval chants, and in particular Gregorian Chant. While we often harken to the Neopagan tribal idea of a Witch as Stone Age mother-goddess worshipping shaman, there is still power and magick in the dark medieval archetype of the Witch from the Burning Times. While Gregorian Chant is obviously not a part of Witchcraft, there is something quite moving about it. For a short while, the New Age and World music scene was dominated by amalgams of Gregorian Chant interspersed with techno dance beats and ambient sounds.

Classical Music: Like Gregorian Chant, there is nothing inherently Pagan about classical music, as much of it was written in the Christian era and often has Christian inspirations, yet many of the European Pagan esthetics ended up in classical music. Even without the Pagan view, there is drama and power in it, making it perfect for ritual drama. Sometimes the references are obvious. Much of Wagner's work, particularly *Flight of the Valkyries*, is clearly Pagan. I'm also partial to *Night on Bald Mountain* by Modest Petrovich Mussorgsky from my favorite Disney *Fantasia* movie experience. Almost anything from *Fantasia* would be appropriate. *The Danse Macabre* by Camille Saint-Saëns. is another favorite, and I'm also partial to the modern classical composer Igor Stravinsky, with *The Rites of Spring* for rituals in the waxing year and *Firebird Suite* for those in the waning year.

World Music: World music is a popularly growing genre showcasing musical stylings and traditions from cultures across the world and a variety of time periods. Depending on the culture drawn upon, the music could have a tribal flair, or pertain to a particular pantheon or time period that is appropriate for your magick. Loreena McKennitt's work is generally considered world music, with Celtic, Middle Eastern, and New Age themes. She is a favorite amongst many modern Witches.

Ambient: Ambient music can be listened to on a number of levels, and can be actively listened to, or easily ignored. The term was coined by Brian Eno. Some consider it simply "mood music." It can be a combination of traditional instrumentation and electronic music.

Celtic: Traditional Celtic music, from folks songs to Celtic harp or other instrumentations , is used in Celtic inspired rituals. Technically the folk music of any culture can be used in rituals influenced by that culture, but the Celtic revival of the last few decades has made the availability of Celtic inspired music easier.

Neopagan: As a new sub-culture, Neopaganism is creating its own music, for both entertainment and ritual, and the line between the two is not always meant to be clear. Neopagan music is typically trance inducing, or at least magickally inspired, and can range from strong drumming tracks to chants and folk songs. Some of it is very modern, while others try to emulate our old world traditional roots. Artists such as Wendy Rule and Frenchy and the Punk are well known in the Neopagan music world. The Witchcraft tradition known as The Reclaiming, based out of the San Francisco Bay area, has made a number of recordings of their chants. I've also composed chants can be heard on *The Outer Temple of Witchcraft CD Companion.*

Dance: While dance music doesn't seem particularly appropriate for a Witch's ritual, I know many Witches and magicians who make a ritual out of a night of dancing. Techno dance music is considered very shamanic by modern practitioners. The pace and rhythms of modern dance music (see **Percussion** following) from disco to the most recent electronica emulate much of our tribal traditions in a new way. A constant rhythmic beat with repeated short melody can be very trance inducing. Although an experience at a club, party, or rave certainly doesn't make you a Witch or shaman, such experiences can be similar to rituals, and we can draw such music into a ritual setting.

Goth: Goth music is another wide range of recordings, usually created by those in the Goth sub culture and marked by a darker or gloomy edge. Some are dance music, but often not of an overtly sexual nature as other forms of dance music, and other times it leans more towards the Neopagan or ambient spectrum, still with this gothic sensibility. While the music of Dead Can Dance is hard to classify, it is often a favorite amongst the Gothic and Pagan subcultures.

New Age: Most music available at metaphysical stores today is classified as New Age music. While everybody knows it when they hear it, it's hard to describe because is covers a wide range of styles. It draws on themes found in ambient and world music, can be either electronic, organic, or a combination of the two, and have influences of cultures considered to influence the New Age, particularly Native American and Celtic, though purists of both will tell you that such New Age renditions are only copying a stereotypical "feel" that is not an accurate portrayal of their cultural music. Sometimes the music includes or is made up of exclusively of nature sounds, including flowing water, animal noises, or other environmental sounds. One of the most popular New Age artists to influence Neopagan circle is Enya, with her slow, moody, relaxing Celtic inspired tracks.

Soundtracks: Movie and television soundtracks select music on the basis of setting an appropriate mood. Programs suitable to the mood of your ritual might have appropriate music already selected. Movies with Pagan, magick, horror, or gothic themes can be quite effective when their soundtracks become the backdrop for ritual.

Popular Music: Any music that sets the mood for you can be used in ritual. I've spoken to a number of experienced practitioners to see what music they have used, and gotten responses including the music of Mannheim Steamroller, Stevie Nicks, Fleetwood Mac, Tori Amos, Alice In Chains and Smashing Pumpkins, to name a few.

Percussion

Our first musical instruments were most likely ritual objects. Drums, rattles, bells, chimes, and other percussive instruments used by indigenous tribal cultures all across the globe that still have an active shamanic tradition. Banging on an object to create rhythm and tone is the simplest musical tool. They are also the simplest instrument to play. Although percussion is an art form in itself, almost everybody has the ability to hit or shake something. It doesn't require a specially developed skill to be functional, as much as an instrument such as the violin or tuba would. You can start right away and have good results, though it can take quite a while to develop the rhythm and style of a true musician.

Drums: Most traditional shamanic drums are made from the wood the tradition or tribe identifies with the world tree. The world tree is the great cosmic axis, envisioned as a tree that maintains the structure of the other worlds in relationship to our physical world. Generally they are described as an upper world in the heavens, a middle world of time, space, seasons, and humanity, and a lower world of powerful and dark initiatory forces, as well as the ancestors. The tree is like a ladder connecting these three worlds. While the Norse called the World Tree Yggdrasil and thought it to be an ash or yew (needle ash) tree, other cultures saw it as other types of tree. The Druids possibly thought of it as an oak. Some Italian traditions might have used the walnut tree. Localized traditions ascribe a local tree. By hitting an instrument made from the same wood, you are resonating with the powers of the tree. The skin of the drum is traditionally made from an animal of power, usually four-hoofed animal, as the drum is said to evoke the shamanic "steed" by which the shaman travels to the other world. The beat is the gallop of the hooves. Today, many modern drums are made with synthetic materials, including a synthetic head. The head can be decorated with power symbols and images of you're your shamanic animal allies. Hand held shamanic style drums can be round or, if not round, usually octagonal. They use a stick with a single padded head. Celtic drums, known as bodhrans, use a double stick, known as a tipper, where both ends are used to strike the drum. Other forms of drums used in Neopagan rituals include the African Djembes and Congas.

Rattles: Hollow objects, such as dried gourds or hollow animal horns can be filled with small pebbles or grains, sealed, and used as a rattle. Animal rattles relate to the animal spirit associated with it, while plant rattles evoke the power of the plant world. Synthetic shakers and rattles are also available for their sound only. My own rattle is a hollowed cattle horn, like a drinking horn, filled with dried maize with a cloth covering over the mouth tied with a cord and fixed with a liberal amount of glue.

Bells, Chimes, and Bowls: While drums and rattles are more prevalent, other instruments in the same vein are often metallic. Percussive yet melodious sounds can be produced from bells and chimes. The bell is used in Witchcraft rituals, usually to clear the space of unwanted energy, much like a sonic equivalent to sage, or saltwater sprinkling, or to return the consciousness back to an alert and aware state. They can be used repeatedly like a rattle as well. Bowls, constructed of metal or crystal, like the Tibetan Singing Bowls and Quartz Crystal bowls, can be struck repetitively to create a rhythm, but more often they are stroked with a wooded stick around the edges, to cause them to vibrate in a pulsating rhythm and a series of overtones. While they are not percussive instruments in the traditional sense, the patterns they create are quite like the patterns created by drumming and rattling.

Nature Sounds: Some percussive instruments emulate the sounds of nature. Rain sticks, now easily available, produce a rain-like sound to help induce trance, even though it is not oriented toward a beat. Another popular item, a wooden block, often carved in the shape of a frog, with a ridged back, and a wooded stick, emulates the croaking of a frog, and is used to induce trance. One Witchcraft teacher I know suggested Witches and shamans use the sounds of the swamp as their music, and this was an attempt to capture that with an instrument.

The simple benefit of percussive instruments, and in particular the drum, is the change in consciousness they create. While most people think that to do meditative work the drum beat must be mellow and gentle, shamanic traditions across the world have one thing in common when it comes to drumming. While the cultural context, rhythms, and symbols are different, the most common timing is roughly twice the relaxed human heart beat. Shamanic drumming usually ranges in the 140 to 250 beat per minute, and this rhythm entrains the brainwaves down from beta to alpha and even theta, to alter consciousness. 210-220 seems to be ideal for most people, and a duration of about fifteen minutes yields the most results, and typically no more than thirty minutes, or exhaustion sets in and the practitioner's attention wanders. In many shamanic traditions, the rhythm changes to over 350 beat per minute, sometimes in an erratic manner, or lapses into a much slower erratic beat, to return the journeying practitioner back to normal waking consciousness.

In the practice of shamanism, the shaman "journeys" to the otherworld, usually envisioning the image of the world tree to climb to the heavens or descend down through the roots, and communes with the gods and spirits. The beat is like a galloping steed, or the overtones of the sound act like "waves," pushing the journeying into deeper levels of consciousness. I've had some students describe it like surfing when I've told them to "ride the wave."

It is a manner of free form pathworking, without much in the way of suggested visions. The tree works as a key to tap into a pattern used by shamans for centuries, and encoded in much of our myth and folklore. Shamanic journeys are most likely the source of our more complex spiritual wisdom that gave us method of pathworking, methods to follow a shaman back to a specific "place" in the otherworld, using the guidance of the same mythic symbols. Trance work with percussion brings us back to the primal mysteries of magick and consciousness exploration. Through percussion, we tap into a technique stretching back to the dawn of our civilization, and used by humans continuously since then, even as our cultures have grown and developed.

Exercise: Shamanic Journey

Prepare yourself and your space by cleansing the area with a purifying incense. You can perform a ceremony to establish sacred space, such as the Witch's circle (see **Chapter Fourteen**) or simply honoring the four directions and the spaces above, below, and center.

The shamanic position most popular in modern core shamanism is laying flat on your back. Some emphasize the palms should be up, in the Hindu Position of the Corpse, Savasana, while other practitioners place no emphasis on the arms or hands.

Either via a recording, or having someone play for your live, listen to a rhythmic beat on a drum or rattle at approximately 220 bpm. I believe it's helpful to start the drum slower, and with a bit of a guided meditation as a "launch" into the spirit world when the drum speeds up. I start with the initial visuals of the World Tree from the Visiting the Inner Temple exercise.

Feel the steady beat of the drum "push" you into the tunnels of the world tree, carrying you up, down or through. You might feel like the beat is a steed, like riding a horse, or other animal, or the overtones are like a wave, and you are riding the crest of the wave into the other worlds.

Eventually the tunnel of the world tree lets out into some otherworld space. Explore your surroundings. What do you perceive? If you have never done shamanic journey before, the typical first step is to seek out an animal spirit ally. You will encounter one animal spirit either in three or four "flashes" of awareness, or hold a steady sense of presence from the animal friendly towards you. You can ask to befriend this creature and it may agree to be your spirit ally. If you have worked with spirits and deities before, you could encounter these allies while on the journey, or find new ones.

At the end of the predetermined time set between you and your musician, or the recording (usually fifteen minutes and no more than thirty) a callback is played. The rhythm will change to an erratic pattern of roughly 350 bpm, signaling it's time to come back to the physical world.

Follow the path that allowed you entry, retracing your steps, unless a trusted spirit ally guides you out another way.

Exit the tree and ground yourself. Open your eyes and return to the physical world.

While the image of the World Tree is most prevalent in Witchcraft and shamanic traditions, some myths have the image of a great mountain, tower, or ladder, which can also be used to travel the otherworlds. If a different image comes to you at the start of your journey, use whatever works best for you.

While it is possible to drum or rattle for yourself and journey, it's not recommended for beginner or even intermediate students. It can be quite difficult to give both tasks the necessary attention to be successful. Though I've been able to drum and journey at the same time, I much prefer another to drum when I need to journey, or the value of a recording to guide us all.

Most shamanic traditions and shamanic practitioners have an animist worldview, meaning they believe everything has a spirit, and magick is often building a relationship with the spirits to aid you, and you must in turn aid them. While most spirits exist beyond the physical realm, many of our allies are the spirits of our "tools" inhabiting and animating the spiritual power objects we use in magick and healing.

One of the first embodied allies found in a power object is the spirit of your musical instrument, your drum, rattle, or any other instrument you use. Traditionally it is the drum or rattle that is "woken" up and empowered. Regular offerings are made to it, to maintain its energy and link with you.

The following exercise is excellent if you are seeking to empower your drum for the first time, and can be used on any instrument or tool before you start using it.

Exercise: Empowering the Spirit of your Instrument

Hold your instrument in your hands before you lay down. You are not using this musical instrument to journey this time. You are using some other method of sound to journey. The instrument you are empowering must be still when you begin this exercise.

Repeat the Shamanic Journey exercise described above, but hold the intention of "awakening" or "capturing" the spirit of your drum or rattle.

Ride the drumbeat while holding your intention, and you will find yourself led to a special place. Sometimes you will feel you are being lead to a time in the past when the "life" of your instrument, or the materials used to make it, was taken. It might be when and where the slaughtering of the animal to make the hide or horn took place, or when the wood was cut or the gourd was picked. At that moment, commune with the spirit, and ask it to empower your instrument. Make a pact to honor it if it will help you to travel, and bring others, to the spirit world. Perceive the spirit entering the instrument in your hands, if it has agreed to help you. If the spirit has not agreed, end your journey and try it again at a later date, to find a different spirit who does agree and want to work with you.

Return as you normally would from the journey. Feel your instrument. Feel its difference from when you began. Thank the spirit. Give it an offering. Different traditions make different kinds of offerings. Flour, corn meal, bread, wine, beer, mead, honey, bread, and tobacco are all forms of offerings. If appropriate, sprinkle some on your instrument. Do this often, particularly before a ritual if possible, when you're going to use the instrument.

I make offerings of olive oil to my drum. The instructions that came with it when I purchased it from a craft dealer was to oil it regularly to prevent the skin from breaking. So I combine maintenance with offering, as oil is a sacred substance.

This process can be used to empower the broom, from the astral travel exercise in **Chapter Two**, or any other magickal tool.

While a simple, fast rhythm is best for most shamanic journey, it is not the only way to induce trance. Slower rhythms have their virtues as well. Slower rhythms may not necessarily be an exhibitory trance technique for profound vision of the spirit world, but they can calm the body, bringing tranquility and focus. A simple heart beat meditation, mimicking the "lub-lub" of the heart, at roughly 70 beat per minute, or even slower, can tranquilize and heal. This is considered the beat of the Mother in many traditions, mimicking the sound we hear when we're in the womb, our own mother's heartbeat.

For those with a more intricate understanding of music, a discussion of time signature can be most helpful. Time signatures are a tool used by musicians to notate rhythm. This signature is expressed as a fraction. The upper number, the numerator of the fraction, is the number of beats in a measure of music. A measure is a way to organize the music. If you are going to count, to keep on rhythm, where would you begin the count again? That is the start of a new measure. The bottom number, or denominator of the fraction, tells you what kind of note gets a beat. It appears at the start of a piece of music, after what is known as the cleft, to tell you the range of the instrument, and the key signature.

The most familiar signature is 4/4. It means that there are four beats per measure, and a quarter note, 4 for the quarter, is what is given a beat in the measure. So music in a 4/4 time signature would be counted **1**-2-3-4-**1**-2-3-4-**1**... etc. The strong beat usually comes down on the first beat of a measure, though different styles of music can change that. Most rock music is in 4/4, but the emphasis is on the second and fourth beat. If you listen to something with a strong rock drum beat, you will naturally count it as 1-**2**-3-**4**-1-**2**-3-**4**-1-**2**... The two is slightly stronger than the four.

In the 3/4 signature, three beats are in a measure, while the quarter note, four, still gets the value of one beat. The waltz is a common piece for the 3/4 signature. **1**-2-3-**1**-2-3-**1**-2-3... Other common signatures are 2/4, 6/8, and 12/8.

While there is no one easily agreed upon series of magickal correspondences for music, some systems associate time signatures with particular magickal correspondences. Music in these time signatures is more conducive to magick in harmony with these associations.

Signature	Elemental Association	Qualities and Uses
4/4	Earth	Grounded, solid, general trance purposes
3/4	Air	Stimulating mind, memories, expression
6/8	Water	Emotional healing, flow, feeling
9/8	Fire	Energy, inspiration, creativity, power

Fig. 9: Time Signature Correspondences

Exercise: Time Signature Exploration

Either with your own drum, or having someone with a steady hand drum for you, listen to rhythms in this various time signatures. Listen to each one for as little as five minutes and as much as ten or twenty. What type of feelings does it evoke in you? What type of ritual does it suggest? If you find associations different from the ones listed here, use what works best for you, and makes the most sense to your own internal rhythms. Explore different tempos to see they make a difference. Notate your experience for future reference and repeat, seeing if the same rhythms evoke the same sensations each time.

Tuned Instruments

Tuned instruments are also quite powerful in our magickal rituals. Like percussive instruments, our first tuned musical instruments most likely have a magickal origin. Many ancient myths cite the gods as the sources of instruments. Pan is said to be the creator of the pan flute, naturally. The seven reeds making not only the seven notes of a traditional sale, but an allegory for the seven notes emitted by the seven planets, the wandering stars creating the "music of the spheres." The Greek lyre, a harp-like stringed instrument, made from the shell of a tortoise, is usually attributed to Hermes, who then gave it to his brother Apollo, trading it for the caduceus. Apollo is patron of music and poetry. From these two myths we have the birth of the family of woodwinds and stringed instruments, (with the rise of brass not coming until later in human development.)

Unlike percussion instruments, where you can make a sound with little or no training, tuned instruments require more knowledge and skill. Though some melodic instruments are also considered percussions, such as the xylophone and piano, they too require knowledge and skill. Some are relatively simple. You can blow through a woodwind, pluck a string and hit a note on a keyboard, but it still takes skill to use them.

Training in any musical instrument is beyond the scope of this book, but if you have knowledge in a tuned instrument, or music in general, you can apply these magickal ideas to your playing and appreciation of music.

To many ancient mystics, the heavens emanated a sound, the music of the spheres. This music was said to correspond to the patterns of the Earth, and in the proportion of not only music, but light, geometry, nature, and even time itself, we could come closer to the heavens. In the west, music was organized around the concept of seven note scales. Sound itself is divided into a twelve-tone scale, a series of half step increments as you play the ascending scale. If you look at a piano, an octave has twelve notes with seven white keys and five black keys before repeating. The simplest scale, the major scale, consists of the seven white notes and sounds cheery and bright until it reaches its octave, the first note in the next set. By altering the notes in the seven-fold pattern, you create various scales with different moods, flavors, and magickal correspondences. You can find the influence of modes giving particular styles of music their flavor. They are basically divided into modes similar to the major scale and those similar to minor scale. Various philosophers and musicians have put forth their own ideas as to how the modes of music influence consciousness.

The modes, or at least their study, originated in Greece, for they are named after ancient Greek subgroups or regions that used them frequently. The modes prevalent in the music of a culture are said to influence that culture. Though their influence has been limited in classical music, they enjoyed a resurgence in modern use through jazz, impressionism, guitar-based rock music and other trends in the twentieth century.

Ionian
Standard Major Scale

Planet: Sun

Most of us are familiar with music played on the major scale. It evokes a presence of clarity, brightness and general happiness. It's used in children's tunes, and brings the power of health, friendship, and good will.

Lydian
Major Scale with raised 4th

Planet: Mars

While occult lore gives Lydian music associations with raising energy or venting any anger or frustrations, classical musical lore describes it as "happy." It is bright and fiery and, depending on the composition, can drive forward your will and intention.

Myxolydian
Major Scale with a lowered 7th

Planet: Jupiter

Classical musical lore describes it as angelic, uniting the feelings of pleasure and sadness in the music. The Greeks used this mode in the worship of Dionysus, as it's said to induce divine ecstasy in those who hear it. It is also used for traditional Jupiter associations, such as wealth, increase, and good fortune.

Locrian
Neither Major nor Minor

Planet: Mercury

The strange Locrian mode has the dreaded dissonant interval known as the tritone, or diminished fifth, made popular in the modern psyche by the theme song of *The Simpsons* cartoon. The Church forbade the use of the interval in liturgical music, considering it the Devil's. It does have a truly strange sound to it, and I've found most Witches like it. It's rare to have music played solely in this scale, but it is a very effective and powerful magickal tool, used to do all forms of magick: open portals to the spirit world and perform magick of invisibility, psychic development, necromancy and spirit summoning.

Aeolian

Natural Minor Scale

Planet: Moon

Traditional musical associations paint the natural minor scale as "sad" or "dark" particularly when compared to the more well known Major (Ionian) scale. In magick, it is calming, soothing, and cooling to the mood and temperament. It opens you to the power of the soul and the touch of the Goddess.

Dorian

Minor Scale with a raised 7th

Planet: Saturn

The Dorian scale is said to be serious and to tame the passions, though it's also used in lot of folk music. It's also found in both Gregorian chant and the chants of many Witches' covens. It's was one of the first modes I began experimenting with while earning my degree in music, and the compositions always took on an occult tone. The magick of the Dorian scale is to evoke a sense of timelessness and antiquity.

Phrygian

Minor Scale with a lowered 2nd

Planet: Venus

In musical lore, Phrygian is considered mystical in terms of the atmosphere it evokes and, strangely for its occult associations with Venus, considered the scale to incite anger. Perhaps it's not anger so much as passion or jealousy, for the sensuality of the scale can be heard in Gypsy flamenco music, as well as Arabic and Hindu music, making their way into American pop music via the 1960s psychedelia.

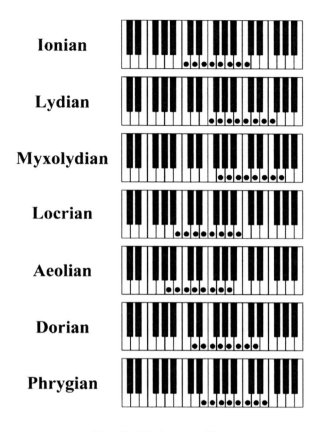

Fig. 10: Modes on a Piano

Certain notes, and thereby the keys to which they are the tonic—or root note of—are said to be influenced by a particular heavenly body. Such lore is a combination of ancient principles, magickal patterns, and speculative science, there is no universal system of musical/magickal correspondences, at least note by note. One of the problems for this is our current musical notation system is not the same as in the ancient world, or even amongst the earliest classical composers. Our measurement of what middle C on the piano is has been standardized, but the standard in the past was not the same. The note A beneath the middle C on the piano is considered 440 htz, though that was not always the case throughout history, adding to the confusion of musical correspondences.

Here are some associations I've found helpful in my own practice:

Notes	Chakra	Planet	Zodiac Sign–Planet
C	Root	Moon/Saturn	Aries–Mars
C#			Taurus–Venus
D	Belly	Mercury/Jupiter	Gemini–Mercury
D#			Cancer–Moon
E	Solar Plexus	Venus/Mars	Leo–Sun
F	Heart	Sun, Earth/Venus	Virgo–Mercury
F#		Mars	Libra–Venus
G	Throat	Jupiter/Mercury	Scorpio–Mars/Pluto
G#		Uranus	Sagittarius–Jupiter
A	Brow	Saturn/Moon	Capricorn–Saturn
A#		Neptune, Uranus	Aquarius–Saturn/Uranus
B	Crown	Pluto, Uranus/Sun	Pisces–Jupiter/Pisces

Fig. 11: Musical Note Correspondence

By playing that note, or a piece of music in the key of that note, you are helping to invoke that planetary power. You can combine the modes, with planetary associations, with particular keys, to emphasize more than one planetary power. If you play the Ionian mode to invoke the Sun, but play C Ionian, the C brings the influence of the Moon, Saturn, or Aries.

Some magicians associate particular instruments to the elements, believing each family of instruments evokes certain associations. People who are attracted to those instruments are working in part with those elemental forces. While I think any instrument with a wide enough range and flexibility in style can embody more than one element, general wisdom associates the following instruments with the elements:

Earth	drums and percussion of all kinds, low toned instruments such as the bass
Water	strings (violin, cello, viola), harp
Air	woodwinds, high pitches instruments
Fire	brass, electric guitar
Spirit	keyboard instruments, harp

VOCAL MUSIC

Unlike tuned instruments, vocal music is a method to create melody that anybody can do. You might doubt your ability, but I spent a while as a part time vocal coach, and found very few people are truly tone deaf. They may not be comfortable with their voice, lack finesse or control, but they can, with some practice, carry a simple tune. Others are naturally gifted and confident, and can belt out a melodic tune with the best of them. Even those who don't feel comfortable singing in ritual can find ways of using voice to empower their magick. As long as you can speak aloud, you can find a way to use your voice to open the gates.

Toning: Toning is a simple technique of making whatever tone, whatever sound, you intuitively feel is appropriate at the time. Toning is usually used for release and clearing. Healers will tone, or have their client tone, a sound, intuiting the sound that will break up the illness in the body. Toning can clear the energy of a space, much like a sonic form of sage or other incense, and it can to be used to transfer energy for any other purpose. It's a very primal form of vocalization, ranging from a simple harmoniously sustained note, to a more unbalanced, unfocused sound. Sometimes the noises created mimic sounds in nature.

Vowel Sounds: Vowel sounding is toning exclusively made from the various vowel sounds of human language. Sometimes these sounds are combined with various consonants to create something akin to a primal magickal word. The planets, as well as the elements have each been associated with a vowel sound, and such sounds can be used in ritual practices to evoke their energy, or to awaken all the powers within you by doing them in sequence.

Planet	Vowel Sound
Moon	A (ah)
Mercury	E (eh)
Venus	A (ay)
Sun	I (ee)
Mars	O (oh)
Jupiter	Y (ü)
Saturn	O (oo)

Fig. 12: Planet Vowel Correspondence

Exercise: Planetary Vowels

Chant the vowel sounds in a planetary sequence. The sequence listed is Qabalistic, starting with the lowest "planet" on the Tree of Life, the Moon, and rising through the Tree to Saturn. You can use this sequence ascending or descending. If you learned to work with the planets in a different order, feel free to use that sequence. Sustain each vowel on one breath, for a total of seven breaths. How do you feel during each sound, and how do you feel at the end? When you change the sequence, do you feel different?

For the elements, I have created a system of invocation and banishing based upon the elemental pentagrams. Originally inspired by R.J. Stewart's four-fold elemental calls found in his book, *The Spiritual Dimensions of Music*. My own calls use the five vowel sounds I associate with the elements. By placing them on the classic Western magick pentagram of the elements, they can be transformed into calls and releases. Magicians and Witches have specific ways of drawing the pentagram to open up to a particular elemental force, or to close down to it and banish it. They are used at the beginning and end of circle rituals.

By toning the vowel associated with the point you are drawing towards, you create a specific call to that element when following an invoking pattern, and a specific sonic release when following the pattern of a banishing pentagram. While I first composed them, I intended each to be done on one extended breath and a single note. The complexity of the calls can be increased by assigning a note from the first given notes of the major scale (Ionian Mode) to each element. If you are familiar with the invoking/banishing pentagrams already, the patterns are easier to understand. Those unfamiliar with such pentagrams might need more time to learn the patterns, vowels and notes to have an effective system.

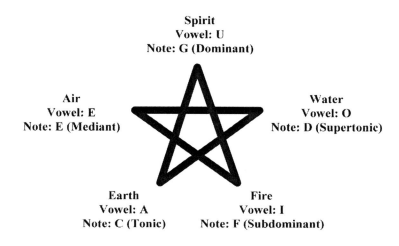

Spirit
Vowel: U
Note: G (Dominant)

Air
Vowel: E
Note: E (Mediant)

Water
Vowel: O
Note: D (Supertonic)

Earth
Vowel: A
Note: C (Tonic)

Fire
Vowel: I
Note: F (Subdominant)

Fig. 13: Elemental Pentagram with Vowel Sounds and Notes

Vowel	Element	Note (C scale)
U	Spirit	G
I	Fire	F
E	Air	E
O	Water	D
A	Earth	C

Pentagram	Vowel Sounds	Notes
Invoking Pentagram of Earth	A-O-E-I-U	C-D-E-F-G
Banishing Pentagram of Earth	U-I-E-O-A	G-F-E-D-C
Invoking Pentagram of Water	O-A-U-I-E	D-C-G-F-E
Banishing Pentagram of Water	E-I-U-A-O	E-F-G-C-D
Invoking Pentagram of Air	E-I-U-A-O	E-F-G-C-D
Banishing Pentagram of Air	O-A-U-I-E	D-C-G-F-D
Invoking Pentagram of Fire	A-O-E-I-U	C-D-E-F-G
Banishing Pentagram of Fire	U-I-E-O-A	G-F-E-D-C
Invoking Pentagram of Active Spirit	E-O-A-U-I	E-D-C-G-F
Banishing Pentagram of Active Spirit	I-U-A-O-E	F-G-C-D-E
Invoking Pentagram of Passive Spirit	O-E-I-U-A	D-E-F-G-C

Banishing Pentagram of Passive Spirit   A-U-I-E-O   C-G-F-E-D

Notice in this system, some note patterns repeat, just as some pentagrams are repeated, and are only differentiated by the intention of the type of element you are trying to summon are banish. Clear intention in their use is what truly makes these calls effective. I use the calls and banishments in ritual and as a focus for trance when I want to work with one elemental realm specifically.

Ritual magician Gareth Knight, in his book *The Rose Cross and the Goddess,* has an entirely different system and set of associations with ritual music tones. Also based in terms of intervals rather than specific keys, he associates the root note of a key with the east and air, the minor third with the south and fire, the fifth with the west and water and the north and earth element with the minor seventh. In the key of C, the notes are C, Eb, G and Bb. Ritual patterns, using chimes, bells or toning are created, starting in the east.

E – S- W – N – E	C – Eb – G – Bb- C	Building the Circle, Raising Power
E – N – W- S – E	C – Bb – G – Eb – C	Releasing the Circle, Powering Down
E – W – N – S – C	C – G – Bb – Eb – C	Energy flow of the Crossed Circle

Mantras: Mantras refer to verbal formulas used to induce different states of consciousness and effect the subtle energy bodies. Though the term comes from the Hindu traditions, variations and adoptions of material can be found in West. They are derived from the great sages and masters in deep meditation, and act as conduits, connecting us to that same level of divine consciousness. Each one has a different meaning, and reflects a different experience of the divine. They can be given, almost like a spiritual prescription, to facilitate a healthy change in a practitioner. Some are strictly devotional, to perfect the soul and merge with the divine. A mantra can be repeated silently as a meditation focus, or spoken or chanted out loud. Some, such as practitioners of Kundalini Yoga, believe that not only does the sound affect your consciousness, but when spoken aloud, the tongue strikes specific points on the palette and, like reflexology, sends energy in specific patterns through the energy system of the body. One of the most famous mantras comes from Buddhism and is quite popular in the New Age, "Om mani padme hum (usually pronounced Ohm mani pame hung)." It is usually translated as "Jewel in the Lotus" possibly referring to the chakras, but there are many interpretations, and it mostly likely is a name or title for the Bodhisattva of compassion, Avalokiteshvara. (The Dalai Lama is an incarnation of Avalokiteshvara.) Mantras from the east are sometimes used in a Neopagan context, but in an effort to find sounds that resonate more with Pagan culture and tradition, there has been a wide range of experimentation. Some use simple syllable sounds from ancient cultures, now associated with elements and planets. I like the modern New Age chant of El-Ka-Leem-Om-Ra for earth-fire-air-water-spirit. I particularly favor the seed syllable sounds for each of the chakras. Qabalistically influenced Witches use the Hebrew names of God associated with the planets and elements. By far the most Neopagan of mantras is using a single deity name, or a list of deity names as a mantra. The "Goddess Chant" of "Isis, Astarte, Diana, Hecate, Demeter, Kali, Inanna" is an excellent Witchcraft mantra for attuning to the power of the Great Mother, energy raising and altering consciousness for ritual and meditation.

Chakra Seed Syllables

Root	LAM
Belly	VAM
Solar Plexus	RAM
Heart	YAM
Throat	HAM
Brow	KSHAM (OM)
Crown	OM (None)

Elemental Syllables

Element	*Egyptian*	*Hindu*	*Tibetan*	*Thelemic*	*Modern*
Earth	Ta	Lam	A	Al	El
Water	Nu	Vam	Va	Nu	Om
Air	As	Pam	Ha	Ad	Leem
Fire	Am	Ram	Ra	Re	Ra (Ka)
Spirit	Sa	Ham	Kha	Ah	Ka (Ra)

Hebrew Names of God

Element	*Name*	*Translation*
Earth	Adonai ha Aretz	Lord of the Earth
Water	Elohim	Gods
Air	Shaddai el Chai	Almighty Living God or Living Mother God
Fire	Yod Heh Vehv Heh Tzabaoth	Lord of Hosts
Spirit	Eihehe	I Am, I Am that I Am

Planet	Name of God	Translation
Earth	Adonai Ha Aretz	Lord of the Earth
Moon	Shaddai El Chai	Almighty Living God or Living Mother God
Mercury	Elohim Tzabaoth	God of Hosts
Venus	YHVH Tzabaoth	Lord of Hosts
Sun	YHVH Eloah Va Daath	Lord God of Knowledge
Mars	Elohim Gibor	Gods of Strength, Gods of Power
Jupiter	El	God
Saturn	YHVH Elohim	Tetragrammaton Gods
Neptune	YHVH	Tetragrammaton
Pluto/Uranus	Eihehe	I Am, I Am that I Am

Exercise: Mantra Experiment

Choose a mantra from any of the systems above, and use it as a meditation focus. Situate yourself just as you did for the Candle Meditation, but rather than stare at the candle, close your eyes and repeat the mantra out loud. Eastern traditions use prayer beads known as *mala* beads, usually one hundred and eight smaller beads with one larger "count" bead. Every time a mantra is said, you finger another bead until you reach the end, keeping count without actually having to count. Witchcraft traditions sometimes use a tool known as a Witch's ladder, a knotted cord.

Exercise: Witch's Ladder

Braid three cords together, using colors that are significant to you (See **Chapter Three**). Popular combinations include the colors white, red, and black for the maiden, mother, and crone, or red, blue, and yellow, for the three primary rays found in the Theosophical traditions. For basic meditation purposes I suggest choosing a number that is significant to you. (I outline a variation for a nineteen month course of study in *The Living Temple of Witchcraft*.) Witch's Ladders are done in sets of nine, thirteen, twenty-eight, thirty three, or forty knots, with forty being the most traditional in older forms of Witchcraft. Use your knots like a rosary or set of mala beads, to keep track of your mantra, chants and other repeated prayers while meditating or doing spell work. It can be used for out loud verbalization, inner silent "chanting" or even to count your breaths.

Exercise: Kundalini Mantra

One of my personal favorite mantras from the eastern traditions is found in the Sikh tradition of Kundalini Yoga. Known as the Shakti Mantra, it is said to tune one into the Divine Mother. Its power is generative and creative, protects the users and fulfills your desires with the primal power of the Goddess. I learned this particular mantra as a call and response, with each line called out by a chant leader or recording, and then repeated by the group.

ADI SHAKTI,
ADI SHAKTI,
ADI SHAKTI,
NAMO NAMO,
SARAB SHAKTI,
SARAB SHAKTI,
SARAB SHAKTI,
NAMO NAMO,
PRITHUM BHAGAWATI
PRITHUM BHAGAWATI,
PRITHUM BHAGAWATI,
NAMO NAMO,
KUNDALINI, MATA SHAKTI,
KUNDALINI, MATA SHAKTI,
NAMO NAMO.

Audible Prayer: Audible prayer, speaking your intentions out loud to the divine, is a powerful and simple way of using sound to change your reality. While we often look for formalized techniques and procedures, the simple, heartfelt conversation with the divine can be the most transformative. You can ritualize your prayers as much or as little as you want. Many traditions believe incense or candle flame take the prayers to the gods more easily, so lighting either or both can help set the mood and intention of the prayer, but are not necessary.

Runic Chant: One can chant the sequence of runes, the names associated with the symbolic mysteries of the Northern Tradition, from either the Elder Futhark or Younger Futhark. The whole sequence can be used to hallow space, raise energy and induce trance, or specific sequences based upon the magickal properties chosen by the practitioner for the intention of the trance. Below is the Elder Futhark sequence.

Fehu, Uruz, Thurisaz, Ansuz, Raido, Kenaz, Gebo, Wunjo

Hagalaz, Nauthiz, Isa, Jera, Eihwaz, Pertho, Algiz, Sowilo

Tiwaz, Berkano, Ehwaz, Mannaz, Laguz, Ingwaz, Dagaz, Othila

Spoken Charm: like a prayer, intentions can be spoken, and are often spoken in rhyme to manifest their desire. The spoken charm both induces trance to open the gates and becomes the magickal focus to speak a thing into being. In the full Wiccan Rede, it says, "To bind the spell every time, let the spell be spake in rhyme." Many Witches believe the recipes, the style of which is possibly preserved in writings of Shakespeare, were mnemonic devices to remember what to do, codes to disguise the herbs used as animal parts and charms that add rhythmic verses when spoken aloud, to induce trance to empower the brew.

> *"Eye of newt, and toe of frog,*
> *Wool of bat, and tongue of dog,*
> *Adder's fork, and blind-worm's sting,*
> *Lizard's leg, and howlet's wing,*
> *For a charm of powerful trouble,*
> *Like a hell-broth boil and bubble.*
> *"Double, double, toil and trouble;*
> *Fire, burn; and caldron, bubble."*
> – Macbeth

Modern and old traditions of Witchcraft use spoken verse to create change. While you can find many examples of it in modern spell books, one of the most interesting ones comes from famous Scottish Witch Isobel Gowdie, who gave a detailed and unprompted confession of her practices and coven. She used the following to shapeshift (see **Chapters Five** and **Twelve**) into a hare or borrow a hare's form and turn back again. Note the mention of the "Devil's Name" is indicative of the Christian time period in which Isobel Gowdie lived, and such magick can be adapted by modern Pagans to reflect their own theological worldview without the concept of the Devil.

Hare Transformation

> *I shall go into a hare,*
> *With sorrow and sych (such) and meickle(great) care;*
> *And I shall go in the Devil's name,*
> *Ay while I come home again.*

Reverse Hare Transformation

Hare, hare, God send thee care.

I am in a hare's likeness now,

But I shall be in a woman's likeness even now.

Ritual Prose: The poetry of ritual has it own meter and rhythm that is conducive to trance. While heartfelt and spontaneous rituals are quite powerful, the repetition of certain poetry is a powerful technique. If you have had a particularly intense past experience, and a poem was a part of that experience, the reciting of that poem conjures your past ritual experience, and helps take you deeper, back to the place you were in the past ritual. In some version of the Eight Paths of Power, ritual knowledge is known as "the Keys" as in the keys to power. Knowledge of how to run a ritual, and particularly what to say along with the appropriate energy work, is a key to inducing trance and bringing one through the gates of power. The knowledge of runes, not specifically the Norse symbol system, but poetic devices, are really spoken charms. You can look to poetry, particularly poetry of the ancient world, for trance inducing patterns. The eight syllable rhythmic pattern found in much of the Finnish Kalevala is quite trance inducing. Even modern translations of ancient prose, such as the Sumerian myth of Inanna translated by Diane Wolkstein and Samuel Noah Kramer in *Inanna: Queen of Heaven and Earth* can induce trance. Three of the most important modern Wiccan pieces of ritual prose are *The Charge of the Goddess*, *The Wiccan Rede*, and *The Witch's Rune*.

The Charge of the Goddess

Listen to the words of the Great Mother, Who of old was called Artemis, Astarte, Dione, Melusine, Aphrodite, Ceridwen, Diana, Arianrhod, Brigid and by many other names:

"Whenever you have need of anything, once in the month and better it be when the moon is full, you shall assemble in some secret place and adore the spirit of Me Who is Queen of all the Wise.

You shall be free from slavery, and as a sign that you be free you shall be naked in your rites. Sing, feast, dance, make music and love, all in My presence, for Mine is the ecstasy of the spirit and Mine also is joy on earth. For my law is love unto all beings. Mine is the secret that opens upon the door of youth and Mine is the cup of wine of life that is the cauldron of Ceridwen that is the holy grail of immortality.

I give the knowledge of the spirit eternal and beyond death I give peace and freedom and reunion with those that have gone on before. Nor do I demand aught of sacrifice, for behold, I am the mother of all things and My love is poured out upon the Earth."

Hear also the words of the Star Goddess, the dust of Whose feet are the hosts of heaven, Whose body encircles the universe:

"I Who am the beauty of the green earth and the white moon among the stars and the mysteries of the waters, I call upon your soul to arise and come unto Me. For I am the soul of nature that gives life to the universe. From Me all things proceed and unto Me they must return.

Let My worship be in the heart that rejoices, for behold – all acts of love and pleasure are My rituals. Let there be beauty and strength, power and compassion, honor and humility, mirth and reverence within you.

And you who seek to know Me, know that your seeking and yearning will avail you not, unless you know the Mystery: for if that which you seek, you find not within yourself, you will never find it without. For behold, I have been with you from the beginning, and

I am that which is attained at the end of desire."

The Wiccan Rede

Bide the Wiccan Laws we must
In perfect Love and perfect Trust
Live and let live,
Fairly take and fairly give.
Cast the Circle thrice about
To keep the evil spirits out.
To bind the spell every time
Let the spell be spake in rhyme
Soft of eye and light of touch,
Speak little, listen much.
Deosil go by the waxing moon,
Chanting out the Witches' rune.
Widdershins go by the waning moon,
Chanting out the baneful rune.
When the lady's moon is new,
Kiss thy hand to her, times two.
When the moon rides at Her peak,
Then your heart's desire seek.
Heed the North wind's mighty gale,
Lock the door and drop the sail.

When the wind comes from the South,
Love will kiss thee on the mouth.
When the wind blows from the East,
Expect the new and set the feast.
When the wind blows from the West,
Departed souls will have no rest.
When the West wind blows o'er thee
Departed spirits restless be.
Nine woods into the cauldron go,
Burn them fast and burn them slow.
Elder be your Lady's tree,
Burn it not or cursed ye'll be.
When the Wheel begins to turn,
Let the Beltane fires burn.
When the Wheel has turned to Yule,
Light the log and the Horned One rules
Heed ye Flower, Bush and Tree,
By the Lady, Blessed Be.
Where the rippling waters go,
Cast a stone and truth ye'll know.
When ye have a need,
Hearken not to other's greed.
With a fool no season spend,
Nor be counted as his friend.
Merry meet, Merry part,
Bright the cheeks and warm the heart.
Mind the Threefold Law ye should,
Three times bad and three times good.
When misfortune is enow,
Wear the Blue Star on the brow.
True in love ever be,
Unless thy Lover's false to thee.

Eight words to the Wiccan Rede fulfill

And ye harm none, do what ye will.

The Witch's Rune

Darksome night and shining moon,

Hearken to the witches' rune.

East, then south, west then north,

Here come I to call thee forth.

Earth and water, air and fire,

Work ye unto my desire.

Wand and Pentacle and Sword

Hearken ye unto my word.

Cords and Censer, Scourge and Knife,

Waken all ye into life.

Power of the Witches Blade,

Come ye as the charm is made.

Queen of Heaven, Queen of Hell,

Lend your aid unto the spell.

Horned Hunter of the Night,

Work my will by magic rite.

By all the power of land and sea,

As I do will, so mote it be.

By all the might of Moon and Sun,

Chant the spell and be it done.

Chanting and Singing: Good old fashioned chanting and singing are effective methods to focus energy and induce trance. Simple songs are also a way of building group consciousness, to get a larger number of people focused at the same time, on the same thing. One of the older traditional chants is a foreign rune, known as the *Bagahi Rune*. Repeated in ritual, it raises power. It possibly originates from the Basque region of Spain, an area known for its association with Witchcraft, and could be a list of deity names now lost and forgotten to us. The foreign feel of the words, no matter what language you practice in, helps add to the mystery of the magick and alter your awareness. It is often used at Samhain in British Traditional Wiccan circles. The most popular modern chant was penned by author and activist Zsuzsanna Budapest (*www.zbudapest.com*)

and is entitled, *We All Come from the Goddess*. Many variations of tune and beat exist, and it's often combined with the Goddess Chant. I've also written a number of seasonal chants for the Wheel of the Year, that can be found on *The Outer Temple of Witchcraft CD Companion* (Disc 4).

The Bagahai Rune

Bagahi laca bachahe	bah-GAH-hee LAH-ka BAH-khah-hey
Lamac cahi achabahe	Lah-Mahk kah-HEE ah-KHAH-bah-hey
Karrrelyos!	Kah-RREL-yohs!
Lamac lamec bachalyos	La-Mahk lah-Mekh bah-KHAH-lee-ohs
Cabahagi sabalyos	Kah-BAH-hah-Gee sah-BAH-lee-ohs
Baryols!	Bah-RREE-oh-lahs!
Lagozatha cabyolas	Lah-Goh-zah-THAH kah-BEE-oh-lahs
Samahac et famyolas	Sah-MAH-HAHK EHT fah-MEE-oh-lahs
Harrahya!	Hah-RRAH-hee-yah!

We All Come from the Goddess (Z. Budapest)

We all come from the Goddess
And to her we shall return
Like a drop of rain
Flowing to the ocean.

Samhain Chant (Christopher Penczak)

Earth and air,
Fire and water,
Goddess Crone,
Mother and Daughter.
Lords of Light,
Lords of Death,
With your love
We are blessed.

A song less popular in modern Witchcraft, but finding it way back to our lore is *Green Grow the Rushes O*. In one of Robert Cochrane's famous letters to Joe Wilson on his traditional craft, he states, "My religious beliefs are found in an ancient song, Green Grow the Rushes O" and it gives us some insight into both his beliefs and a song that can capture the spirit of those beliefs for ritual.

Green Grow The Rushes O

I'll sing you one, O
Green grow the rushes, O
What is your one, O?
One is one and all alone,
and ever more shall it be so.
I'll sing you two, O
Green grow the rushes, O
What is your two, O?
Two, two lily-white boys
clothed all in green, O
One is one and all alone,
and ever more shall it be so.
I'll sing you three, O
Green grow the rushes, O
What is your three, O?
Three, three the rivals!
Two, two lily-white boys
clothed all in green, O
One is one and all alone,
and ever more shall it be so.
I'll sing you four, O
Green grow the rushes, O
What is your four, O?
Four for the four wind-makers,
Three, three the rivals!
Two, two the lily-white boys

clothed all in green, O
One is one and all alone,
and ever more shall it be so.
I'll sing you five, O
Green grow the rushes, O
What is your five, O?
Five for the symbol at your door,
Four for the four wind makers,
Three, three the rivals!
Two, two the lily-white boys,
clothed all in green, O
One is one and all alone,
and ever more shall it be so.
I'll sing you six, O
Green grow the rushes, O
What is your six, O?
Six for the six proud walkers,
Five for the symbol at your door,
four for the four wind makers,
Three, three the rivals!
Two, two the lily-white boys,
clothed all in green, O
One is one and all alone,
and ever more shall it be so.
I'll sing you seven, O
Green grow the rushes, O
What is your seven, O?
Seven for the seven stars in the sky,
Six for the six proud walkers,
Five for the symbol at your door,
Four for the four wind makers,
Three, three the rivals!
Two, two the lily-white boys,

clothed all in green, O
One is one and all alone,
and ever more shall it be so.
I'll sing you eight, O
Green grow the rushes, O
What is your eight, O?
Eight for the April Rainers,
Seven for the seven stars in the sky,
Six for the six proud walkers,
Five for the symbol at your door,
Four for the four wind makers,
Three, Three the rivals!
Two, two the lily-white boys,
clothed all in green, O
One is one and all alone,
and ever more shall it be so.
I'll sing you nine, O
Green grow the rushes, O
What is your nine, O?
Nine for the nine bright shiners,
Eight for the April Rainers,
Seven for the seven stars in the sky,
six for the six proud walkers,
Five for the symbol at your door,
Four for the four wind makers,
Three, three the rivals!
Two, two the lily-white boys,
clothed all in green, O
One is one and all alone,
and ever more shall it be so.

Another poem found in the traditions associated with Robert Cochrane and in the writings of William G. Gray, the short, nursery-like style of *This is the Taper that Lights the Way,* can also reveal beliefs on other forms of Witchcraft, and be used as ritual poetry and chant.

This is the Taper that Lights the Way

This is the taper that lights the way.
This is the cloak that covers the stone
That sharpens the knife.
That cuts the cord
That binds the staff.
That is owned by the Maid.
That tends the fire.
That boils the pot
That scalds the sword.
That fashions the bridge.
That crosses the ditch.
That compasses the hand.
That knocks the door.
That fetches the watch.
That releases the man.
That turns the Mill.
That grinds the corn.
That bakes the cake.
That feeds the hound.
That guards the gate.
That hides a maze.
That is worth a light.
And into the house that Jack built.

The "original" full song from where Isobel Gowdie's Hare incantation song can be found in Robert Graves' *The White Goddess,* and has been used as ritual poetry in whole or part in a wide variety of modern Witchcraft traditions. The shape shifting animal pairs are seasonal, and are used in Sabbat rituals, but it also speaks of a deeper initiation cycle similar to the shape shifting hunt of Ceridwen and Gwion Bach/Taliesin, or the punishment of Gwydion.

Cunning and art he did not lack;
Aye, her whistle would fetch him back.
O, I shall go into a hare

With sorrow and sighing and mickle care,
And I shall do in the Devil's name
Aye, till I be fetched hame.
-Hare, take heed of a bitch greyhound
Will harry thee all these fells around,
For here come I in Our Lady's name
All but to fetch thee hame.
Cunning and art he did not lack:
Aye, her whistle would fetch him back.

Yet I shall go into a trout
With sorrow and sighing and mickle doubt,
And show thee many a merry game
Ere that I be fetched hame.
-Trout, take heed of an otter lank
Will harry thee close from bank to bank,
For here I come in Our Lady's name
All but to fetch thee hame.
Cunning and art he did not lack;
Aye, her whistle would fetch him back.

Yet I shall go into a bee
With mickle horror and dread of thee,
And flit to hive in the Devil's name
Ere that I be fetched hame.
-Bee, take head of a swallow hen
Will harry thee close, both butt and ben,
For here come I in Our Lady's name
All for to fetch thee hame.
Cunning and art he did not lack;
Aye, her whistle would fetch him back.

Yet I shall go into a mouse

And haste me unto the miller's house,
There in his corn to have good game
Ere that I be fetched hame.
-Mouse, take heed of a white tib-cat
That never was baulked of mouse or rat,
For I'll crack thy bones in Our Lady's name:
Thus shalt thou be fetched hame.
Cunning and art he did not lack;
Aye, her whistle would fetch him back.

An excellent resource for modern musical correspondences by a musician is *The Goodly Spellbook: Old Spells for Modern Problems* by Lady Passion and *Diuvei. I've found this book enormously helpful for new ideas on music and magick, including correspondences with vowel sounds, letters and the modes. The phonetic aid for the Bagahai Rune is also from *The Goodly Spellbook.*

Exercise: Spirit Drum & Chant Circle

Musical circles can be an excellent way to raise energy for other magickal uses. Shamanic groups start rituals with a drumming, rattling and chatting period, to build the energy in the sacred space, and then use that energy for ritual journey, letting the energy propel them into the otherworld, or to experience different states of consciousness in this world. Energy can also be harnessed and charged for a specific act of magick, such as healing. Create your sacred space to contain the energy generated, and then begin to make music. I suggest having several "leaders" with a predetermined order of leadership, so as one gets tired, another can seamlessly take over. Usually the more experienced drummers set the pace for the others to join in, and more experienced chanters lead the chant until other join in. You can do this circle with both percussion and chant, or just one, depending on your group and the feel of the circle. Once you have generated sufficient energy, move onto the next part of your ritual.

POWER OF SILENCE

Silence is the shadow to words and sounds. Yet of all the shadows of the paths, it is one of the most powerful, potent, and safe to explore. While trance induced by sound is a powerful technique, sometimes the lack of sound, the silence, or simply the ambient sounds of nature and life, can provide a focus for meditation. There is power in silence and the ability to listen, rather than fill the background.

The only time silence should be cautioned against is when it results from horse-ness of voice, from overexerting your own speaking and singing voice, and the silence is forced and not chosen. If you plan on doing a lot of ritualized chanting and singing, it is worthwhile to learn proper breathing and vocal technique, to support your vocal chords rather than strain them. Repeated strain will only result in injury.

If you use a lot of sound in your magick, take the time to explore the power of silence. The path of silence is also be explored more in discussing isolation techniques in **Chapter Six**.

AIDS FOR THE PATH OF MUSIC

Keep the following in mind when exploring music, drumming, and chant:

Make Noise: Don't be so afraid of not sounding "good" that you don't make a sound at all. Music for ritual can be beautiful, but it must be heartfelt first and foremost. No one, including the gods and spirits, is judging your musical ability. If you don't attempt it, you can never get better.

Imitate: Imitate those you like as you learn to find your own style and manner of doing things. Our first songs were likely imitations of animal calls, bird songs, and other noises in nature. Imitation has a long and rich history. If you find someone who has a style you like, sing along, play along, learn to mimic and copy. As you learn to do this with several influences, you begin to build your own style.

Listen: Listen to the music that has influenced your peers and teachers. The following is a list of artists who have been inspirational to a number of modern Pagans. If it has worked for other Pagans, then such music might aid you, too. Thankfully with the Internet we often have an opportunity to sample music before we purchase, so you can find what artist and songs are appropriate for your own rituals.

Amethystium	Dragon Ritual	Horne, Fiona	Nox Arcana
Azam Ali	Drummers	Inkubus Sukkubus	Reclaiming Chants
Bjork	Emerald Rose	*Interview with a*	Rhea's Obsession
Blackmore's Night	Enigma	*Vampire* Soundtrack	Roach, Steve
Bush, Kate	Enya	Jethro Tull	Rule, Wendy
Carol, Shawna	Faith and the Muse	Kelianna	Spiral Dance
Clannad	Fleetwood Mac	*Labyrinth* Soundtrack	Spiral Rhythms
Conti, Al	Frenchy and the	Mannheim	Steeleye Span
Copland, Aaron	Punk	Steamroller	Stravinsky, Igor
Coyle, T. Thorn	Gaia Consort	McKennitt,	Thiel, Lisa
Cure, The	Gerrard, Lisa	Loreena	Vox
Dark Muse	*Gladiator* Soundtrack	McLachlan, Sarah	*The Wicker Man*
Dead Can Dance	Godsmack	Medieval Babes	Soundtrack
Delerium	Gypsy Enchantress	Merlin's Magic	
Doors, The	Heart, Micky	Nicks, Stevie	

CHAPTER FIVE:
THE SACRED DANCE

Some say the universe began as a slow and intimate courtship dance between the Goddess and the God. Each moved to and fro, drawing close and ebbing away from the other, creating the patterns and pulses that lead to our world's creation. Their courtship set creation in motion, bringing the world we know into form.

Since that time, we humans have used movement, posture, and dance to connect to that divine impulse of creation. Dance, like music, has been a part of almost every culture, and particularly a part of religious culture. Dance emulates the ecstasy of the divine, ever moving, ever changing, and evolving toward some unseen and unknown conclusion. Dance has become a ritual in itself. One of the reasons why dance is so universally popular, both for religious reasons and secular enjoyment, is that it is a path of power that leads to the center of consciousness.

BODY POSTURES

Some of techniques of body magick could only be called dance in the most rudimentary way, meaning they are movements, but not necessarily what we think of as dance. Moving the body into specific postures and positions is said to facilitate the shift in consciousness within us, and has become the basis of many of our metaphysical practices, including a variety of forms of yoga and marital arts. While they are not what we typically classify as dance, they have a dance-like manner to them.

Mudras

Mudras are a simple form of body posture from the Hindu tradition, usually involving holding a hand or finger position, rather than a full body position although some mudras involve the whole body. They are ritual gestures seen in Hindu and Buddhist artwork, being held by the gods and gurus. They are considered sacred "seals." Holding such positions is said to confer particular connections to divine consciousness.

In Witchcraft, the first mudra I learned was my Instant Alpha Trigger. While in a meditative state, I crossed my index and middle fingers and programmed that position to automatically bring me to a light meditative state where I can do all my magick. Called the Instant Alpha Trigger in the Cabot Tradition, I call it the Instant Magick Trigger in my *Temple of Witchcraft* series of books, and I, at first, assumed that it was solely a post hypnotic command, programmed into our consciousness through meditative trance. I later found out that the specific hand position suggested by Laurie Cabot was actually an Eastern mudra for balancing the male and female energies within you, and could grant wishes. In other words, give you access to your natural magick. While the programming helps reinforce it, the position itself has a magickal quality to it.

Mudras are described as like buttons in our energy system. By putting pressure on certain points, we create shifts in our energy. Change the points touched, you change the quality of the energy flowing, and thereby alter the result in your body and in your consciousness.

Some of my favorite mudras are simple, involving only the fingers and thumb. By bringing together the thumb with each of the four fingers, you emphasize the energy of four different planets within you. In Aryuvedic lore, as well as Palmistry, each finger is ruled by a different planet, and the mudra of each confers different blessings.

Finger	Mudra	Title	Planet	Attribute
Index	Gyan Mudra	Seal of Knowledge	Jupiter	Wisdom
Middle	Shuni Mudra	Seal of Patience	Saturn	Patience
Ring	Surya Mudra	Seal of Life	Sun	Energy
Pinky	Buddhi Mudra	Seal of Clarity	Mercury	Communication

Fig. 14: Mudra Correspondences

Generally placing the fleshy part of the thumb to the fleshy part of the finger is considered the inward focus. The qualities you generate will circulate within you. If you want to be projective with the energies, broadcasting them to the area around you, touch the fleshy part of the thumb to the nail of the finger.

One of the most common meditation positions is the thumb and index finger together, to gain greater wisdom and knowledge in meditation. Simply by holding the thumb and middle finger together, you gain more patience. Hold the thumb and ring finger together for a burst of energy. When negotiating or communicating with another in a difficult situation, hold the thumb and pinky together. If you seek to meditate on any of these qualities, to integrate them into your life, holding the mudra helps you make a natural connection.

Exercise: Mantra-Mudra Meditation

A simple Kundalini Yoga Mantra-Mudra meditation mixes the paths of breath, sound, and movement in a very easy manner. Get into a comfortable position and inhale, and think Sa-Ta-Na-Ma, while holding the thumb and index finger together on the Sa, thumb and middle finger on the Ta, thumb and ring finger on the Na and thumb and pinky on the Ma. Exhale and think Sa-Se(Say)-So-Hung, repeating the mudra pattern of index, middle, ring and thumb on each of the four syllables. This mantra is said to invoke the healing nature of your soul, the undying part of your self. If you are comfortable with the internalized version of it, you can chant it out loud. A popular and beautiful rendition of this chant is set to Pachelbel's Canon (Canon in D Major). This meditation is quite a powerful rejuvenator and healer of the body, mind, heart, and soul.

Though they are not specifically called mudras in other cultures, you can find similar movements in mythic art and stories. Another used in Celtic traditions of Witchcraft and magick, as strange as it might sound, is putting your thumb in your mouth, like sucking your thumb as a child. It is considered a symbol of inspiration, and mythic figures such as Taliesin are known to hold this gesture. The origin goes back to Taliesin's own initiation. In his previous life as Gwion Bach, servant of the goddess Ceridwen, he burns his thumb on the potion of inspiration, and sucks his thumb to soothe the burn. Gwion inadvertently swallows the power of the potion of inspiration, and begins an initiatory chain of events resulting in his transformation into the bard Taliesin.

Another popular meditative mudra, particularly for Witches, is to place the corresponding fingertips of each hand together with a slight pressure, to balance the five element forces within. This can be held similar to an outstretched prayer position at the chest level. Each finger is said to correspond with a different element, through sources usually disagree with each other on the assignment of which element to which finger. Generally I think of the elements, based on the planetary associations as index-Jupiter-water, middle-Saturn-earth, ring-Sun-fire and pinky-Mercury-air, with the thumb as spirit.

Yoga

Most people in the western world think of yoga as the form of exercise where you put your body in strange and uncomfortable positions. Yoga really covers a wide range of practices and traditions, only some of which include forms of exercise. Yoga is usually translated in the west as either "yoke" or "union" referring to practices that "yoke" you to the divine. The physical positions prepare the body and consciousness for deeper states of awareness. Many of the positions from the various forms of yoga are named after natural phenomenon, such as animals, plants or nature. Popular poses are called Mountain, Tree, Half Moon, and Cobra. Some yogic practices are sequences of positions that attune to nature, such as the Salutation to the Sun and Salutation to the Moon.

While Yoga comes from the Vedic traditions of India, and is ideally practiced in that cultural context and tradition, it has been introduced to the west in a non-religious, non-dogmatic way, becoming a part of exercise programs at the gym and yoga studios where those exploring mystical traditions and philosophies can find support. It is here where many Pagans and Witches have found both yogic philosophy and the power of yogic body positions, pranayama, mudras, mantras, and yantras. Though the eastern philosophies are not a complete theological match for Witchcraft, there is a common Indo-European root to both, and many modern Witchcraft traditions have claimed Hindu terms and concepts, such as karma, dharma, chakras and reincarnation. The association of the yogic positions with natural phenomenon is another link between the two traditions, and many Witches use yogic techniques as a part of their own meditative and spiritual practices. I've found the Salutation to the Sun sequence and the Five Tibetans quite helpful in my own practice.

Exercise: Salutation to the Sun

Also known as the Sun Salutation Surya Namaskar, this is a series of twelve postures returning you back to center, used to strengthen, loosen, and align the muscles of the back and spine, as well as align the practitioner with the powers of healing and vitality from the Sun. Ideally it is done as the Sun is rising, facing east, to align with the solar orb, spiritually, and physically.

Fig. 15: Salutation to the Sun

1. Begin standing upright (usually facing east), feet together, looking forward, with your arms and hands in prayer position at the heart. Acknowledge the Sun and its power in our lives.
2. Inhale and reach up with your arms, keeping the palms of your hands together. Reach backwards lightly from the waist, looking up to the heavens. Acknowledge the stars as other Suns.
3. Exhale and bend your body forward, stretching until your hands touch your feet. If you are not flexible enough to reach your feet, touch your ankles or shins. Draw the light of the Sun and stars down as you reach down and breathe out.

4. As you inhale, your right leg steps backs. Arch your back up and lift your chin, facing toward the "Sun." Feel yourself connecting deeper to the Sun.
5. Exhale and step your left leg back. Straighten your body into a plank, spine, neck, and legs straight, and support your weight on your hands and feet. Feel the light of the Sun giving you support and strength.
6. Holding your breath still, first lower your knees down to the floor, then your chest to the floor and finally your forehead to the floor. Keep your hips up and curl your toes under. In this pose your are humbling your inner Sun, your inner light, before the Sun.
7. Inhale and stretch forward while bending back. Press your hips down and straighten your toes while keeping your arms straight. This is the position of the cobra, rising up to greet the Sun.
8. Exhale and curl your toes under so you can press down on your heels, As you press on your heels, also press on your hands, lift your hips and lift your body up from the Earth.
9. Inhale and move your left leg back. Feel the top of the foot stretched out flat on the floor. Your right foot is between the pillars of your arms. Lift your chin and gaze at the Sun.
10. Exhale and bring your left foot up in line with the right, reach forward and touch your feet, joining Sun and Earth, as you did in Step 3.
11. Inhale and stand upright. As you continue into inhale in one fluid motion, stretch your arms up, keeping the palms of your hands together. Reach backwards lightly from the waist, looking up to the heavens. Acknowledge the stars as other Suns as you did in Step 2.
12. Exhale and gently come back to starting position. Circle arms around to prayer position at the heart, while straightening the back to an upright position. Feel the power of the Sun within you.

There is also a modern Salutation of the Moon, sometimes called the Chandra Namaskar, a series of twenty movement performed to align with the powers of the Moon, and its effects are more cooling and clearing. It's predominantly found in the Americas and from the Kripalu style of yoga, while the Sun Salutation has more associations found in traditional yoga.

The Five Tibetans are not a traditional Vedic yoga practice, although they are yogic in nature. They are supposedly from Tibet, though their history and practice are filled with controversy, as they are not found in any traditional Tibetan lore, and some associations conflict with traditional Tibetan lore. The exercises are said to enhance the seven chakras, yet in the Tibetan forms of mysticism, only five chakras are recognized. When such a discrepancy has been pointed out, it has been theorized that perhaps they come from India or Nepal, rather than Tibet, or they are the clever deception of a charlatan. I tend to favor a more mystic origin, even if it's not Tibet, as I've found great benefit from regularly practicing these exercises. I was first introduced to them in the work of ceremonial magician Donald Michael Kraig, specifically in his classic book *Modern Magick*.

These exercise were popularized by an American Peter Kelder in 1939, based upon his meeting a retired British Colonel, who was said to have learn the five rituals while traveling in Tibet. The benefits of practice are said to be a "fountain of youth" effect, rejuvenating the body and spirit, curing ailments, improving eyesight, increasing memory, and promoting hair growth when suffering from hair loss. Even with their controversial and unknown origin, they have grown in popularity in the western world, both in alternative health and in forms of ceremonial magick. I've found the Five Tibetans to not only have a healing and exercise benefit, but to be a great preparatory rite to precede meditation and ritual. I'll often perform the Five Tibetans, also known as the Five Rites of Rejuvenation, before I do my evening meditations.

Exercise: The Five Tibetans

The Five Tibetans are a form of exercise and despite the health benefits, can aggravate certain conditions of people not used to regular physical exercise. If you suffer from any heart problems, severe arthritis, high blood pressure, any conditions that make movement difficult or painful, or if you are pregnant, please consult a doctor before attempting these exercises to see if they are suitable for you. Ideally each of the five exercises is meant to be done twenty-one times in a daily session. Build up to twenty-one repetitions slowly and gain strength over time. A variety of material has been printed in books and online with variations to the exercises for those with physical impairments. Research the variations that work best for your body.

First Tibetan: Stretch your arms out from your sides, parallel with the floor, palms facing down. Spin clockwise with the arms stretched out, inhaling and exhaling as you spin. You might get slightly dizzy.

Second Tibetan: Lie flat on the floor facing up. Place your arms at your sides fully extended with the palms facing down, fingers close together. Inhale and raise your head off the floor, tucking your chin to your chest as you simultaneously lift your legs, knees straight. Exhale and slowly lower the legs, keeping the knees straight, while lowing the head gently to the floor.

Third Tibetan: Kneel on the floor with the body straight up. Place your hands on the backs of your thighs. Curl your toes so they can touch the floor if possible. Arch forward slightly with the neck bent. Inhale and arch backwards, letting the hands support the back. Exhale as you return to the starting position.

Fourth Tibetan: Sit on the floor with your legs straight before you with about a foot between your feet. Keep your trunk erect and straight, only bending at the hips. Inhale and drop the head backward while at the same time raising the body up so the feet become flat on the floor, knees bent and the body becomes straight, like a "table." Tense the muscles and hold for a moment. Exhale and return to the starting position. You might feel your head and chin slightly tuck in toward the chest before the next thrust backward.

Fifth Tibetan: Lie face down with your arms by your sides, palms down toward the floor slightly ahead of your shoulders, and with your toes curled in to the floor. Inhale and press down on the palms and toes, raising the body up and arch the spine, looking down at the feet. Exhale and lower the body down, arching the head and spine back.

Fig. 16: Five Tibetans

Ritual Gestures

Witchcraft and ceremonial magick are filled with ritual gestures. Sometimes they are simple, and others times complex, but they bear a striking resemblance to the spirit, of not the actual positions, of yoga. In fact, many call western ceremonial magick, based upon the Qabalah, the "Yoga of the West," meaning it has the same level of spiritual depth and complexity as eastern forms of yoga, along with physical body positions and training.

In modern Wicca, the two most prevalent positions are known as the Goddess Position and the God Position. The Goddess position emulates the Nile River Venus statue, with arms outstretched over the head, somewhat like a crescent. Ideally one stands with feet slightly apart, supporting your weight. This position is done to release the cone of power through ritual, and send that power out to manifest your magick.

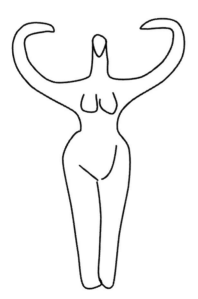   

Fig. 17: Nile River Venus   **Fig. 18: Goddess Position**

The God position emulates the position of Egyptian Pharaohs in their tombs, and the god Osiris. The arms are crossed over the chest, with the feet close together. The God Position follows the Goddess, as a grounding and centering position after raising the Cone of Power and releasing energy from the ritual. It is a reflective position, where can then receive information and wisdom conducive to fulfilling the intentions of your magick.

Fig. 19: Osiris   **Fig. 20: God Position**

Another position used in Wicca is known as the Star Position. It is found in old grimoires giving each limb an association with one of the planets, as a man's image is inscribed in the pentacle. It can be done standing up or lying down. The standing version is energizing, while the lying down version is used to attune to the earth and meditate.

Exercise: Star Position

When done standing up, the arms are outstretched horizontally, with the left palm up and the right palm down. (If you are left handed, reverse this). The legs are spread wide and the head is tilted back slightly. You look like a five-pointed star standing up. By standing in this position, you receive "cosmic" energy flowing from the heavens down into you. It enters your upward turned hand and the top of your head. Feel it fill your body and exit from your feet, the base of your spine, and through your down turned hand. When you stop the position, the remaining energy flows through you and the continuous flow stops. Even though you are a conduit for cosmic energy to the Earth, a portion of it remains within your system to heal and energize you.

In the lying down version of this meditation, you do exactly the same thing, lying outstretched like a star on the ground, yet you can have both palms facing up, both palms facing down, or emulate the standing position, with your left palm up toward the sky and right palm down to the earth. This position attunes you to the cycles of nature and the consciousness of Mother Earth.

Witchcraft also has a number of hand positions like mudras. Many of them are used in blessing and cursing forms of folk magick. In the Italian Strega tradition such gestures are known as *gettatura*. A sign of blessing is known as the *Mano Pantea* is formed by thumb, index, and middle finger extended upward, stiffly pressed together with the ring and pinky folded downward toward the palm. It is used for blessing and as a protection from the evil eye. For hexing, the sign of the fig, also known as the *Fare la Fica* is used. A feminine hex sign formed by making a fist and placing your thumb between the index and middle finger, a form resembling the feminine genitals. A variation places the thumb between the middle and ring fingers. The masculine hex sign is called the *Mano Cornut,* or Sign of the Horns, formed by the thumb being tucked under the middle and ring finger, and the pinky and index finger are extended, to form two horns. Another variation has the thumb over the middle and ring fingers. The image is often made into a charm of gold to be worn on a chain for protection from hexing.

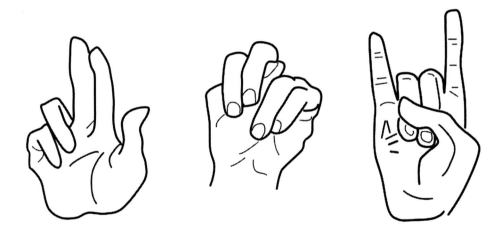

Fig. 21: Mano Pantea   **Fig. 22: Fare la Fica**   **Fig. 23: Mano Cornut**

One of the most prevalent gestures in the modern Craft is The Triangle of Manifestation, held with the thumbs and index fingers of each hand touching their corresponding digit. The "triangle" is held up to the heavens to frame the Moon and draw its light down.

Fig. 24: Triangle of Manifestation

Modern ceremonial magick contains even more formalized gestures and positions. Four of these most helpful for us to explore are the four lower grade signs of the Order of the Golden Dawn. Each one is associated with an element, and embodies that element when held in ritual. They are also associated with various ranks in the order, associated with the elements and a specific position on the Tree of Life.

Fig. 25: Sign of the Zelator Grade – Earth   **Fig. 26: Sign of the Theoricus Grade – Air**

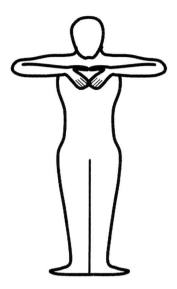 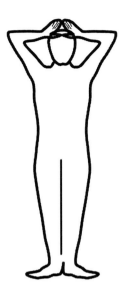

Fig. 27: Sign of the Practicus Grade – Water   **Fig. 28: Sign of the Philosophus Grade – Fire**

I've been to a modern Neopagan group that mixes more traditional Wiccan techniques with these elemental gestures when calling forth the four elements in the quarters of the magick circle.

Ecstatic Trance Postures

One of the most exciting areas of posture exploration for the modern Witch is the research into ancient ecstatic trance postures. Those interested in both ancient cultures and neural science have been exploring the art forms left by ancient cultures, particularly hunger-gatherer and horticultural societies, and believe a variety of art left by these cultures is not just art, but ritual instructions on how to hold your body during a shamanic trance. Research has revealed many of these positions key specific types of shamanic journey and spiritual contact. Much like how yogic positions key the body and energy field into a certain level of consciousness, the entering and remaining in particular positions facilitates a specific experience, as if these poses are specific "settings" within our psyche, or specific keys to the otherworld. Some would even personify the positions as individual spirits, named for the artistic piece depicting their ritual position. The trance position is like a specific call to the spirit embodied by the ritual art.

While some of this information has been used by shamanic practitioners before—emulating cave paintings and other works of art left by shamanic oriented cultures—it has recently been gaining a greater understanding in the mainstream metaphysical community involved in shamanic trance work through the body. These body postures are actually said to activate DNA information in our bodies held from our ancient ancestors who also used them. The posture creates a thread of continuity to the past wisdom.

Much of this work has been pioneered by Felicitas D. Goodman and brought to my attention by the writing of her student Belinda Gore, and can be found in detail in the books *Ecstatic Body Postures: An Alternate Reality Workbook* by Belinda Gore, *Where the Spirits Ride the Wind: Trance Journeys and Other Ecstatic Experiences* by Felicitas D. Goodman, and *Ecstatic Trance: New Ritual Body Postures* by Felicitas D. Goodman and Nana Nauwald. Through their research at the Cuyamungue Institute, they have divided the ritual postures into seven possible categories: Healing, Divination, Metamorphosis, Spirit Journey, Initiation, Living Myth, and Celebration.

Fig. 29: Bear Spirit Posture

Bear Spirit Posture

Type: Healing

Position: Stand with your feet six inches apart, parallel and pointing straight ahead. Keep your knees only slightly bent to prevent them from locking and causing strain on the back. Hold your hands as if you are cupping an egg in each palm. Bring them into the solar plexus area. Touch the first joint of each of the index fingers until they form the apex of a triangle shape. Your thumbs are one in front of the other, not on top of the other. Gently tilt your head back as if you were looking just above where the wall and ceiling meet. Close your eyes. During trance, you might sway or shake.

Magick: Bear Spirit Posture is one of the most global postures, found in the art of many cultures and times. Its use conjures the spirit of great healing, often in the form of a Bear Spirit who either performs healing on you, or shows you how to do it yourself. Other times, other animal spirits or specific colors of energy are conjured.

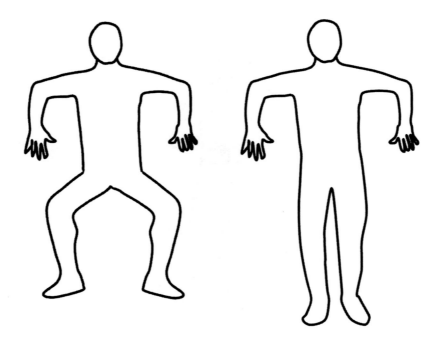

Fig. 30: Hunter Diviner Posture (and variation)

Hunter Diviner Posture

Type: Divination

Position: Place your feet about a foot apart, with your left toes pointing outward to the left side and your right toes pointing outward to the right side. Bend your knees until they are over the toes. Square your shoulders and extend your right arm out to your right side and your left arm out to your left side. Maintain your elbows at shoulder level, but allow your lower arms to drop, hanging down from the elbows, with the palms facing backwards. Stretch your fingers as wide as they will stretch and face straight head with your eyes closed. If you can't hold the feet and legs apart, a less powerful variation is to bring them closer together.

Magick: This is one of the most difficult but, in my experience, most powerful, of the ecstatic body postures. Those who can hold it gain great insight. It conjures the power of the hunter-gatherer societies, and gives us a journey that divines the answer to a question or problem. It's best to ask your question clearly before starting the journey. It can answer questions on health, home, love, money, or anything else you desire, as it "hunts" out the answer in the spirit world with you.

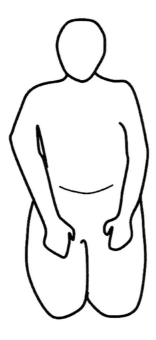

Fig. 31: Corn Goddess Posture

Corn Goddess Position

Type: Metamorphosis

Position: Kneel with your buttocks resting upon your heels. Place your hands palm down upon your thighs, with the heels of your hands resting at the point where your thighs meet your torso and hips. Keep your fingers together and point the tips of your fingers down towards your knees, resting upon the thighs. Keep your arms close to your body, shoulders stiffened and slightly raised. Face ahead, closing your eyes.

Magick: Drawing from Aztec and Southwestern Native art and lore, this position is strikingly powerful for modern Pagans as well. It is a posture of shapeshifting, but not just animal shapeshifting. It is a position that restructures your body, self perception and boundaries. One's very molecules appears to reorganize, with shifts into the plant, insect, and fungus world as well as animals. It's a shapeshift through the cycle of life.

Fig. 32: Priestess of Malta Posture

Priestess of Malta

Type: Spirit Journey

Position: Stand with your feet six inches apart, parallel and pointing straight ahead. Keep your knees only slightly bent to prevent them from locking and causing strain on the back. Keep your right arm stiff and straight at the side, with your right elbow locked. Hold your left upper arm close to your torso, bending the left elbow at a 90-degree angle. Place your left palm flat on your waist and look forward with your eyes closed.

Magick: The Spirit Journey of this posture is not to the upper or lower worlds of the shaman, but across the middle world, across Earth. It is a position used in burial and psychopomp work. Dr. Goodman speculates that the Priestesses of Malta used this form to remind the dying of their homeland before departing this world for the next. Those who use it often experience the sense of being "dead" or at a funeral rite.

Fig. 33: Venus of Galgenberg Posture

Venus of Galgenberg

Type: Spirit Journey

Position: Stand tall with the left leg straight and the left foot facing forward while the right leg is slightly bent at the knee and the right foot angles slightly away from the body to the right. Hold a stick (or wand) in the right hand, with your forefinger extended along the shaft, pointing it down towards the ground. Hold your left arm up to form a 37 degree angle. Cup your left hands and face the palm towards the body. Turn your head to the left, raise it, and gaze towards your left hand, then close your eyes.

Magick: This posture brings the user to the World Tree and can facilitate a journey to either the upper world and/or the lower world. It generates a great amount of energy in the physical body of the user, sometimes manifesting as intense heat or an electric feeling coursing up and/or down the body. Some people's skin reacts to the energy, causing a temporary rash or blotches upon the skin.

Fig. 34: Venus of Laussel Posture

Venus of Laussel

Type: Initiation and Rebirth

Position: Stand with your legs close together, feet parallel with each other, toes forward and knees locked. Hold your left arm close to your torso and put your left hand just above the naval. Move the angle of your hand so your first two fingers point at the navel itself. Spread your fingers. With your right hand, hold a horn, or ritual facsimile (you can make one out of cardboard if needed) The horn should be between your thumb and your fingers. Face your fingers forward. Raise the horn to shoulder level, holding your right arm out to the side of your torso, bending at the elbow. Create a 37 degree angle between your upper arm and lower arm. Face left with your eyes closed.

Magick: A familiar form to many Pagans, this Venus holds a bison horn with twelve notches carved on it, like the twelve Zodiac signs. Originally she was carved in a cave wall near Bordeaux in France. Like many other hunter-gather postures, the Venus of Laussel holds a 37 degree angle, a special form that seems to trigger a primal consciousness. Unlike the journey postures, this form appears to initiate the user into the ways of the Goddess through death and rebirth, returning to and being renewed by the Goddess and the land.

The positions listed here are the some of the ones with the most research and experimentation, and are all positions I've had personal experience using. I find the prospect of researching more ceremonial positions, looking more into the sacred art of the Celts, Norse, Saxons, Egyptians, Sumerians, and other, more "witchy" cultures quite fascinating. Perhaps images such as the figures on the Gunderstrup Cauldron, The Sorcerer figure from Trois-Frères, France, medieval woodcuts and drawing of the Witch's Sabbat, and even the modern positions of Wicca and Ceremonial magick will lead to a new vein of ecstatic trance research. I've found the Goddess position to facilitate middle world and upper world journeys, while the God Position facilitates underworld positions on the mysteries of death. The Star Position can help facilitate an upper world meditation as well.

Fig. 35: Gunderstrup Cauldron

Fig. 36: The Sorcerer

Seidr

Seidr or *Seidhr* (usually pronounced Seeth) is a form of magick found in the traditions of the Northern Germanic culture, and particularly associated with the Norse. It is differentiated from the other major form of Germanic magic, Galdr, or runic magick, which uses the symbols systems known as the runes in pictorial form as well as speaking or singing the rune names. The two most popular forms of runic systems known to modern Pagans today are the Elder Futhark and the Younger Futhark. While we know it was different from runic magick, we are not exactly sure what Seidr really was as a practice.

The Norse god Odin knew both forms of magick, even though Seidr was considered "darker," more"shameful" or "lustful" than Galdr, and not something many men aspired to practicing. He was said to teach it to some of his followers. Women who practiced it were known as Seidkona and men were Seidmard, though they might also be involved other magickal or religious practices. From lore, we believe seidr could be used to divine the future fates of men, change the future, cause illness and death, healing, enchanting objects, protection, travel via spirit, change the weather, fishing, and guide ships at sea. It's possible that seidr was simply a name for sorcery, for magickal practices found in the Norse culture that were not runic. Due to its dark associations, its quite possible seidr practices are influenced by the Sami people of the northern region, renowned for their powerful sorcerers and wizards.

Today modern magicians speculate on a whole range of practices seidr might have included. Modern heathens have reconstructed various versions of "oracular seidr" pioneered and popularized by priestess and author Diana Paxson. The focus of such rituals is prophecy via communication with the spirits of the Nine Worlds of Norse cosmology, and in particular, speaking with the spirits of Hel. It often involves invocatory procedures where the spirits speak through the body of the priest/ess, much like a Pagan tribal form of channeling.

Another take on seidr practices, first brought to my attention by the author Jan Fries and his innovative book *Seidways*, is the use of shaking, shivering, and swaying to induce trance for a variety of magickal purposes. He is quick to point out that we do not know if this what the ancient Germanic people did in their seidr practices, but makes a very reasonable case for it, and details the shaking and swaying practices of several magickal cultures and traditions. The uncontrollable shaking of the epileptic is considered in many traditions to be a mark of a potential shaman, and epilepsy a "sacred" disease. During the Inquisition, it was considered a sign of demonic possession or Witchcraft.

The word seidr is also associated with heating food and drink as well as fermentation, and such actions provide a good analogy of what happens to the body when such practices are put into use. We heat up and often feel as if we are bubbling or boiling from the inside as we enter trance. Shaking and shivering make an ideal technique for people of a northern climate, where the cold is prevalent, and yet, the technique can also keep one reasonably warm. Fries also associates these practices with the serpent mysteries, as swaying produces a snake-like action, and snakes can also be found in strong association with sorcery. While traditionally written as seidr, today many refer to the technique as "seething."

Many experimental magicians and Pagans are using such seidr techniques in their ecstatic practices, making it a perfect path to discuss in the gateway of movement, mixing both the old potential practices with a new interpretation. Today, seidr techniques are used for:

Psychic Travel: Including forms of astral travel, remote viewing, and shamanic journey to spiritual worlds.

Spellcraft: Practitioners sometimes report more developed visualization skills in seidr trance, and use that additional ability to envision the goal of their magick, performing a "wyrdworking" or altering their fate to a new future in alignment with their will.

Energy Raising: Shaking and shivering heats the body as well as raises energy for any ritual working that requires the generation of energy, including the Wiccan "Cone of Power."

Divination: Trance induced with seidr practices can intentionally or spontaneously lead to divination experiences, perceiving the past, present and future, either directly and literally, or through a symbol system open to interpretation.

Magick Persona: A seidr trance easily lends itself to breaking with the traditional everyday persona and summoning the magickal persona for ritual.

Shapeshifting: Shaking and shivering aids in the experience of shapeshifting the self image into another form, particularly animal totem forms.

Invocation: Today seidr is very much associated with rituals of invocation, bringing a spiritual entity fully into the body, to speak through and move the body. Many of the other uses of the trance can be enhanced through proper invocation by an experienced practitioner.

Attunement: One can attune to the land and land spirits of a particular place, the genius loci, by dropping into, or expanding out around, the land where the ritual occurs.

Celebration: Just as one can attune to the space, a particular moment, particularly a seasonal or astrological moment, can be attuned to and celebrated using a shaking trace.

Healing: All forms of trance can be healing on their own, or used in ritual specifically with healing spells and energy techniques, but seidr has the added benefit of both generating internal energy as heat, and through its movement, breaking down the places of personal "psychic armor" and holding found in the body that prevent life force from flowing, as described in the teachings of Wilhelm Reich and Reichian Therapy.

Seidr trance can have a wide range of manifestations. On the most gentle level, it can involve slight swaying, back and forth or side to side. Many people naturally enter this rhythm during certain forms of meditation and prayer. I've found myself entering an almost steady "gallop" pattern of movement, as if I'm riding a shamanic steed. It's more physical than the swaying, but still meditative. Actual shaking movements can range from a slight shiver, like on a cold day, to more vigorous shaking, like the idling of an engine. The most intense forms of shaking trance look more like convulsions or fits.

Though this is a chapter dedicated to movement, many find the use of sound helpful, particularly in the less intense swaying and shaking trances. The use of humming, hissing, or even whistling can be quite effective in inducing a trance and additionally at keeping the mind occupied from feeling too silly.

Exercise: Seething

Make sure you are properly prepared for the practice. It's a fairly advanced technique used for people who are in relatively good physical shape who engage in regular exercise. If you are unused to physical movement, then seidr might not be the place to start. If you have any doubts, speak to your health care practitioner and if you feel ready for the practice, start slow and for only short periods, building your strength.

Prepare your space. Set it up as a ritual space, be it a magick circle ritual or other ritual format. Incense, candles and all the traditional accoutrements of ceremony aid in setting the mood and focusing your will. While music is not necessary, I find it often helps. Music with a strong beat, but something that is not too rhythmic, but off beat, is helpful. Anything with disjoined sounds can also be effective, though practitioners report using rock music as well. Make sure you are wearing loose clothing, (or possibly none at all). Don't seethe on a full stomach, but it takes a lot of energy, so do not fast either. Make sure you've taken in enough calories to sustain you, and it's often a good idea to eat a bit, albeit lightly, afterwards to help ground. Since it is so physical, and the rhythm takes on an almost involuntary quality to it, it's important to make sure you visit the bathroom and relieve yourself before beginning. When you are ready to begin, stretch and warm up as you would for any physical activity.

Start with a loose posture. Generally seething trances are done standing, knees bent slightly. Some find it helpful to put their hands on their knees for some support. (If you are intending a more gentle swaying or rocking trance, it can be standing or sitting. For swaying trance, I like to sit in the yogic position known as "rock pose" with knees bent as if you were kneeling in prayer, buttocks on the heels.)

Start to tremble in the legs. At first it can seem awkward or silly, but soon you will get the hang of it. For some, the tremble starts in the arms and it's brought into the rest of the body.

Move the pulsation upward through the body, from the legs into the trunk. Feel the trunk shake and shiver. It might spread to your arms, head, and neck. Some experience more stability in the legs as the trembling is raised, others feel their entire body tremble.

Vary the pulsation of the trembling. Speed it up, as if you are bringing water on the pot to boil. Turn it down as if you are turning down the heat and stopping the boil, but keeping the water at the edge, near boiling. You can use the boiling pot as a visualization, or find other visualizations that work for you. Jan Fries gives a very effective dragon visualization in *Seidways* that is worth exploring. Allow yourself to go into trance, and notice the different quality of the trance at each level. If you;re up to it, vary between light, moderate, and intense shaking to see what kind of experiences you have with each. Once you understand your own mind-body-spirit connection, the more you can "aim" for the type of trance you desire in the future.

When done your trance work, you might find that you collapse. While this is acceptable, you might want to try to slowly bring your shaking to an end. Bring your ritual to an end, performing all necessary closing and banishings, and ground yourself as necessary.

EXERCISE

While it's not seen as particularly spiritual, any type of physical activity can be used to help alter consciousness and enter a trance state. Exercise is a method where those not involved in the arts of ritual can experience the physiological change that occurs through ecstatic movement, without necessarily signing up for a religious or mystical ceremony. I had a yoga instructor who told us of her experiences running at night, comparing it to flying. As she described it, she had the same sensations and realizations during her evening jog as I do when I perform shamanic journey.

Any form of repetitive exercise can trigger a trance state. If you perform any manner of cardiovascular exercise like aerobics, walking, running, the variety of cardio machines in the modern gym, or repetitive martial arts routines, pay attention to your thoughts before, during and after. Do you notice a difference? Have you ever tried meditating, doing journey work or other forms of ritual after exercise? It can prepare you for a deeper experience much like a yogic session or ritual dance. Perhaps it is because the cardio heartbeat is roughly the same rate as the shamanic drum pace, so we, in essence, are drumming for ourselves with our own hearts when we experience the cardio heartbeat in exercise and dance.

TRUE DANCE

True dance is the heart of this path. Ecstatic movement, bringing together posture and motion, is a powerful method for altering awareness. Like music itself, dance has been a part of most major cultures. It's a natural form of human expression, and it's also a natural, intuitive key to expanded states of consciousness.

Until I started studying Witchcraft, I found it strange that repressive cultures and regimes would restrict dance. Art, literature, theater, and music I understood. Ideas contrary to the regime can be expressed overtly and subtly in such art forms, making people think and question their surroundings. Art can be challenging to the status quo. I didn't give dance the same credit. It's creative and expressive, and perhaps professional dance of the high art world would symbolically present artistic ideas, but why restrict individuals from recreational dancing?

In many ways, dancing is liberating and therefore more dangerous than any form of visual or literary art. Rather than be a spectator, or require language skills and context, dance gives you a direct experience, and through that direct experience, you can touch, feel, and even dance with, the divine. Dance is a gateway to gnosis, whether you know what gnosis is or not. When you experience the liberation found in such an experience, it is difficult to be oppressed, or at least assume an oppressed and beaten mentality, ever again. Many slave cultures and peasant classes found great power and pleasure in dance. It requires no real tools, no education, and no major skills, other than a willingness to move your body with passion and spirit and thereby take your consciousness with it.

Dance harkens back to our tribal preliterate cultures, where ecstatic movement is a major form of spiritual worship and experience. Within the dance there is power, and a part of us remembers it, even if we have consciously lost the connection between dance and spirit. The universe is often described in terms of a dance: the divine dancing with itself, or the gods, dancing the universe into manifestation. Shiva from the Hindu Pantheon is said to be the cosmic dancer when depicted as Nataraja. He is primary god of destruction or dissolution, but also the god of regeneration. The planets are named after various gods in most systems of astrology, and their movement across the heavens can be seen on Earth as a cosmic dance. When we dance, we tap into the same cosmic forces, emulating them on the microcosm as they dance in the macrocosm.

For the purposes of opening the gates to greater consciousness, dance can be divided into several different forms. First it can be divided into the number of participants actively engaged in a similar or complimentary movement and intention. Dances can be solo, partnered, or group dances. Each can bring its own power and challenges. Dance can also be divided into forms based upon style:

Walking: Somewhere between true dance and repetitive exercise, walking can be a part of sacred movement. The "walkabout" of journeying while holding a sacred intention, like a moving vision quest, is a powerful technique. Also simply walking in places in nature, or even in urban environments while paying attention to energy and to spirits, is a powerful technique. The repetition of steps is likely to induce a trance technique as much as drumming, if you pay attention to it and use it.

Exercise: Widdershins Walk

The Widdershins Walk is a simple technique, and there are many variations, most notably using a spiral pattern or figure-eight motion to literally "walk between worlds" when consciousness shifts. The basic technique is simple. While outside, construct a circular path, either in your mind, marking where the circle falls mentally, or literally marking it out with stones or other natural objects. The circle should be fairly wide, at least the size of a traditional nine-foot diameter Witch's Circle, though I've found much larger to be more beneficial. If you can perform this around an actual stone circle, if you are fortunate enough to have one in the vicinity, or to construct your own stone circle, all the better.

Walk widdershins, or counter-clockwise around it. The counterclockwise direction is contrary to most Wiccan traditions, but for some Witches, this is the motion of turning into the land, or underworld, walking toward the left. It is the direction of the stars, and moving against the "natural" motion of the deosil (pronounced jed-sil or jesh-il) or clockwise motion, the resistance can generate quite a bit of energy to go into the otherworld or for spell casting. After many revolutions, sit in the center of the circle and feel yourself sinking deeper into the land. Journey with the spirits of the land, or the deep earth and underworld.

When done, its best to repeat this process in reverse, to walk clockwise several times, to bring yourself back "up" from the depths. Ground as needed.

Free Form: Free form dance refers to spontaneous, unplanned movement with no formal pattern. Simply move your body to a rhythm, being as stylish and creative as you desire. A lot of modern club dancing is in this style, as well as much of what we consider to be neo-tribal dancing at Pagan festivals. It mixes both group and individual characteristics, as you can do it alone or in a group, but even if you are doing it in a group, your dance is not necessarily based upon, or interacting with, anybody else's dance, unless you so choose. Two or more dancers can move in and out of each other's space, playing off each other's moves, or simply ignore each other. Because there are no rules, this can be the most liberating form of dance to induce an altered perception. The drawback to this form of dancing is there is no guidance. There is no reference point to start. If you are shy or inhibited, there is nothing to help you begin, other than watching others who are less shy and inhibited. Even though there is no specific instruction, an understanding of basic movement and anatomy gives us several types of movements to reflect upon before, during and after our dance. These movements are based upon the various "axes" of the human body. You have the vertical axis, parallel with the spine. You have the left-right horizontal axis and the front-back horizontal axis. Chaos magician Steve Wilson does an amazing job of encouraging readers to explore these three movements in his book *Chaos Ritual*. The Vertical Axis involves dancing in a small circle, or spinning like the archetypal Whirling Dervish

Sufis. It's interesting to note that many of Gardner's time, including author and High Priestess Doreen Valiente, thought there was a Middle Eastern Sufi influence on Wicca as they knew it. The Vertical Axis is associated with the Snake. The Horizontal Axis of Left-Right is associated by Wilson with the Elephant and lunar qualities. The Horizontal Axis of Front-Back is associated with the Gazelle for a totem figure, and the planet Mars. Such leaping and thrusting moves are found in African and Native American style dances. Wilson also describes a shaking move without an axis, similar to Seidr, and associates it with the peacock; a rooster-Uranus dance of free from movement but with the head moving randomly, as if you were a chicken who was scared; and the Angel Dance, another free form dance with the head movements of the heavy metal headbanger going forward and back.

The free form style can raise a tremendous amount of energy during the dance if held in a sacred space, and even more so if the space is contained, like a circle. Those with an ability to sense and manipulate both ambient and personal energy can move and "weave" the energy around them in patterns, building its power and directing it towards spellcraft.

Exercise: Dancing With Energy

Simply dance in whatever manner you choose, but while you do, be conscious of the energy around you. Imagine moving and weaving the energy. Use your arms, hands, and fingers in particular, but do not ignore your legs, hips, back, and entire body. Feel the energy flowing both within you and through the environment around you. The next time you do ritual, try this technique as a means of manipulating energy for ritual and spellcasting.

Formal: Formal dancing is what we consider traditional dancing, be it famous dance steps such as the waltz, or folk dancing specific to a region or culture. Formal dances can be solo, duo, or group, depending on their nature. Many of the folk dances of Europe are associated with particular holidays, celebrations and locations, and arguments can be made for their Pagan origin and significance. Formal dance steps must be learned and executed in a specific pattern. Although each dancer brings their skill and personal artistry to the dance, there is only so much open to interpretation and variation, until one dance is transformed into something new. Authors Dorothy Morrison and Kristen Madden align several goddess archetypes to more well known dances in their book *Dancing the Goddess Incarnate.* Gerald Gardner gives instructions for the Meeting Dance in the Gardnerian Book of Shadows:

The Maiden should lead. A man should place both hands on her waist, standing behind her, and alternate men and women should do the same, the Maiden leading and they dance following her. She at last leads them into a right-hand spiral. When the center is reached (and this had better be marked by a stone), she suddenly turns and dances back, kissing each man as she comes to him. All men and women turn likewise and dance back, men kissing girls and girls kissing men. All in time to music, it is a merry game, but must be practiced to be done well. Note, the musicians should watch the dancers and make the music fast or slow as is best. For the beginners it should be slow, or there will be confusion. It is most excellent to get people to know each other at big gatherings.

In the book *Light from the Shadows*, author Gwyn relates dances aligned with the eight sabbats of Witchcraft, but does not give specific instructions on how to perform them.

Yule	Dance of the Flaming Wheel
Imbolc	Broom Dance
Ostara	Snake Dance
Beltane	May Pole Dance and Spiral Dance
Litha	Hobby Horse Dance
Lammas	Sword Dance
Mabon	Chain Dance
Samhain	Maze Dance

Some of these dances will be quite familiar to most modern Pagans, such as the May Pole dance and Spiral Dance. Others can be found in the traces of folk traditions still surviving, such as the Dance of the Flaming Wheel and the Hobby Horse Dance and Sword Dance. By exploring the surviving cultural folk dances of Britain, modern Witches across the world can adapt them for their rituals. While they will not necessarily be the same as those rural folk traditions unless you find explicit instructions or someone to teach you directly, you will still resonate with the ancestors' ways of the past and find the keys to go deeper through ritual, and seasonal, dance.

Exercise: May Pole Dance

A May Pole, or May Day dance requires a vertical pole, known as a May Pole, to be constructed with ribbon streamers hanging from it. Traditionally the May Pole is made from a tree (often Maple, Birch, Hawthorne or Oak) cut down by the men of the community, while the women dig the hole for the pole to be placed. The imagery is an obvious suggestion of the God of the Woods entering the Goddess of the Earth for the fertility of the land. The Pole itself should be taller than the tallest dancer. If you have a large community, the pole can be quite tall, with communities competing to get the tallest May Pole. The custom has roots in Germanic Paganism can be found across Europe, but the version found in England and America is usually shorter than their Northern counterparts in Scandinavia. Ribbons are fastened to the top, in equal number, of two different colors. Usually men and women of equal number dance, each holding a different color ribbon and alternating in the circle. Men face in the clockwise direction around the circle, while women face counterclockwise, and together they weave in and out, women first going under, then men, repeatedly until a woven pattern is created on the pole. Often a floral wreath is placed at the top, over the ribbons, so when the ribbons are held taut by the dancers, the wreath remains, and slowly descends as the dancers wind the ribbons. The dance ensures the fertility and health of the community and the relationship they have with the land.

Exercise: Spiral Dance

The Spiral Dance has been popularized in modern American Wicca through the Reclaiming Tradition and specifically the work of Starhawk, who wrote a book of the same name. It's a powerful ritual dance that can be done with a large group, ideally at least thirty. Smaller groups are not well equipped for an extended dance. The group starts in a large circle, holding hands. The leader of the dance frees the left hand from the circle and spirals inward, clockwise, facing the center of the circle. Upon creating about three loops (more if the group is larger) the leader turns to face the person holding her right hand, and follows the spiral outward, counterclockwise. The pattern repeats with inward and outward spirals resulting in people facing each other, gazing into each others eyes, often accompanied with a chant being sung such as "We All Come from the Goddess." It's a powerful spiritual experience to gaze at the divine within the eyes of every person in the ritual thereby altering consciousness, and also a way to raise energy for other magickal work.

Fig. 37: Spiral Dance

Exercise: Maze Dance

The Maze Dance might refer to traversing a labyrinth. One of the most popular labyrinth images in modern Paganism today goes back to Ancient Crete. The seven turned Cretan labyrinth, when carved on stone and used as a meditative device, was known as a Troy Stone in Britain. The image might serve as the root of the Maze of the Minotaur in Greek myth. William G. Gray, in his book *Western Inner Workings,* described a Pagan group's performance of the Maze technique as follows:

"The Maze was a more complicated performance. A maze-pattern usually of the circular kind had to be traced on the ground. The leader entered it first with sort of skipping motion and the rest followed in single line chanting a wordless tune mostly in vowel sounds. Steps and directions kept changing with the patterns and they continued to go back and forth through the Maze for a considerable time until they felt, as they described it, "different" and ready to "enter the Castle." This might be only a momentary experience of consciousness with their Inner Selves, or they could be lying or sitting around for quite a while, but they usually "came to" after some minutes and joined the feast round the fire afterwards when they felt inclined."

The Cretan labyrinth can be constructed quite easily if you have the space and bare earth for marking its borders. Some will create semi-permanent "mazes" with rocks, twigs, sawdust, and/or candles.

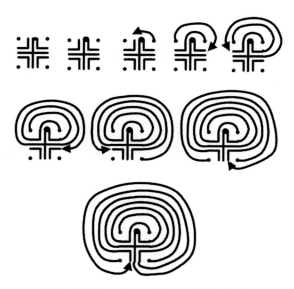

Fig. 38: Creating a Cretan labyrinth

Exercise: Drawing Down Dance

My husband and coven-mate Steve Kenson designed a "Drawing Down" dance using some of the principles of axis and movement outlined in the Free Form sections above to draw down the power of the Sun, or the Moon by a group, via dance for a magick circle ritual. Have your group of dancers stand in a circle, facing clockwise. Walk three steps, following the line of the circle, the turn the body counter clockwise, rotating on the vertical axis. Then repeat, taking three steps again and a counter clockwise rotation. Repeat a third time but rather than rotate counterclockwise, reach up with the arms, draw the energy down and crouch down to the ground, hands touching the floor. Bounce up and repeat this tri-fold pattern. This can be done in a 6/8 time signature. We have found it helpful to count out when learning (Step–2(step)–3(step)–turn–2–3–Step–2–3–turn–2–3–Step–2–3–Up–Down–Up. Repeat.)

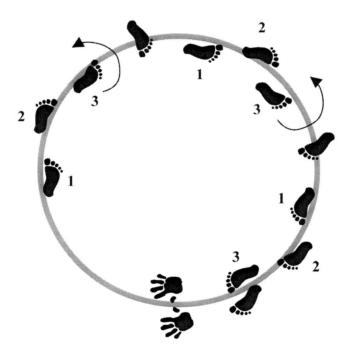

Fig. 39: Drawing Down Dance Steps

Metamorphosis: The dances of metamorphosis are those of shape shifting and transformation. They can be either free form or formal, or a mix of the two. Many tribal cultures have specific animal dances, movements to help a new dancer commune with the spirit and experience of a specific animal. Other animal dancing traditions encourage direct spirit contact and a transformation of energy to better match the spirit of the animal, and spontaneous movements to reflect this change. I believe many spontaneous shapeshifting experiences are then taught, becoming codified into a specific dance, yogic posture or marital arts form.

Exercise: Dancing Your Animal

Dancing is always facilitated with music appropriate for the mood of the ritual. Pick music that you associate with your favorite animal or, more appropriately, the animal you identify as your "power" animal or "totem" animal. Imagine yourself becoming that animal. How would it move? How would it act? Do your best to emulate the movements, sounds and, eventually, the mindset of the animal. Each dance and each dancer will be different, although later traditions have codified specific animal dances. For the purposes of this exercise, don't try to create dance steps, but a ritual of imagination to become more like your animal. I prefer to do it, when appropriate, around a fire, dancing in a circle as I imitate my animal. After a while, the imitation stops, and I feel more like my animal, spiritually and physically. Dancing your animal spirit can be facilitated through the use of animal ritual masks (See **Chapter Twelve**), costuming or, if appropriate, animal skin. Certain ecstatic body postures, while not dances, do facilitate similar metamorphosis experiences.

Circle Dance: Circle Dance is perhaps the most appropriate for Witchcraft rituals, particularly those involving a group. Our rituals are held in a circle. We move in a circle already. Strengthening the flow of energy and inducing trance by keeping with these traditions makes the most sense. Circle dance is just that, dancing in a circle. At its most basic, it's moving everyone around a central vertical axis, imagined at a central point embodied by a fire, altar, cauldron, reflective white stone, or staff/stang planted into the ground. Usually circle dance refers to the group moving in a circle with some specific arranged steps, often holding hands. While the Spiral Dance can be considered a form of circe dance, the circle is obviously broken to form the spiral motion, while circle dances usually maintain the form of a circle.

Fig. 40: Stang

Exercise: Grapevine Step

A simple form of circle dance that can be done deosil or widdershins is the grapevine step, because it emulates the snaking movement of the growing grapevine. Participants stand in a circle, facing inward, holding hands, right hand on top of left hand. In synchronous movement (for a clockwise dance) the right leg is moved over the left, leaving the legs crossed momentarily with the right foot to the left of the left foot. Then the left leg and foot are brought to the left side of right foot. The right leg is then brought behind the left foot, leaving the legs crossed momentarily again with the right foot to the left of the left foot. Then the left leg and foot are bought to the left side of the right foot. The steps are repeated to move the circle. The same motion is followed for a widdershins dance, but the directions are reversed.

Exercise: Group Cord Dance

The cord dance is performed by a coven, using their cingulums, or Witch's cords. Most often used as a corded belt for robes, the cords are linked together like the spokes of a wheel. The first person makes a loop with the cord, holding both ends. The second passes their cord through the loop and holds both ends in one hand, creating the first two "spokes of the wheel. Other members pass their cords through and hold both ends in one hand, creating additional spokes, until a full wheel of many spokes is formed. Move in a circular motion, usually clockwise, faster and faster, until the energy is raises. The leader of the group, who may or may not be in the dance itself, give a signal for everyone to let go of one end of the cord, releasing the wheel and allowing it to be used for journey or spellcraft.

Exercise: Solitary Spiral Circle Dance

Gareth Knight espouses the benefits of not only studying the spiral pattern, but physically moving in that pattern and, in *The Rose Cross and the Goddess*, shows us another form of "Spiral Dance." This is a solitary dance emulating the image and movement of the spindle. Start in the center with a rod, such as a staff or stang, firmly in the ground, with a cord warped around it. Then in a clockwise direction, slowly unravel the cord from the rod, tracing with your steps a spiral that culminates in a circle. Through this work, you are aligning with the great Weaver goddess, and the mysteries of the spindle and loom. Your "partners" are the Fates themselves, as you hold one end of the cord and they hold the other.

Treading the Mill: Dancing or treading the mill has been one of the most interesting and powerful ritual dances I've learned. Technically a form of circle dance, it really requires its own section, for its lore is deep and magickal. The "mill" is not one set of steps, or really any one dance. It refers to a concept found in non-Gardnerian derived forms of Witchcraft. I first came across in through the writings of Doreen Valiente, in references to the teachings she learned from Robert Cochrane and his Clan of Tubal Cain. I have later experienced it through several different sources, including a group of Welsh descended traditional Witches and through the work of faery seer and author Orion Foxwood. The mill is representative of the turning forces of the universe. The turning mill is in the stars, but also in the living land. It is the wheel of destiny from which our life threads are spun, and the grindstone of the gods that grinds the universe down to dust. The dance steps are ways of moving the energy of the mill to not only induce trance and raise energy, but commune with the forces of nature to make your magick. While the mill can be a part of sacred space, it is sometimes confused with the more Wiccan magick circle. It's not a magick ritual circle in the formal sense of a boundary, though Foxwood does teach that is has four points to it. These points are not the four well known elements of the magick circle, but four celestial forces – Sun, Moon, Planets and Stars.

Exercise: Mill Dance

The actual dancing of the mill can be done in many ways. Some Witches perform it clockwise, or deosil, while others performing it counterclockwise, widdershins or *tuathal*. For many, turning to the left, counterclockwise means descending into the underworld, while others see it rising to the stars. Clockwise is the motion of life on the surface of our planet, the middle world of space and time. The dance can be done holding hands, doing something similar to the grapevine step detailed previously, holding shoulders facing each other's backs, with cords or with no physical link at all. For some of the dances, participants would face in, others face out or in the direction of the circle's movement. Often it is a slow shuffle around the circle done for a very long time. The monotony of it helps induce trance. The general characteristic of the dance is an energetic feeling of "grinding" or "friction" raising the energy to alter consciousness and do the work. Chanting and singing can be done, with specific words, or simple tones. The Mill of Magick chant is obviously a popular chant for this working. Two versions exist, one considered "traditional" and the other known as the Devonshire Witch's Mill Chant. Though they are not credited and listed as traditional, some believe them to be written by, or at least reworked by, high priestess Doreen Valiente.

Mill of Magick (Traditional)

Air breath, Air blow,
Make the Mill of Magick go.
Work the will for which we pray
Io, Deo, Ha He Hey.

Fire Flame and Fire burn,
Make the Mill of Magick turn.
Work the will for which we pray,
Io, Deo, Ha He Hey.

Water bubble, Water boil,
Make the Mill of Magick toil.
Work the will for which we pray,
Io, Deo, Ha He Hey.

Earth without and Earth within,
Make the Mill of Magick spin.

Work the will for which we pray,
Io, Deo, Ha He Hey!

The Devonshire rendering of the chant ends each stanza with "Eman hetan, hau he hu!" instead of the "Io, Deo, Ha He Hey!"

One of the most powerful versions of the dance I participated in involved simply aligning people on opposite sides of the circle, as if they were on the same "spoke" and dancing silently counterclockwise. We synchronized our out breath by overemphasizing it, helping to create group consciousness. The leader of the group heightened the pace faster and faster, until we all dropped to the ground, linked hands right over left, and began a séance style underworld journey as a group. The breathwork and dancing facilitated a strong group consciousness.

EXHAUSTION

Exhaustion is the shadow to dance, a necessary component to the path, but an edge that should be walked carefully. While the dance itself is trance inducing, most Witchcraft practices dealing with the other worlds use the dance to build energy prior to a collapse and visionary journey. The exhaustion preceding the collapse is what helps open the inner gateway to travel, and the energy generated by the dance ritual helps propel participants through the gateway. It's a powerful method found in many cultures, but it does have its drawbacks. While it can be used, it isn't always the wisest method to use regularly. If you keep a regular spiritual practice, it can be quite difficult on your whole body to dance yourself to a manic exhaustion and collapse into a journey every night. The path of dance and other strenuous movements should be reserved for major workings, when the extra energy is needed, and the body's strength should be built over time with more regular exercise, particularly yogic and martial art forms of exercise.

If you do pursue techniques that induce exhaustion, be careful of over exerting yourself over the long run. Make sure to take care of your physical body. Nurture it with good food, regular moderate exercise and fresh air. If your body is your instrument, it must be finely tuned. Don't push yourself to the breaking point as a regular practice, while still challenging both your body and your psyche. Build your strength and power so you can go further longer. Do not abstain from regular exercise to build up your energy, and then attempt a major dance ritual and injure yourself. Just like performing a marathon, train to build up your strength in smaller ways, before tackling the larger workings. The positive use of exhaustion will be somewhat covered in the **Chapter Six** and **Chapter Nine**.

Aids for the Way of Dance

Sacred movement and dance can be enhanced if you keep these points in mind:

Lose Your Inhibitions: Those involved in the ecstasy of the dance don't care how they look to other people. They aren't worried about being laughed at. They are in the moment, stepping out of their self-perceptions in flow with music, motion, and spirit. If you are inhibited, worried about looking foolish or embarrassing yourself, you will never reach that gnosis point through dance. Lose your inhibitions. Dance until you don't care any more, and the magickal gate will open.

Group Dance: Group dance can be less intimidating in ritual than solo dance, as you can lose yourself in the group and use the "good" dancers as inspiration while you move. Find those who seem to successfully use dance and magick together, and by observing and emulating them, you will find your own inspiration and work the magick of dance.

Do What Feels Good: Do what feels good to your body. Though dance can be challenging athletically, and exhausting after a time, find what works for your body. If your body just doesn't want to move in certain ways, don't force. Push yourself, but don't push yourself beyond safe limits. Injury is not conducive to the way of movement.

Perfection: While technique is important, depending on the type of sacred movement, there is not an emphasis on getting things "right" in most forms of sacred dance. The feeling, attitude, and doing your best within the parameters of the movement are what matter most.

CHAPTER SIX:
THE LONELY ROAD

As we continue onward through the eight original paths, they become more fraught with difficulties. The lonely road, the path of isolation and asceticism, is not an easy choice for most Witches.

Strangely, we associate many of the practices of this path with being truly "spiritual," as the path fits many of the dominant notions, preconceived or otherwise, of both Christian traditions and Eastern spiritual traditions. Yet they are only one path, not *the* path, as some would have you believe. In our effort to embrace body-positive approaches to spirituality, we tend to neglect the harsher paths. While some would think monastic techniques have no place in Neopaganism, if we look to the orders of priests in the ancient world, we find monastic lifestyles are not restricted to the Christian or the Buddhist.

The path of isolation and asceticism can be found in the ancient Pagan world. First and foremost, our tribal ancestors, with shamanic cunning men and wise women, would most likely had such healers and priests living at the edge of society, accessible, but somewhat isolated from the tribe. Surviving tribal people with a shamanic practice often have their medicine practitioners living at the edge of society, part of the tribe, yet separate, in a state of between-ness that marks them as otherworldly. This is similar to the rural Witch of medieval Europe, living at the edge of the village or edge of the forest.

As the tribal societies of the hunter-gatherers gave way to the rise of agrarian communities and our first urban settlements, organized temple traditions of priests and priestesses, acting as community clergy, arose. In many of those cultures, the clergy lived on the temple grounds, and undertook lifestyle practices, including periods of seclusion, silence, and specific dietary restrictions separating them from the mainstream society. Such practices of the temple traditions eventually developed into the more familiar monastic life of discipline we find in mainstream Christianity and some eastern sects. Many modern Pagans speculate that Celtic brotherhoods and sisterhoods of Druids and Druidesses, bards, and seers were more easily absorbed into Christian orders because their practices were not so different and were thereby able to influence the development of the Celtic Christian Church. The priestesses of Bride made a fairly easily transition into the Nuns of St. Bridget.

I've found the path of isolation not to be a technique for everyday use, but for when a particularly powerful and intense form of trance is needed. It is best used for rituals of a life changing nature – initiation, vision quests, atonements. While aspects of it can be used for more common rituals, such as sabbats or esbats, yearly or lunar rituals, multiple techniques from this chapter should only be combined when you are intending a particularly vital ritual.

If you have little experience with these techniques, start slowly and in small steps, and make sure the technique is something you are capable of, both mentally and physically. Many magicians and Witches do not always have the physical stamina for some of the techniques. There are many paths to the center, and this is only one, so if it is not for you, don't feel you are forced to explore this way.

While many of our techniques before have been simple, you do them when you want to enter trance, the path of isolation takes more of a build up. Simply using a technique for twenty minutes, or even a few hours, will not create the necessary shifts to your consciousness. They need to be done over a period of several hours, if not days, depending on the technique.

ISOLATION

Isolation is the key component of this path. You set yourself apart from the normal, the everyday, through your desired trance state. One of the most profound ways to create this magickal separation of consciousness is to actually separate yourself from the normal, ordinary, and mundane. A spiritual retreat of some sort, self-imposed isolation, does strange things to the consciousness. By removing yourself from day-to-day concerns, your internal dialogue shifts. You are less focused on the presentation of how you wish things to be, both to yourself and others, and more focused on what simply is. Isolation can be done moderately or dramatically. Usually it requires a change of location, such as literally taking a retreat without the modern amenities, particularly the amenities of communication. Phone, television, computers and the like bring us right back into the normal, un-isolated consciousness, defeating the purpose. Going to a cabin retreat is an excellent start. Others simply sequester themselves off while remaining in their home

– taking time off from work, electronics, and other connections. More serious isolation practices include performing it outdoors, away from people, or in taking an overnight vigil. Set an allotted amount of time and spend it away from civilization, even if its only a short hike into the woods, or an afternoon in a lonely field. Perform your magick there, and notice how the lack of human companionship and, in fact, the lack of all signs of civilization, can induce a new awareness, taking you back to the ways of your ancient ancestors, often being "alone" in the wild.

SILENCE

Silence is exactly what it appears – being quiet. While much of ritual focuses on the sounds we make, the words we speak, and rhythms we make, there is a power in silence. Particularly there is a power when we are silent ourselves, not just existing in a quiet environment. Stopping the flow of vocal power forces the energy within our consciousness, and can open the gates to new perceptions and introspection. The lack of outward communication to anyone restricts our interactions and allows us to focus on our own energy.

Stopping verbal communication also makes us aware of the thousands of sounds, and thousands of currents of energy, that we ignore every day, because we are too busy projecting, rather than receiving. The sense of hearing can actually become more acute during periods of silence. You can become more appreciative of the sounds already in your environment, and these sounds can help induce gnosis. If you are combining silence with outdoor isolation the sounds of the wind, birds, water, insects, all combine to add to your deepening awareness.

Exercise: Vow of Silence

Take a vow of silence for twenty-four hours. Arrange your schedule so you have no responsibilities that require you to speak. If not combining this with isolation, inform your family and friends you are exploring an aspect of your spirituality that requires no verbal contact for twenty-four hours. If family obligations do not allow the luxury of a full twenty-four hours, then pick a shorter time and stick with it. This is a ritual of discipline as well as isolation. Take your vow of silence for the time period and observe your thoughts and feelings through the day. Silence includes all verbal noise, not just talking to people – no talking to animal, plants, or yourself. No humming, signing or other noises. Conserve the verbal energy. Do some form of magick or meditation at the culmination of this period. Did the silence effect your experience? Journal about the experience, detailing what you felt, thought, and did during your period of silence, and how it altered your consciousness.

SLEEP DEPRIVATION

Sleep deprivation is another powerful (and dangerous) technique for altering consciousness. When the human body does not experience enough sleep, particularly when we don't experience the dream state, physiological, emotional, and psychological changes occur. This process can be used to our advantage on the path of isolation, for lack of sleep isolates us from the dream world, and from normal humanity. It differentiates us from the norm, and in that state of altering consciousness and perception, new realizations can occur. Older texts warn that a sleep deprived mind will start to hallucinate, and while that might be true, the Witch, shaman, and magician would question if such experiences are hallucinations, or trance induced visions. Is there a difference? Perhaps the only difference is the benefit the vision grants its viewer and the fear and discord the hallucination grants its viewer. The main difference between the two is that one is controlled, intentional, and done with purpose, while the other is haphazard and outside of a sacred ritual context. The boundary of ritual is an important demarcation between practices that would generally be considered ill-advised and those of a magician.

One of the most powerful ways of using sleep deprivation is in keeping a vigil. In a religious context, a vigil consists of staying awake beyond the bounds of normal sleep, often to precede a religious service, festival, or ritual. Though vigils can be done in a group context, usually silent vigils, most Witches find them more effective in solitary practice. It's a powerful method for the solitary to heighten the experience before a major working. The vigil can be held in the confines of a sacred space such as a magick circle (**Chapter Fourteen**) or in an outdoor location deemed appropriate for the working, but without the specific boundaries of a circle. Vigils are sometimes combined with fasting and other isolation techniques from this chapter.

FASTING

Fasting is way to restrict your energy and interactions with others. Restricting the amount of food, and what kinds of food, you take in. By changing the type and amount of "fuel" your body receives, you change its working. Many believe that by consuming very little, you are giving your internal organs a rest, and also an opportunity for such energy to be turned inward. You are clearing the body, purging chemicals and waste from the digestive tract and organs. Your body operates as efficiently as possible when fasting, and removes unwanted diseased cells and generally clears all body systems. As you physically clear the body, you are also clearing the psyche. On a physiological level, the lack of food makes you less grounded. Such a state facilitates otherworldly contact and sensitivity to energy. Most use the technique of fasting in part of a larger ritual for personal revelation, healing, and initiation.

One famous Cunning Man who used fasting as a method of practical gnosis was the Wise Man of Stokesley, John Wrightson. He was the seventh son of a seventh daughter, but claimed he was no wiser than the next man ordinarily. He simply received knowledge when he fasted and was known to cure animals, find lost or stolen possessions and know the happenings occurring at other locations by some psychic means. Rather than a deep philosophical gnosis on the mysteries, he used his fasting trance state for practical purposes and was known as quite an aid in his village and surrounding areas, well respected by the populace.

There are many kinds of fasts, and not all of them are right for all types of people. In fact, many people probably shouldn't fast, at least without the supervision of a trained medical professional. Some people simply have body chemistry types not conducive to restricted food intake. If you have any doubts, consult with a health care practitioner before embarking upon a fast.

Water Fast: A period of abstinence from all food. Fluids are consumed for both thirst and for bodily requirements. It is possible for a person to fast for forty days on water without suffering a deficiency of proteins, vitamins, minerals, and fatty acids if otherwise healthy and not exposed to harsh elements or other debilitating conditions. At least two liters of water should be drunk per day. Distilled water is best for cleansing, though spring water can be used. Tap water should be avoided unless it is thoroughly purified. Water fasts work aggressively in the body. Generally a few days of the Juice Fast precedes the Water Fast, and then a few days of the Juice Fast after the water fast, to help re-acclimate your body to digestion. If the water fast is too harsh for the body, it can be alternated with the juice fast, for example having three days on juice and then two days of water, then five days of juice and three days on water. The juice can be used when you are more intensively working, and the water fast for when you have weekends and days off.

Juice Fast: A juice fast refrains from all solid food, but fruit and vegetable juices in addition to water. Ideally the fruits and vegetable juices are as fresh and pure as possible. Some versions of this fast also include herbal teas, vegetable broth, barley greens, wheat grass juice and health food supplements. The intensity of the fast depends on how much juice you drink. Generally drink when you feel hunger developing and drink until pleasantly full and satisfied, rather than stuffed. Juice can also be diluted with water.

Raw Fruit & Vegetable Fast: A variation of the Juice Fast abstains from all solid foods except raw fruits and vegetables, and their juices. The reduction of heavy processed foods and meats from the diet both alters the digestive process and gives some of the benefit of a true fast.

Shamanic Diet: The Shamanic Diet is from the teachings of South American shamans who primarily work with the plant entheogen of ayahuasca, though their diet format is similar to several other magickal traditions. It's not a true fast, but a method of eating that facilitates spiritual contact, and is done in conjunction with rituals, meditations, songs, and herbal remedies to help prepare the practitioner for spirit contact. This diet is undertaken during the shaman's apprenticeship, and repeated before major workings or teachings.

No salt
No alcohol
No spices or condiments
No pork
No fats
No coffee or other stimulants
No citrus fruit, particularly lemon or lime
No shellfish or "bottom feeders"

Mainly eat rice, fish, and unseasoned vegetables. While poultry is allowed, it is not encouraged. Grains other than rice or not specifically prohibited, but do not seem to be encouraged. Nuts are generally avoided. No sex is allowed on this diet as well, as the plant spirit as an ally is often seen as a lover, and gets jealous if your attentions stray to another. To break the fast once the spiritual working is complete, have salt, or a lemon with salt. Gradually resume normal eating. William Gray's work confirms this was not just a South American practice, reporting in *Western Inner Workings* that Pagans he knew refrained from salt for several days before any major working. Salt is said to banish spirits. One of the underlying ideas of such a fast with bland food and no sex was to diminish the practitioners connection to the physical world, to heighten the connection to the spirit world.

Plant Spirit Fast: The same conditions are followed for the Shamanic Diet, but one of the allowed foods is a strong brew of a particular plant, seen as a teaching spirit. In this method, you are drinking your "teaching" to facilitate a deeper contact with that plant spirit.

Master Cleanse: The Master Cleanse Fast, also known as the Lemon Cleanse Fast is one of my favorites and the fast I have the most personal experience using for health reasons, and have successfully combined it with trance inducing techniques. The Master Cleanse consists of drinking the following throughout the day:

2 Tablespoons of Fresh Squeezed Lemon (1/2 Lemon)

2 Tablespoons of Organic Maple Syrup, Grade B or C

1/10th or more teaspoon of cayenne pepper

10-14 Oz of Pure Water (Spring, Purified or Distilled)

This mix gives you enough calories to work normally, and enough cleansing properties to detoxify the body. The radical change in digestion also works well for trance inducing fasts. Drink at least twelve 8 oz glasses of this "lemonade" and make sure you drink a lot of pure water besides. To go off the fast, start with vegetable broth and fruit juice before resuming a normal diet.

Black Fast: The Blast Fast is not a health regime, but a bit of magick I first came across in the writing of Doreen Valiente. Rather than purging the body of toxins, or inducing a state of gnosis, the Black Fast directs all your psychic energy to a particular goal. Sadly, it is usually the purpose of a curse, but I've used fasting techniques similar to the Black Fast for more constructive purposes. Basically one vows not to eat anything but bread, water, and salt until a certain condition or action occurs. All your mind and body's resources are directed toward that goal due to the fast, and make the magick more potent. The Black Fast is also referred to in Catholicism, with its own guidelines and direction, omitting the cursing or spell craft. It was one of the most strict types of fast, undertaken during Holy Week or before ordination, but gradually grew out of favor with the Church.

Fasts are done for varying time periods. If you have no experience in fasting, a single day long fast is the best place to start. For trance-inducing effects, one to three days of fasting can be more than enough to alter perceptions. Simply fasting for the day of a ritual working, esbat, sabbat, or other gathering is sufficient. For medical fasting, to heal, cleanse, and cure illness, varying periods are recommended. For the water fast, ten days has become a standard. For the Juice Fast, twenty to thirty days is the standard. The Master Cleanse is performed for eight to forty days. It's best to determine a set time for your fast and stick to it, starting small if you are not experienced in fasting. Eating should be resumed in a very gradual and gentle manner. Keep your first few solid meals light and easily digestible, and gradually return to a normal diet. You might find that your tastes and needs have changed after an extended fast.

Be mindful of dizziness or blackouts during fasting. Headaches are common within the first few days of fasting. Though many report having more energy, faster reflexes, and feeling more cognitively sharp then when eating normally, be cautious in operating any heavy machinery or placing yourself in any other life threatening situations. You can experience cold or flu-like symptoms, as well as diarrhea, constipation, itchiness, and a range of symptoms as your body cleanses over an extended fast. You can even experience a healing crisis of a mental, emotional, or spiritual nature. As part of the process of altered perspective and energy, repressed issues can come to the surface and must be faced.

All fasts assume you will refrain from all drugs, nicotine, and alcohol during the fasting period. Some programs use herbal teas, but most do not. If you have a prescription that must be taken daily, please talk to your health care provider before performing a fast or suspending your medication. If you have hyperglycemia, hypoglycemia, diabetes, abnormal thyroid functioning, kidney disease, liver disease, chronic heart conditions, or any mental illness or chemical imbalance, consult with a fasting expert before undertaking a fast.

This is not a book on medicinal fasting and cannot possibly cover the range of everyone's medical and health needs. If you desire to perform an extended fast beyond the normal trance inducing techniques, please consult with appropriate resources and experts.

CELIBACY

Restricting the use of sexual energy, specifically refraining from partnered or solo sexual activity, is a potent way of gathering energy. Many traditions of spiritual devotion, ranging from Catholicism and Eastern asceticism, to Pagan and shamanic traditions, use abstinence, temporarily or as a life style, to gather and transmute spiritual power. Orders of celibate nuns, monks, and priests are still traditional today. Modern Paganism and most shamanic traditions use only temporary celibacy, refraining from sexual activity prior to magickal or religious workings, to persevere the energy and purify it for the ritual. In some shamanic traditions, the spirits, particularly plant spirits, are seen as lovers, and any sexual activity before imploring their aid is taken as unfaithfulness, resulting in jealousy from the spirit. Refraining from sexual activity for days, or even weeks prior to a major working helps facilitate the energies of the ritual.

RESTRICTED SPACE

Another method of isolation is specifically restricting your area. Rather than simply being in a place to avoid the mundane world and social contact, marking out a specific boundary, and not straying from that boundary is an excellent way to enhance that isolation. Restricting yourself can be a simple as limiting your area to your home, a specific room, or a specific area outdoors. You can use the natural marking of a hilltop, a riverbank, a field or clearing to be the bounds of your space. Restricted space is much like creating a magick circle. Not only are you containing your self to one area, but creating a sort of vessel for the energy of consciousness, preventing it from dissipating in a million different directions and distractions. Like all parts of the lonely road, this technique force you to be present with what is, right there with you, and everything you brought in psychically to the space, rather than focusing on the future, past, or social conventions.

Vision Quest

A vision quest, most commonly found in Native American traditions, and specifically in Lakota culture where it is known as a *Hanblecheyapi* (Crying for a Vision) is a method that combines many of the techniques above, including isolation, silence, sleep deprivation, fasting, and space restriction. Traditionally it is done under the supervision of a tribal elder or medicine man, and usually done for the first time in the early teenage years, to receive a vision to guide one in life. Modern Witches with leanings towards Native Traditions have adopted and adapted the technique.

Hanblecheyapi is not unlike the Northern tradition of *utiseta*, or "sitting out." While the term appears to simply mean to sit outside for a marked time, it has a deeper meaning of sitting "outside" of all things, outside of your world, your society, expectations, to being outside of your own self, thoughts, and ego. Only then can you see clearly and have proper contact with the spirits. Utiseta might be combined with other northern trance techniques, such as runic magick or seidr.

Generally the quester finds a place and marks out a predetermined circle, much like the Witch's traditional nine foot diameter circle, usually in stones, bringing nothing from "normal" society into it other than water. Sacred items might be brought into the circle. Only water is drunk and usually vigil must be kept, without sleeping. The quester prays, meditates, chants, performs ritual and does journey work to go within, asking for a vision. Spirit contact, particularly contact with a totemic or guardian animal ally can occur, or a message can be received from the spirit world in a dream. The seeker discusses the experience with the elder to receive a proper interpretation of the vision without ego or delusion to cloud it. An object from the site is often collected and placed into the seekers "medicine bag" of power objects, to retain the power of the vision for their lifetime.

The vision quest can last from one to four days. Sometimes a mentor or friend checks in on the seeker, directly or covertly, particularly in cases of extreme weather. Cleansing rituals, to prepare for the event, are not uncommon, such as the sweat lodge (see below). If you decide to undertake a vision quest type of experience, here are some points to keep in mind:

Food: Even if you choose not to make a fast a part of your quest, prepare for the experience by reducing your caloric intake at least a week prior to your ritual. Eliminate things like caffeine, alcohol, sugar, tobacco and all non-prescription/medicinal drugs you can reasonably eliminate and remain safe and healthy. Eat a diet consisting of whole foods such as fresh fruits and vegetables, foods with more fiber, lots of pure water, and detoxifying herbal teas. Purification baths prior to the vision quest also prepare you. When you are going to your vision quest, make sure you have lots of fresh water. If you are eating, bring simple foods like fruits and nuts.

Mental Preparation: Prepare for isolation a week prior to the event by limiting the people you see socially, only doing what is necessary for family and work commitments. Reduce your intake of electronic media such as television, radio, and the Internet. Refrain from gossip. Withdraw from that which is not necessary and will distract you.

Ritual Tools: Have whatever ritual tools you feel necessary for the trip. Have offerings for the spirits of the land and your allies. In Native traditions, cornmeal, sage, and tobacco are usual offerings. Incense, musical instruments and even a pen/journal are appropriate. Usually tents and sleeping bags are foregone in such rituals, but bring a blanket and appropriate clothing to protect you from the elements.

Location: Choose a remote location, away from the sounds, sights, and smells of modern society, yet one accessible to you. Do not choose a location beyond your body's capability to travel. You can often loose the traces of human civilization in local woods and parks without traveling too far away. If you don't have someone physically checking up on you at the location, make sure someone knows where you are exactly, and when you should be home in case something goes wrong and help is necessary. Check the local history and myth of the area if possible. Choose places that are "neutral" or generally benign psychically. If the location was a place of battle, crime, or other violence, avoid it.

Duration: While a vision quest can go on for four days, if you have never experienced such a ritual, and do not have an experienced teacher guiding you, I believe a six hour vigil is the best way to start, working your way up to an overnight solitary vigil.

Ritual: create sacred space in whatever way you want. Usually you mark the four directions and your boundary of sacred space with a powder like cornmeal, or using stones from the location. Make your offerings and invite your spirit allies, ancestors and deities to join you. If you have a specific intention for the vision quest, state it. Do ritual – prayer, drumming, chanting, meditation, etc. Be aware of everything that occurs, inside of your consciousness and outside of your body. Look for synchronicities between your thoughts and feelings and signs from nature – the passing of an animal, the cry of a bird or a change in the weather. Nature, along with the spirit world, will often respond to your cry for a vision.

Record and Discuss: Record your experience and while you might clearly understand your vision and experience, traditionally it is best to go over your vision with a wise elder or teacher who will guide you. It's easy to become zealous in such states of heightened awareness, and misinterpret things to be more flattering to our ego than necessary.

Sometimes the sitting will not be "out" but in, as in the form of a natural cave or other underground restricted space, usually lacking light. The *fogous* is a man made underground ceremonial structure found in Cornwall, while the *souterrains*, or "earth house" is its equivalent in Brittany. Most magickal practitioners believe they were used for ceremonial purposes, but they could have been dwelling shelters or storehouses as well.

Sacred Pilgrimage

The sacred pilgrimage is not restricting space, but restricting yourself from daily life and typical movement. The pilgrimage is a journey, usually solitary to a sacred site, though the tradition of the "walk about" is to simply wander, following intuition and omens, until the ritual purpose of the journey, such as the answer to a life question, is complete. It often follows a path followed by pilgrims in ages past. The Celtic term "turas" can denote specific pilgrim paths usually associated with Celtic saints, or a general term for sacred pilgrimage. In her sensational book, *The Camino*, actress Shirley MacClaine describes her own personal pilgrimage in Spain, following a traditional train believed to be aligned with a "ley line" upon the Earth (See **Chapter Ten**). Many of the same prohibitions in a Vision Quest are followed in such a Sacred Pilgrimage, such as isolation, simple food, simple clothing, silence (or at least minimal communication) and attunement with nature. The journey might be culminated with a ritual or meditation at the last stop.

RESTRICTED SENSES

After restricting the space you occupy, the only way to further your isolation is to restrict the senses through which you perceive the space. With less sensory input, your consciousness is turned even further inward. You focus on the worlds beyond the veil, for the world of flesh and blood is blocked to your senses.

Elements	Senses
Fire	Sight
Air	Smell
Water	Taste
Earth	Touch
Spirit	Hearing

Sight: Blindfolds, veils, hoods, and eyeless masks can be used to block out light. Ritual areas that naturally block out light can also be used. In a natural setting, caves and dark forests grant virtual blindness. A temple room with the light blocked from the windows and doors will also serve. Absolute darkness can conjure up vivid images, where journeys, myths and stories take on amazing realism. Some modern practitioners conjecture this was a technique for the ancient bards and Druids to memorize their tales and grow in magickal power. The three darknesses of Taliesin in his rebirth myth with Ceridwen (the dark hut stirring the cauldron, the time within Ceridwen's womb, and the sea journey in the dark leather bag) mark three periods where the bard was immersed in total darkness, seeking a vision. While such darkness can conjure journeys due to the sensory deprivation, sometimes a single illumination, such as a candle or lamp, can serve as a powerful focus, blocking out all other visual information and focusing on the one source of light. Sometimes simply obscuring one eye with a veil or hood can also help induce trance, imitating the one eyed god Odin/Wotan on his search for magick and power.

Sound: Earplugs, cotton, earmuffs, and head wrappings can be used to isolate sound from your senses. White noise generators, while technically sound, block out all other noise, and can be used via speakers or with headphones. The lack of external noise forces you to focus on the internal "noise."

Touch: Removing any dramatic tactile objects from the ritual context – from soft fur or feathers, to hard and cold iron or stone, reduces the tactile sensory information. Some would suggest working in a simple robe or other loose fitting clothing, others would suggest working nude, or skyclad, though skyclad can heighten the sensation of touch and temperature.

Smell: While it can be very difficult to block out the sense of smell, strong scents from oils or incense can block out other scent information and eventually become part of the olfactory background, no longer noticeable but not allowing other information through. The chosen scent depends on the individual, and should also be magickally conducive to the operation (See **Chapter Seven**). Camphor, along with having a strong overpowering scent, is also conducive to working with other levels of consciousness.

Taste: If not combining this restriction with fasting, keeping food to the barest minimum, such as bread or other grains, water and a simple protein, with no spices or flavors, helps reduce the intake on taste information, and open our senses to other information, including psychic information.

Modern sensory deprivation chambers are the ultimate extension of this concept, and I've known quite a few people who have had profound spiritual experiences while immersed in the floating water of the deprivation tank. Ancient world "deprivation tanks" would include caves and catacombs. If you explore such dark places, please use caution, as you never know when a dangerous animal has set up residence in such a cave or tunnel. Work with someone who knows the land well and can point out signs of habitation or danger.

RESTRICTED MOVEMENT

Restricted movement refers to not only restricting the space you are in, and possibly restricting the senses, but physically restricting your ability to move. Many forms of bondage can induce trance states, as the restriction can direct the consciousness into an altered state, as the usual outlets for energy to be released are no longer available. Sometimes the restriction is done to promote a particular position, and that position is more conducive to a trance state, much like the ecstatic body postures of the previous chapter.

In the original eightfold path, blood control, via the Cords, is one of the paths to power. It is sometimes referred to as *Warricking*. A Warrick is a screw used to tighten chains or rope around a wagon or around timber, but in the context of Witchcraft, it refers to the control of blood flow. (Sometimes its is confused with warlock or warlocking, but it is not the same word.) The restriction and binding can alter the flow of blood and patterns of breathing, resulting in an altered state of consciousness. In some versions of the eightfold path, the cords are also linked with breath control as one path for this reason, yet they are two distinct paths. One is measured, controlled, and conscious breath control, while the other is involuntary, caused by the ritual tool of the cord.

The use of the cord is found most prevalently in the initiation rituals of British Traditional Wicca. Some point to the use of the garter as the first historic example of a length of cord restricting the flow of blood in Witchcraft. A cave painting in Spain seemingly depicting a shamanic figure with a cord or garter tied under each knee, surrounded by nine women in pointed headdresses as an example of our Stone Age Witchcraft ancestors practicing this tradition. Other examples have been found in ceremonial magick and secret societies and orders. The Cathars, Templars, and Waldensians are all known to have use cords or girdles. The garter was associated with Witchcraft, and might possibly be indicative of membership in a coven or a specific rank and level of initiation. King Edward III of England established the Most Noble Order of the Garter, also known as the Order of the Knights of the Garter, and it has been speculated that he was a Witch, or had sympathy for local Witch groups while in power. Edward sought to return England to a time of chivalry reminiscent of the legends of King Arthur, and many modern Witches today see a connection between the old mysteries, Witchcraft, and the garter order of King Edward. Others claim the link is entirely fictional.

In modern British style Wicca initiation, cords are used in two ways. One is used to take the measure, measuring out the body proportions of the initiate through knotting the cord, making a sympathetic link to the initiate. Originally this measure is kept by the initiator, as "insurance" should the initiate ever break oaths with the coven. Having a talisman perfectly aligned with the initiate can be used in retributive magick to ensure oaths are kept. A practice believed to be started by the Alexandrian line of Witchcraft, and adopted by many progressive traditions, gives the measure back to the initiate, as a sign of trust and adulthood. In this way they keep with the old customs but understand that no one is another's keeper and we must all bear the responsibilities of our actions to the gods first and foremost. Often the cord itself is thin string, not useful for true binding, but simply for measuring.

The second way the cord is seen in initiation ceremonies is through the actual binding of the initiate during the ceremony. While there are other methods to bind one with cord to control the flow of blood and induce trance, the initiate binding is one of the most prevalent and carries both magickal significance and physiological support.

When we hear binding and blood control, we think of practices that can restrict the blood too much and cause damage. No one is attempting to cause harm or injury to induce trance. The blood flow slows, but is not tied off. Likewise, the windpipe is not compressed to the point of not breathing. Many tales in the news media have been told about unfortunate practitioners of auto-erotic asphyxiation. This is not the goal of the Witch. Any binding that restricts one to the point of physical detriment is counterproductive to the making of magick. The process slows down physiology, but does not prevent blood flow or induce unconsciousness. One of the reasons this method is done with another, or a group, is there is a safety net of experienced practitioners to relieve the pressure or give aid in case the one being bound approaches black out or inappropriate discomfort.

The sensation of the binding is meant to direct our energy and awareness. It can act like a "pressure cooker." Things are uncomfortable, but not necessarily painful. Many of us don the ritual garb of formal wear for a variety of occasions. The businessman's stiff collar comes to mind. The pressure of the collar and tie produces is conducive to the pressure of the business environment he works in. (One could argue how conducive that environment is in the long term, but the effect of modern business and health would be the topic of another entire book.) The restriction matches the tenor of the "ritual" of work, and can make one more alert, ready and productive in that work capacity. When work is done, the collar is unbuttoned and the pressure and energy is released. Choker style necklaces also serve a similar function.

The initiation binding is described in the Gardnerian Book of Shadows as part of the "Properly Prepared" section:

…For initiation, tie hands behind back, pull up to small of back, and tie ends in front of throat, leaving a cable-tow to lead by, hanging down in front. (Arms thus form a triangle at back.) When initiate is kneeling at altar, the cable-tow is tied to a ring in the altar. A short cord is tied like a garter round the initiate's left leg above the knee, with ends tucked in. Another is tied round right ankle and ends tucked in so as to be out of the way while moving about. These cords are used to tie feet together while initiate is kneeling at the altar and must be long enough to do this firmly. Knees must also be firmly tied. This must be carefully done. If the aspirant complains of pain, the bonds must be loosened slightly; always remember the object is to retard the blood flow enough to induce a trance state. This involves slight discomfort, but great discomfort prevents the trance state; so it is best to spend some little time loosening and tightening the bonds until they are just right. The aspirant alone can tell you when this is so…

Traditional blood restriction also aids the use of plant magick when applying ointments. The area anointed with an herbal entheogenic ointment is restricted and is absorbed where the blood has been slowed, and when the cord is released the substance flushes the system faster, rather than a gradual introduction into the system when no cord is used.

The binding of the hands prevents us from feeling we need to "do" something and we can tune inward towards the trance or towards the objective of the magick. The cords across the neck can be more problematic for Witches, as many of us believe we have past lives where were hung, and a cord ritually placed around the neck can trigger those traumatic past life memories, feelings, and energies on a deep level, yet such practices help us with those memories move through the limits of our past lives and experience the blessings of such same practices. Beyond the simple set up with the initiate posture, the cords around the neck can be done like a necktie, easily slid off and granting only the same amount of pressure a tie would cause, or with other forms including a quick release knot. The cord around the neck does cause most of us to react to the pressure by standing up straight, arching backwards and altering the capacity of the lung, to help induce trance. Having the tow cable in the front, makes most of the pressure on the back of the neck, not the windpipe, alleviating any concerns of asphyxiation.

While this might seem extreme to an outside observer, any amount of restriction, even a minimal amount, can create a change in the mindset and activate the magickal mind. We do it all the time with formal dress, neckties, jewelry, high heels, girdles, watches, and other conventions of society.

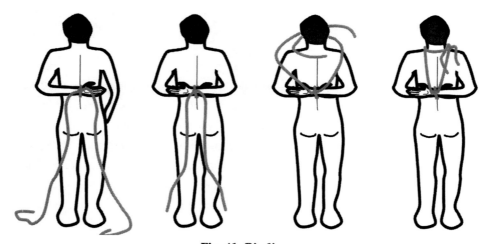

Fig. 41: Binding

Exercise: Corded Jewelry

One of my favorite simple and safe methods of using binding cord is in the process of ritualizing cord as jewelry. I was taught this method by a friend who is an initiate of the African Ifa tradition. He would make beaded or threaded necklaces for a particular Orisha he was working with, and keep it on continuously until that inner spiritual work is over. Siberian shamans would tie a red thread around the neck of a patient, attaching a healing or protection spirit to that patient that would stay only until the thread wore down and fell off, and then would return to the shaman. In South American folk magick honoring Pachamama, white and black wool threads are woven on the first of August, tied to the ankles, wrist and neck to avoid the "punishment" of Pachamama.

Out of thread, yarn or thin cording, make a talisman to be tied around a wrist, ankle or neck. It can be three strands braided, single strands knotted or anything else you can create. Make it with intention. Is there something you are working on manifesting in the outer world? Are you doing it to create a shift in your relationships with yourself, the spirits or gods in the inner world? Are you doing it to remind you to do something, or prevent you from taking a harmful action, perhaps breaking a bad habit? Make it with intention and, either by yourself or with the aid of a trusted confidant, ritually tie the binding around you. Continue to work on it until it naturally wears itself off your body, or after a specific and predetermined length of time. While the cord will not necessarily restrict you or your blood flow, it will produce a psychic pressure, a constant awareness to help you direct and focus your energy to achieve your goal.

The Witch's Cradle

The Witch's Cradle is one of the most intense and serious isolation techniques found in our tradition. I must admit no first hand knowledge of it, and know very few people who do. Supposedly, it was originally a method of torture to elicit confession of a Witch during the Inquisition. In its simplest form, the Witch was tied up in sack, and hung form a tree limb, and set to swing. The sensory deprivation along with the disorientation of the movement produced "hallucinations" that added to the confessions. Other versions of the Witch's cradle appear to be racks where the Witch is wrapped up, strapped in with leather, and the entire rack is hung and set to swing, similar to the sack. Raymond Buckland and Carl Llewellyn Weschcke are two of the few modern Witches to discuss the use of the Witch's cradle.

My only intriguing second-hand experience on a similar method was in discussion traditions with a Witch from Basque Spain currently living in the United States. Decidedly not from a Wiccan background or practice, but seeking community, she befriended members of her local Pagan community and happened to hear me while I was on tour. I said enough about trance techniques different from her own Wiccan group in the United States that she asked me more questions after the lecture, and shared with me some of the outer facts of her own initiation in Spain. She told me that a bull was killed and the skin made into leather straps as part of the initiation, and one would be wrapped in the leather straps, and hung from a tree during the night. Your body would fight against the stress and pressure of the leather until you finally submitted and hung there, completely relaxed, having an out of body experience and communing with the spirits and gods, who would give you your Witch name and share the secrets of magick. But the trick to induce this state of consciousness was in the hanging. I told her what little I knew about the Witch's cradle, and she agreed they seemed very similar, though she felt the sacrifice of the bull, and the tanning of the leather by the initiate made it that much more important and energized for the initiation.

Fig. 42: Witch's Cradle

Exercise: Death Shroud

While it is not as disorienting as the Witch's Cradle, and form of sensory deprivation and restricted movement can be found in a simpler technique I tend to reserve for initiatory journey and intense rebirthing rituals. I first found it in the work of John Matthews, specifically *The Celtic Shaman*, and have used it successfully both for myself and students.

The one to journey lays down on the floor, either in the Hindu death pose, flat on the back with palms up, or the Egyptian style God position, arms crossed over the chest like a mummy. A shroud, colored to suit the intention of the magick, but often black, is placed over the journeyer, and several rocks are placed near the body, over the shroud, to "pin" the cloth down, preventing the journeyer from easily getting up. A shamanic journey or meditation is taken while covered in the shroud. The helper to this ritual must then take the rocks and shroud up, aiding in the "resurrection" process.

The process can be more intense if truly treated like a death and burial, with the journeyer stripped naked and bathed, as if preparing for a funeral. Herbs of burial and purification can be used, such as salt, myrrh, fumitory, sandalwood, tansy, cypress, yew, roses, periwinkle, oak, parley and lemon balm. The journeyer is then wrapped in linen, much like a mummy. Simple clean sheets can be used. Make sure the journeyer can breathe easily, but otherwise movement is severely restricted. One must be "unwrapped" at the end of the journey to awaken to the world again.

The Witch's cradle and the initiatory binding are similar to many practices of BDSM – bondage and discipline, sadism and masochism—sexual fantasy practices exploring roles outside the norm of everyday society. While many in the Pagan communities enjoy BDSM practices, and many in the BDSM communities experience altered states of consciousness in their practice, even profound spiritual insights, such practices go beyond the scope of this book. They are not necessarily a part of the Witchcraft tradition, though practitioners have adopted and adapted them to suit our rituals. If you feel drawn to such practices, please seek out training with those who have experience and can do so safely and securely with you, rather than try to experiment on your own with no understanding or education of the techniques and safety guides to bondage.

Sweat Lodge

The last, and possibly most physically intense of the techniques outlined here, is the Sweat Lodge. Traditionally associated with Native American purification rituals, the process of purification and altering consciousness through sweat is found in Europe too. While many modern Pagans conjecture at European versions of the lodge, we find a rich history in the use of the sauna in Finish shamanism and culture, bearing a striking resemblance to the Native American sweat lodge until the rise of the modern sports center oriented sauna. In older traditions, the sauna was connected with nature, and believed to have it's own "elf" or gnome spirit that helped those in the sauna. One behaved in the sauna as if it were "church" according to old customs. The sauna is a sacred place. Due to the popularity of Native American traditions in modern Neopagan setting, the practices of the sweat lodge have been adopted into many Pagan traditions, trying to claim the more tribal associations of the sauna in a ritual context. While the sauna is known for it's health benefits and relaxing properties, the sweat lodge is more often thought of as a ritual of endurance and purification.

Generally a lodge is built, either temporarily or as a permanent structure, like a small hut or dome on the bare earth. Willow, or another supple wood, is bent over to form the dome, and wet blankets, canvas or animal skins are placed over it, to form the walls of the lodge. The hut is aligned to the four directions, usually with a fire on the outside, in the east, and the door to the lodge facing the fire. In many ways the lodge is symbolic of the womb and the fire of the male power. Stones are heated in the fire, and moved with deer antlers, pitchfork or shovel, to the central pit in the lodge, where they glow red hot in the darkness. They are much like the male power entering the womb. The leader of the lodge pours water and makes offers and prayers to the fire, as the stones are seen as elders and entities in and of themselves. Usually four rounds of stones and steam are performed, and some traditions have signing, drumming, rattling, prayers, and offerings, while others are done in silence. Participants leave at the end of one cycle, also known as a round, like children exiting the womb, reborn and renewed. Often there are four rounds for each of the cardinal directions. The power of the darkness, heat, steam, sweating, fasting, and offerings of herbs and prayers, become a feat of endurance that alters consciousness, can bring profound realizations, spirit contact, and transformative experiences. The rituals of the lodge mix the spirits of humans with fire, earth, water, air, animal, and plants together, and in Native traditions are said to give direct communion with the creator, the Great Spirit. They are prayers, purifications and a chance to heal and be whole.

Sweat lodges are a long and involved practice, and should only be undertaken with a trained and experienced group leader, be it in a traditional setting or modern Pagan setting.

FEAR

Perhaps not so much the shadow, but the partner to isolation is fear. Many initiatory practices use some form of isolation, in actually or perceived, and the purpose of this isolation is to induce fear. When reduced to a fearful, almost pre-verbal state where we are concerned about our safety and survival, much of our societal conditioning falls away, and in the context of the ritual, we can see things as they truly are, not how we, or those in society who have programmed us, think they should be.

Such fear can be a great teacher, assuming the ritual context gives us the skills to build ourselves back up again, with our new insights and awareness. intact While exploring fear ritually is powerful, of all the paths, with the potential exception of the paths of poison and pain, it is most important to have an experienced practitioner or mentor guiding you through the process, to ultimately provide the safety net needed to work through this fear. It doesn't mean the fears are not real, or your facing them is not real, but you have a container in which to face it, and a method to resume life, rather than running blindingly into the wilderness. While the archetype of the mad hermit is a romantic one for a short time, the reality is less. So modern rituals compress the time of fear and madness, so the initiate can recover and reintegrate.

If you are intrigued by the path of isolation, you might find your best course of action is to seek a mentor, teacher or lineage path of initiation to teach you these ways.

AIDS FOR THE LONELY ROAD

Keep the following thoughts in mind as you walk the lonely road:

Listen to your Body: Listen to your body, not your mind. There is a difference between the signal from the body that it is in pain, or has reached a limit, and the thoughts of the mind telling you something is impossible. The body is telling you the truth, while the mind is echoing your own doubts and fears, not necessarily reality. Part of this work is to move through the ego mind and connect with a wisdom greater than your individual personal self. Learning to distinguish between the two is critical on this path.

Isolation is not for Everybody: Isolation is not a path for everybody. Don't feel you have to try it to be a Witch. Many Witches work just fine without exploring the darker paths of isolation, poison, and pain. Don't force yourself to do something beyond your personal bounds unless you are truly ready for it, and really want to do it.

CHAPTER SEVEN:
THE PATH OF POISON

Out of all the ways of power, the path of poison most fits the archetype of the classic Witch, with cauldron bubbling, potions brewing, and herbs harvested and hanging from her cottage rafters. While we might call it the path of poison, the name is a bit misleading. What is "poison" can sometimes be subjective. Depending on the dose, everything can be a poison. Depending on the dose, everything can be a cure. The magick is in how you use it. The goal of this path is not to poison yourself, but in skirting the edge of danger with very powerful substances, it's important to remember the reality of these powers, and the potential to poison ourselves physically, but also mentally, emotionally and spiritually.

This is called the path of poison for many reasons. Many are fearful of the plant world, and what it offers. Many of us readily take all manner of pharmaceutical poisons, yet shun the plant world fearing it's too dangerous. While plants are medicines that should be respected, and allies that should be courted, they are far less toxic and far more willing to help than most of the chemicals that pass for food and medicine in the modern American diet. Fear prevents many people from opening the gates of magick, and this is one of the reasons Witches and shamans are feared by their own people; we go where others fear to tread. Don't let societal fear of the green world prevent you from seeking wisdom. At their heart, plants are allies and friends seeking to commune with us to balance not only ourselves, but our relationship with the world.

While we often work with plant substances that are not technically classified as poisons, poisons are the purview of the Witch. The poisoning we most talk about on this path is the poisoning of the rational mind, the mental guard that keeps us locked in ordinary reality by dismissing our intuitions and daydreams. All the gate techniques of the Witch and mystic are really ways to trick, command, control, sedate, or partner with the guardian that keeps us in normal consciousness and learn to control the opening and closing of the gateway itself. This is not a dismissal of the guardian spirit found in many traditions, but of the ego guardian using logic to mask fear. Our path of poison drugs the guard into pleasant euphoria, sleep, or ecstasy, so we may travel to the realms between.

The path of poison might be called the path of entheogens or path of psychedelics, though most of the substances we cover here are not technically considered psychedelics or entheogens. Psychedelic is a term often used in place of hallucinogenic, because users of these substance disagree that their experiences are hallucinations, or falsehoods induced by the plant. They believe, rightly so, that these substances have opened up their psyche, their soul, to another reality. Entheogens are substances that release the "god within" helping you realize your own divinity, and many practitioners feel this is an even truer definition for the substance, replacing psychedelic.

The toxicity aspect comes into play because many of these substances are potentially lethal, and even more so in the classic lore of the Witch. Powerful toxins such as monkshood, hemlock and belladonna are staples of the medieval Witch garden. All psychedelic or entheogenic substances open up new perceptions of the world, either sending your perception "out" or sending it deeper "in." There is a fine line between going out/in on a temporary journey, or leaving permanently.

Because of this danger, and the fear associated with the path of poison, modern Witches know relatively little about this path. Though it is listed in the Book of Shadows, few receive training in it beyond the very basics. It seems until relatively recently, herbal lore has not be a major part in the modern Witchcraft renaissance. To the British Traditional Wiccan, the path includes not just plant "drugs" but also incense, oils, and wine, all used to release the spirit and open the gates to new awareness. The term drug has fallen out of favor, because most use it to refer to illegal substances, as in America's "War of Drugs," not herbal medicines. It has often been combined with movement and dance, as one of the Book of Shadows "Various Aphorisms" tells us "Enhance thy trance with drug and dance."

One wonders what experiences the founders of the modern Witchcraft movements had with this path. Gerald Gardner has quite a warning on the use of hemp:

Note. One must be very careful about this. Incense is usually harmless, but you must be careful. If it has bad aftereffects, reduce the amount used, or the duration of the time it is inhaled. Drugs are very dangerous if taken to excess, but it must be remembered that there are drugs that are absolutely harmless, though people talk of them with bated breath, but Hemp is especially dangerous, because it unlocks the inner eye swiftly and easily, so one is tempted to use it more and more. If it is used at all, it must be with the strictest precautions, to see that the person who uses it has no control over the supply. This should be doled out by some responsible person, and the supply strictly limited.

In *Pentagram Magazine*, a short run British Pagan publication, an author writing under the pen-name "Taliesin" wrote that he spoke with Gerald Gardner about the fly agaric mushroom, and Gardner told him that he knew nothing of it, and that he doubted its role in the Old Religion. Taliesin claimed knowledge of living traditions that still used it. Doreen Valiente, former High Priestess of Gardner, and in many ways the mother of the modern Witchcraft movement, later wrote that Gardner was simply being discreet with someone new, and that she knew Gardner and his New Forrest coven had knowledge of the fly agaric and other herbal preparations. Perhaps his warning in the Book of Shadows is also his way of being discreet, in case the BOS reached the hands of a non-initiate.

Other Witches of the era of Gardner also used the traditional Witch's herbs and potions. Besides Taliesin, Witchcraft teacher Robert Cochrane, of the Clan of Tubal Cain, was infamous for his magickal potions. He died of an overdose of belladonna, and we still speculate if his death was a suicide, willing sacrifice, or terrible accident. In this way, Cochrane is an excellent teacher to remind of us the dangers of powerful and terrible plant allies and, no matter our level of mastery, knowledge or experience, there is always danger.

It's interesting to note that much of our talk of "drugs" as a path tends to focus on the sensational, either the toxicity of such plants, or the illegality. Strangely though some, like hemp, are considered illegal in many countries, the far more dangerous ones are quite legal, and you can find them growing in your backyard garden as a wild or ornamental plant. And much of our discussion completely ignores the variety of plants that are both relatively safe and legal, and a variety of safer techniques to work with the more dangerous ones.

Plants on the path of poison can be worked with in a variety of ways. While consuming the plant is often the best way to directly interact with it, there are many plants where it would be unwise to consume, even if you are an experienced plant magician. There are safer options to put you in contact with the plant spirit, and induce trance.

Ingested Potion: Ingested potion includes any mixture you consume and digest. This would include herbal teas (infusions made in water), tinctures in alcohol, herbal cordials, wine, beer, philters (powders dissolved in water) or any other form of ingested elixir.

Topical Potion: Topical potions include oils (ranging from pure essential oils, blended essential oils in a base, and infused herbal oils), ointments (oils and wax), creams, washes (infusions used topically, often preserved with salt) and magickal fluid condensers.

Incense: The use of incense and smoking herbs is a subset of the path of poison—the path of smoke or the bridge of smoke—as such mixtures seem to not only open the gates, but also provide a tenuous footing to the otherworld. Herbs can be burned to release their power, either to inherently release their spiritual energy, or the smoke is breathed in so its scent induces trance via its chemical components when entering the bloodstream. Burning alters the chemical composition of the plants, and some are more conducive to trance with such heat. Incense usually consists of a mixture of resins, woods, herbs, and oils, though herbs can smoke singly or in a blend without mixing in the more sticky substances.

Charms: Herbs can be made into charms, physical objects to be held, carried in daily life and used in ritual. Charms can be herbs carried in a pouch or capsule, sewn into dream pillows, put into bottles, roots carved into fetishes or made into other decorations.

Cultivation: Growing your own herbs in your garden is a powerful way to ally yourself with the most toxic plants. If you not capable of keeping a garden, wildcrafting and identification can also aid in building a relationship with the plant spirit.

Meditation: Simply meditating next to a growing plant is way to commune with its spirit. Some of my most profound trance experience have been communing with a plant or tree, simply lying down beneath the plant.

Dreaming: Much like meditating with the plant, one can make effective contact while dreaming with the plant. In many shamanic traditions, its difficult to tell when a teacher is speaking about shamanic journey, or literally sleeping and dreaming. If you can't dream under the living plant, dreaming with a charm of the plant, in a pouch or pillow, can serve as a physical contact point for deeper dream magick.

Strewing: Scattering herbs on your path, around your home or in your environment, inside or out, helps you connect with the energy and effects of the herb. You can make a dust of ground herbs, and create a physical ring for your magick circle, surrounding yourself in the plant's energy.

Food: Herbs that are non-toxic in nature can be used in food, ranging from seasoning the main course to flavoring baked goods. Ingesting an herb as part of your daily routine integrates its spirit with your own. Sampling fresh leaves in the garden is an excellent way to attune to its spirit, and the art of culinary magick, combining herbs with various food groups, is an amazing and often underrated technique of magick, healing and trance. Sacred meals of particular flavors, herbs, spices, colors, and textures can to stimulate the senses and create a different, magickal, atmosphere.

Bathing: Using baths of non-toxic herbs is another method to commune with herbal energy. Infusions of the herbs are added to the bathwater, and the practitioner is immersed in the herbal brew to receive its blessings. Herbal baths can be used for purification before ritual, or as rituals themselves.

Flower Essences: Flower essences and vibrational remedies are a modern form of ingested potion pioneered by Dr. Edward Bach, though they resemble older forms of magick using dew from flowers or water collected off standing stones. They are diluted solutions of plant matter, bordering on a homeopathic remedy without the same dilutions and potentization process. Flowers are soaked in water, imprinting their energetic signature upon the water, and the water is then preserved and diluted as a remedy for mental, emotional and spiritual ailments. Flower essences are a very safe way to ingest the energies of more toxic herbs, as very little, if any, physical plant matter is consumed.

Many plants not considered psychedelics can have powerful effect when used with knowledge, intent, and preparation, or in various combinations with other herbs. They include common plants found locally, in your garden or even in your own spice rack. They can open the gates in a variety of ways, not with the danger of toxicity, yet they change the body chemistry in other ways conducive to magick.

PLANT SPIRITS

The most important part of working with plants on this path is to consciously work with the plant spirit. Many Witches, shamans, and magicians believe each plant species has its own governing intelligence, sometimes referred to as its deva, daimon, angel, faery or simply its spirit. Through a relationship with such spirits, Witches of old learned how to walk the green path and find cures and poisons. Through communication with the plant spirit, they learned how to prepare and how much of a dosage to use, to transform a poison into a guardian of the gateway and teacher of wisdom.

While all plants have a spirit, and each spirit has its own, arguably objective, personality, the plant spirits associated with Witchcraft are, as you'd expect, witchy. The are seductive and dangerous, and more often than not, feminine. They can appears as plants or as beautiful ladies, particularly belladonna and datura.

One of the common points among the plants of Witchcraft is the propensity for five petalled flowers. Many of our sacred herbs flower with five petals to a bloom, much like the pentagram. The five petalled flowers hold a special purpose in the green world. They are most likely to open and close gateways of life force. They represent a spectrum of powers.

On the right side, we have plants such as St. John's wort and vervain. Both are known as protective and healing herbs. Both have been used as charms, as shields, to block harm and herbally to nourish and rejuvenate from all manner of illness. Their five pointed star brings energy into the world, into the incarnated body for healing and protection. They are the shield of the pentacle.

On the left side we have the deadly poisons of nightshade, datura, henbane, and mandrake. They kill and must be handled with care. They open the five-pointed gate to send your spirit to the underworld, the realm of the dead. They open and release, and pull life force away. They are the gateway of the pentacle, to open the door to spirit.

Yet when you change the dosage of each herb, lowered from the medicinal or toxic dose, you have herbs that create a doorway that swings both ways. They allow you to fare forth from the material into the spiritual and back again. Yet it is having a relationship with the plant spirits themselves that allow the wisdom to know what dose, and in what combination of other herbs, is right for you. I believe this relationship is essential to truly walk the path of poison in a safe and responsible manner.

Fig. 43: Five Petalled Flowers

Exercise: Plant Spirit Journey

Pick a plant that you feel an affinity towards. It does not necessarily have to be one of the toxic plants on the path of poison. It can be a flower, bush, or tree from the garden, or your favorite herb. Ideally, go somewhere you can find the living plant, or if doing this in the fall or winter, you can hold the dry plant in a charm bag, or burn it as incense as you do this working.

Perform the Shamanic Journey Exercise from **Chapter Four**. You do not have to ingest the plant at this time. In fact, it might be good in your preliminary journey *not* to ingest the plant, as you can first establish a spiritual connection with it, to make sure it wants to work with you. Spirits are like people, and some want to work with you, and others do not. Working with plants you can establish a relationship which makes things more effective than trying to work with those plants that do not resonate with you. Go into the journey with the intention of meeting the spirit of the plant and see how that spirit manifests to you. After repeated journeys, it will reveal its mysteries and power to you, if it chooses to work with you.

Repeat with this process with several plants. Learn to discern the nature of the various plants from one another and build relationships with several before experimenting with them in any trance inducing technique.

PLANT TRANCE

Like other trance inducing techniques, plant allies can be divided into inhibitory and exhibitory. Inhibitory plants naturally calm the body, clear the mind and senses, or lower body functions. Exhibitory plants have a tendency to excite, stimulate, and raise body functions. For some plants, the line is not so clear, depending on circumstances they can be used in several ways.

Inspired by the pentacle mandala created by Dale Pendell, in his ground breaking trilogy *Pharmako/Poeia, Pharmako/Dynamis* and *Pharmako/Gnosis,* exploring the effect of plant allies with people, dividing them into categories, and placing the on points and paths of the pentacle, I found myself constructing my own mandala of plants on the pentacle, specifically focused for the practicing Witch, rather than the modern psychonaut. Instead of looking across the world to a variety of exotic plant substances, I looked to what is already in the repertoire of the modern Witch, in terms of both plants and their uses. Different plants are best for different types of magick. Here I share part of the mandala, focused on inhibitory and exhibitory purposes for trance. The entire mandala, to be featured in one of my future books specifically on herbs, will include practical magick, ceremony and herbal medicine.

The paths of the star involve five basic categories considered more active and exhibitory. The lines of the pentagon, in which the pentagram is inscribed, details five more inwardly directed magickal intents.

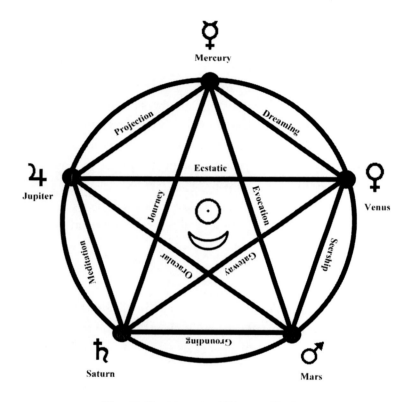

Fig. 44: Pentagram of Trance Herbs

Exhibitory Trance – Pentagram

Evocation – Mercury to Mars: The process of evocation is to summon a spirit to manifestation. Spirits are conjured and make their presence known. Sometimes the manifestation is only perceived by the psychically sensitive, while others come with more tangible manifestations, such as a gust of wind or a change in temperature in the room. Some forms of evocation have manifestations in smoke or flame.

Evocation Herbs: Wormwood, Dittany of Crete, Tobacco, Sweet Grass, Thistle, Patchouli, Mastic, Oregano, Mullein, Parsley, Dandelion, Rowan, Yew, White Willow

Oracular – Mars to Jupiter: Oracular herbs are those used not for evocation, the manifestation of a spirit outside of the body, but invocation, the manifestation of the spirit inside the body. These are the herbs of possession and trance channeling, for the spirits and gods to speak through the practitioner. An oracle is one who classically divined the future and offered counsel while in trance. The Oracle of Delphi is probably one of the most famous of these ancient oracles, possibly using both herbs and the release of subterranean gases from a crevice in the oracle chamber.

Oracular Herbs: Bay, Angelica, Tobacco, Basil, Lobelia, Coltsfoot, Cedar, Oak, Cinnamon, Juniper, Dandelion, Galangal, Anise, Marigold, Poppy, Hops

Ecstatic – Jupiter to Venus: Ecstatic herbs excite the body into an ecstatic trance. While many think of ecstasy as a sexual pleasure, it truly refers to a level of consciousness, to be "free from flesh" or simply having an expanded awareness beyond the flesh, reaching out through both space and time. Ecstatic herbs are used for trance involving dance, shapeshifting, energy-raising, sex magick and inspiration.

Ecstatic Herbs: Licorice, Bay, Calamus, Damiana, Henbane, Star Anise, Allspice, Lobelia, Ginger, Tea, Wine, Beer

Gateway – Venus to Saturn: Gateway herbs are those that induce trance to open a gateway, a portal of consciousness where connections can be made. They can open the way to travel to other realms, or facilitate contact from those other realms to us. Though categorized as exhibitory, some can be considered inhibitory. Herbs of this path are also often associated with bewitchment and fascination, as they make connections between people. While most Witchcraft entheogens are considered gateway plants, these in particular hold the characteristic.

Gateway Herbs: Datura, Belladonna, Mandrake, Cinquefoil, Foxglove, Lotus, Pomegranate, Elder, Blackberry, Camphor, Willow, Elm

Journey – Saturn to Mercury: Journey herbs are those that facilitate shamanic journey. While some can be considered inhibitory trance inducing, generally this refers to visionary journey done intensely through ecstatic posture or repetitive sound. Journeys of a shamanic variety include psychopomp work, guiding spirits between worlds, as well as personal, tribal and planetary healing.

Journey Herbs: Scotch Broom, Nutmeg, Damiana, Hemp, Hemlock, Solomon's Seal, Pokeweed, Angelica, Yarrow, Anise

Inhibitory Trance – Pentagon

Dreaming – Mercury to Venus: Dreaming herbs are those inducing a slumbering trance state. They are the medicinal relaxants, calmatives, and sedatives. Through a dreaming trance, we can receive prophecy of the future, have spirit contact, and in particular spirit contact with our ancestors, and can even set our slumbering mind toward solving the problems of the everyday world.

Dreaming Herbs: Scullcap, Oatstraw, Milky Oats, Hops, Lavender, Valerian, Wild Lettuce, Agrimony, Rose, Marigold, Poppy, Jasmine, Camphor, Lotus, Vervain, Ash, Apple

Seership – Venus to Mars: The herbs of seership are the herbs of sight, but go far beyond the simple view we have of psychic sight. They induce clairvoyance in many, true, but also bring the other psychic gifts of clairaudience, clairsentience, psychometry, and telepathy. They open us to information, for a true seer "sees" on many levels, and receives whatever information is needed. They are the herbs of divination, of seeing patterns, predicting the future and answering questions.

Seership Herbs: Mugwort, Eyebright, Nettles, Damiana, Catnip, Thyme, Periwinkle, Queen Anne's Lace, Raspberry, Blackberry, Hibiscus, Frankincense, Morning Glory, Blueberry, Seaweed, Camphor, Jasmine

Grounding – Mars to Saturn: The herbs of grounding close the gates. They link you with your body, clear the energy channels of excess power and help center and stabilize you. They are often protective and preserving, helping shelter you as you return form a more vulnerable psychic state to the waking world.

Grounding Herbs: Myrrh, Patchouli, Flax, Potato, Comfrey, Solomon's Seal, Dandelion, Cedar

Meditation – Saturn to Jupiter: Plants associated with the powers of meditation are either peaceful or hypnotic. They do not induce the sleep of sedative herbs, but bring peace and clarity to a busy mind and agitated body. They are more tonic in nature, without a strong chemical effect.

Meditation Herbs: Sandalwood, Passion Flower, Horse Chestnut, Lungwort, Juniper

Projection – Jupiter to Mercury: The herbs or projection are similar in overall function to the exhibitory herbs. In fact, many would suggest the arts of shamanic journey are no different from those of astral travel. But in practice, there is an exhibitory intensity to the journey technique associated with drums, rattles, dance, and exciting herbs, while other plant allies help us with the more meditative remote viewing, astral travel, and mental projection. Truly they are two sides of the same gift, but practitioners approach them differently. Workings labeled astral travel often tend to be more cerebral in nature, detached, while shamanic journey can be more primal.

Projection Herbs: Benzoin, Anise, Catnip, Cornflower, Yarrow, Pennyroyal, Lemongrass, Hemp

CRAFTING POTIONS

Potions are the easiest way to work this path. Teas, tinctures, washes, oils, and ointments are all methods of blending plant spirit magick for a specific purpose, and have been a huge part of the Craft. Many of our first magickal arts go back to the craft of potions, of making healing elixirs and knowing the deadly poisons.

Having the herbs in your system, via digestion or absorption through the skin, even in minute doses, is one of the best ways to build a relationship with them, and open the gates.

Brew: The simplest form of ingested potion is a tea. The names tea, brew, and infusion have been used synonymously, though tea tends to reflect a social drink, brew a magickal drink, and infusion a medicinal aid. Such mixtures are usually made exclusively with water and herbal matter, extracting the water soluble parts of the plant. Generally one tablespoon of dry, powdered plant matter is used with one cup of boiling water to make a brew. If the herb is fresh, then two tablespoons of herb to one cup of hot water. Let it steep for anywhere from five minutes to fifteen minutes, or to gain a truly strong brew, overnight in the dark, with a covering. Brews are best used fresh, as they spoil easily over time, even if refrigerated.

Sacred Dance Tea

2 Parts Black Tea
1 Part Ginger Root
1 Part Licorice Root
1 Part Calamus Root
1/2 Part Damiana Leaf
1/2 Part Coriander
1/2 Part Star Anise
Honey to taste

Mix the herbs together and then put one tablespoon of the dry mixture to one cup of hot water and let it steep, covered, for at least ten minutes. Drink before or at the start of the ritual, about a half hour before one needs to be ecstatic.

Datura Journey Tea

5 Datura Seeds
1 Slice of Fresh Ginger Root or 1/2 Teaspoon of Dried Root
1/2 Teaspoon of Lemon Balm
1/2 Teaspoon of Vervain
1/2 Teaspoon of Cinquefoil
Honey to taste

This is a controversial formula, as it involves the use of Datura seeds, which are considered toxic, so use at your own risk. If you are otherwise healthy adult with no specific allergies to Datura, this can be quite a potent tea for the experienced Witch and pose no long term ill effects. It can cause nausea, so the ginger is added to settle the stomach. Grind the seeds with a mortar and pestle and mix them with the herbs. Add 1.5 cups of boiling water (12 oz.) and let it steep covered for at least an hour. Add honey to make it more palatable and drink in ritual. Wait at least a half hour before it is adequately through your system. At this dose, it doesn't necessarily create a "trip" like recreational drugs, but when used with intention to journey, it can make the experience clearer and more powerful.

Communion with Nature Tea

1 Part Lady's Mantle
1/2 Part Rose-hips
1/2 Part Blackberry Leaf
1/2 Part Mugwort
1/2 Part Lemon Balm
Local Honey to Sweeten

Drink a cup of this tea before communing with the spirits of the plants, land, nature, and the elementals. It makes you more attuned with the spirits of nature and better able to be accepted by them and commune with them. Use local honey to help attune to the spirit of your location.

Tincture: A tincture is an herbal extract created in alcohol, usually vodka. Most alcoholic liquids are a mixture of both water and true alcohol. The ratio of water to alcohol creates the "proof" of the substance: 100 Proof means 50% alcohol. The mix of water and alcohol extracts both the water soluble and alcohol soluble portions of the plant, potentially making a more potent mixture, and each of the chemicals do different things. Some formulas need only the water soluble portion to be effective. The simple method of making a tincture is take a mason jar, fill it 1/3 with the dry herb, or full of the fresh herb, and then fill the remaining space with at least 80 proof alcohol. (100 proof is even better.) Cover with plastic wrap before screwing on the lid, to prevent the metal lid from coming in contact with the mixture. Shake regularly and let it extract for four to six weeks, if not longer. The liquid will change color. Strain out the herb. I like to make tinctures on the new moon, if possible, go through the next new Moon, and then in two more weeks decant them on the Full Moon.

Meditation Tincture
2 Parts Passion Flower
1 Part Nettle Leaf
1/2 Part Lavender
1/2 Part Lemon Peel

Mix the herbs together and steep them in alcohol before straining. Take 10-20 drops under the tongue prior to meditation. It is particularly helpful in pathworking and guided meditations.

Spirit Work Tincture
2 Parts Wormwood
1 Part Mugwort
1/2 Part Lemon Balm
1/2 Part Passion Flower
1 Pinch/5 drops of Lobelia

Take 5-20 drops under the tongue or in a ritual drink when you seek to commune with the spirits. It is particularly helpful in communing with the ancestors, spirits guides, and masters. If mixing tinctures already made, use a Tablespoon as one "part" and add 5 drops of Lobelia. If you are making it as a complete tincture from dried herbs, add just a pinch of lobelia. It helps open the way for the spirits to speak, and for you to speak to the spirits. If you want to particularly attune to the angelic realm of spirits, add some angelica root. If you want to attune to the faery realm, add elderflower or elderberry. My coven used this formula in our Samhain workings and people who notoriously have difficulty communicating with spirits have amazing visions, messages, and insights.

Divination Tincture

3 Parts Mugwort

2 Parts Star Anise

1 Part Nettles

1 Part Thyme

1/2 Part Nutmeg

Take 5-20 drops of this tincture before doing any type of divination work, including reading tarot cards, runes, or crystal scrying.

Alcoholic Beverages: While a tincture is usually seen as a medicinal potion, herbs can be brewed into beverages usually seen as more social drinks. Herbs can be quite easily made into sweet cordials. Various recipes for beers and wine use additional herbal constituents, to both change the flavor and add to the magick. Herbs can be quite easily mulled in wine to make a magickal drink.

Samhain Journey Wine

1 Teaspoon Chamomile

2 Teaspoons Mugwort

1 Teaspoon Scullcap

2 Teaspoons Vervain

3 Teaspoons of Cinnamon

1 Pinch of American Mandrake (May Apple Root)

This mixture I created for a Samhain ritual years ago, and it's been a favorite among my students and friends. Though not working with any of the more toxic and chemically active plants, their mixture to the wine creates a powerful brew helping one talk to the ancestors, journey to the underworld, and experience spiritual guidance through divination. Pour a bottle of red wine into a simmering pan, and add the herbs one at a time. Allow the mixture to simmer on low heat, covered for at least thirty minutes, stirring frequently. Strain out the herb. Let it cool and bottle it. Take a few sips to a full wine glass before or during ritual to enhance your magickal experience. If European Mandrake root is available, by all means use it instead of May Apple.

Oils: In modern magick, ritual oils usually refer to blends of essential oils, the volatile chemicals of a plant distilled from the plant matter, mixed with a base oil to dilute their chemical potency for use on the skin or inhalation. Medicinal aromatherapists usually use a ratio of 1/8 oz of base oil, such as grape seed, apricot kernel, jojoba oil or even olive oil for short term potions, with 5-9 drops of pure essential oil. Older occult recipes often use a ratio of 50/50, or in their recipes, a half dram to dram ratio. A dram is an imprecise measurement of 20 drops, and they formulate with 10 drops of a base oil and 10 drops of essential oil mix, and have a magickally and chemically potent oil. Such ratios should not be used by people with sensitive skin, or with topically strong oils such as cinnamon.

Though sight, taste, and texture can all be used as mnemonic triggers, the sense of smell holds the strongest connection to our memory. One powerful technique of magickal traditions is to use a scented oil or incense in dramatic, well crafted rituals. The student then associates that particular scent with intense magickal experiences, and subsequent rituals might not be as intense, but the use of the scent takes the student back to that time and place, and that level of intensity. When I first started my practice, I used a horrible synthetic oil of frankincense and myrrh, but I didn't know it was not real at the time. To this day, the scent of it still induces a feeling of magick, even though the substance lacks any true plant connection and smells nothing like real frankincense and myrrh. Mixing scent with plant spirit makes an even more powerful connection.

Psychic Sight Oil

10 Drops of Base Oil
5 Drops of Sandalwood Essential Oil
3 Drops of Mugwort Essential Oil
2 Drops of Frankincense Essential Oil

Anoint your brow with this oil before doing any psychic working. Jasmine is also traditionally found in lunar based psychic oils but, due to the high cost of authentic jasmine oil, it can be prohibitive for many of us. Hemp or Hemp Seed infused oil another traditional ingredient. If you have access to either, feel free to use add a drop of Jasmine, or use the Hemp infused oil as the base oil.

Meditation Oil

10 Drops of Base Oil
4 Drops of Sandalwood Essential Oil
2 Drops of Frankincense Essential Oil
2 Drops of Myrrh Essential Oil

1 Drop of Lavender Essential Oil

1 Drop of Lemongrass Essential Oil

Use a few drops of this oil before meditation or ritual. It has both relaxing and protective qualities, to help you keep focused and centered upon your meditation practice. Traditionally you can anoint both wrists, the brow and the back of the skull where the head and spine meet.

Gardnerian Anointing Oil

The Gardnerian Tradition has its own recipe for anointing oil, made with infused oil rather than essential oils, used for a variety of effects, from blessing and protection to trance-inducing. Thyme, one of the main ingredients, is used in classic formula to see faeries. The Book of Shadows formula is:

To make the anointing ointment, take some glazed pans filled half full with grease or olive oil. Put in one sweet mint, marjoram in another, ground thyme in a 3rd, and if you may have it, patchouli, dried leaves pounded. Place pans in hot water bath. Stir and cook for several hours, then put into linen bags, and squeeze grease through into pans again, and fill up with fresh leaves. After doing this several times, the grease will be highly perfumed. Then mix all together and store in a well-corked jar. Anoint behind ears, throat, armpits, breasts, and womb. Also, for all ceremonies where the feet are kissed, they should also be anointed.

Washes: A wash is used for anointing, blessing, bathing, or even literally washing the floors and windows, to change the energy of a place. They are made like a brew, but are not ingested, and can be preserved with a bit of alcohol, vinegar, or sea salt if kept over the long term. Usually they are made as needed. Some washes have essential oils added to them to improve the overall scent. In ritual, they are asperged—sprinkled with the finger, tree branch or other ritual tool— around the ritual area or over the altar.

Faery Wash

Willow Leaf or Bark

Elder Flower

Marigolds

Nettles

Lavender

Rose Petals

This wash is for those who wish greater contact with the Faery realm. It can be used as a bath, foot wash, or asperged to create a ritual space conducive to faery work. Mix these herbs with warm water. Use fresh herbs if available.

Ancestor Wash

Yew Needles
Rosemary
Myrrh Essential Oil
Pennyroyal Essential Oil

Like the Faery Wash, this mixture creates a conducive atmosphere for the ancestors It should not be used as a bath or a wash on the body, but asperged in a ritual area to welcome the ancestors. It works best outdoors, but if working indoors, it should be thoroughly cleaned from the floors before people or pets come into contact with it. It should most definitely be avoided by those who are pregnant, as pennyroyal is an abortificient.

Unguents: Unguent is a fancy old world name for an ointment, a mixture of oil and wax, or perhaps other fatty substances, to get a gooey mix that can be applied to the body. Usually the herbal matter is extracted into an oil, and mixed with melted wax, with other oils or essences added to it and allowed to cool. The resulting ointment is smeared on the body. The classical Witch's flying ointment was believed to be applied to the sensitive areas of the body: the genitals, anus, and beneath the arms, where the skin would most readily absorb the herbal chemicals. The flying ointment herbs were notoriously toxic to ingest, and this is one way they could be used safer, but this use still has many dangers.

Classic Flying Ointments

Here are some classic historic examples of the Witch's Flying Ointment. They are quite toxic and are presented here for historic purposes only. These recipes should *not* be attempted. They contain the sensationalist elements of "baby's fat" or animal blood which are not part of the modern Witch's work.

Flying Ointment No. 1
Boiled Fat in a Copper Vessel
Parsley
Aconite
Poplar Leaves
Soot

Flying Ointment No. 2
Water Parsnip
Sweet Flag
Cinquefoil
Deadly Nightshade
Bat's Blood
Oil

Flying Ointment No. 3
Baby's Fat
Water Parsnip Juice
Aconite
Cinquefoil
Deadly Nightshade
Soot

Modern Flying Ointment

Here is a variation of a recipe I used as my own modern Flying Ointment. It's perfectly safe as long as you are not pregnant or specifically allergic to any of the plants used. Personally I prefer to add a few datura seeds to the mix, but datura is one of the plants I have a strong spiritual connection with.

1.5 Oz. of Mugwort Infused Oil
1.5 Oz. of Lemon Balm Infused Oil
1 Oz., by weight of Beeswax
5 Drops of Mugwort Essential Oil
3 Drops of Lemongrass Essential Oil

2 Drops of Lavender Essential Oil

13 drops of Mugwort Tincture

10 Drops of Wormwood Tincture

7 drops of Cinquefoil Tincture

5 drops of Vervain Tincture

3 drops of Elder Flower or Elder Berry Tincture

1 drop of Mandrake Tincture (Label Poisonous!)

1 Acorn, if possible – on the twig or seed of the tree you consider to be the world tree.

To make an infused oil, place either a full canning jar of the fresh herb, or 1/4 of the canning jar filled with the dry herb, fill the rest with an oil such as olive or sunflower seed oil and let it steep in the warm sunlight for at least four weeks. Cover the mouth of the bottle with plastic wrap before you screw on the metal lid. Strain out the plant matter, as its medicinal and magickal properties have transferred to the oil. If in a rush, you can warm the oil and plant matter in a crock-pot or double boiler for a few hours to speed the infusion. Heat the oil again in a double boiler and add the tinctures to mix. Add the beeswax and let it melt. Pour off into a sealable ointment jar. Add the essential oils to the cooling jar and stir them in quickly, and cover the jar, not to loose their scent or chemical power, as they are quite volatile.

THE BRIDGE OF SMOKE

The path of smoke is considered to be a subdivision of the poison path of green magick. The plants' effects are taken in through the inhalation of smoke rather than ingestion or topical application. The three main methods of working with the path of smoke are through incense, pipe smoking, and fire burning.

Incense: Incense is the most common of the three in modern Witchcraft. Witches have been crafting their own herbal blends to burn on charcoal, in a thurible, or other vessel since the dawn of temple traditions. Today's Witch can easily obtain self-igniting charcoal from occult shops, and use them in an incense burner or cauldron to burn a variety of incenses. Generally incenses consist of several parts, including a resin or wood as the bulk of the incense, to make a pleasing smell when burning. The remaining incense mix is a combination of roots, leaves, stems, seeds, and flowers. Those with a higher concentration of essential oils burn with a more pleasing smell than others. Gently heating the wine or a wine/honey mixture helps the process. The resins, woods, and other plant matter are ground together in a mortal and pestle, or other grinding device. Sometime a "base" mixture is used, such as bamba powder (bamboo sawdust) colored with vegetable dye, or another wood powder, such as sandalwood. The mixture is bound together with oils, often essential oils of the herbs already in the mixture. It can also be bound with honey or wine. The blend is allowed to dry and then stored for approximately a moon cycle away from the light, to let the scents mellow and mingle together.

Pagan Ritual Incense

This blend was reportedly used by Pagans known to author William G. Gray, and found in his book *Western Inner Workings*. Though it doesn't name the group, we can speculate based upon his life and social contacts that it was mostly like the Clan of Tubal Cain with Robert Cochrane or a group associated with Patricia or Arnold Crowther. This recipe doesn't list proportions, but generally the further down on the list the ingredient, the less was used. I haven't used this exact formula myself, due to some difficulty in getting all in the ingredients, but a variation. Gray seems less concerned with exact formulas and more that these are particularly good plants to use in such otherworldly workings. He adds that wormwood, agrimony, rosemary, and vervain can be added to improve the scent of the blend.

Henbane Root
Birch Bark
Willow Bark
Apple Gum
Pine Gum
Deadly Nightshade Roots
White Bryony Roots
Sunspurge Leaves
Cinquefoil Leaves
Foxglove Leaves
Bracken Seeds

Meditation Incense

2 Parts Sandalwood
1 Part Frankincense
1 Part Myrrh
1/2 Part Lavender

A simple incense used to aid meditation practices of all kinds. It clears the space and practitioner, but also quiets the mind.

Opening the Gates Incense

3 Parts Willow Bark

2 Parts Elder Flower

1 Part Frankincense

1 Part Datura Leaf

1 Part Cinquefoil

1/2 Part Foxglove Flowers and/or Leaves

1 Part Honey

Opening the Gates incense is great for rituals where you are opening the gateway to the spirit word, either to invite the spirits to your space, or to make journeying to their realm easier. It helps create a sacred space between that bridges the worlds.

Spirit Work Incense

2 Parts Myrrh

1 Part Dragon's Blood

1 Part Willow Bark

1 Part Wormwood

1/2 Part Mugwort

1/2 Part Eyebright

1/8 Part Datura Seeds

13 Drops of Myrrh Essential Oil

Use this incense whenever calling the spirits to you, to enhance manifestation, communication, and your relationship with them. Like the Spirit Work tincture, it can be adapted to work with specific kinds of spirits by adding Angelica Root (for angelic contact), Elder Flower (for faery contact), or Henbane flowers/seeds (for ancestor contact).

Journeying Incense No. 1

1 part Sandalwood

1 part of Orris Root

1 part of Frankincense

1 part of Benzoin
1 part of Star Anise
1/2 part Mugwort
1/2 part of Broom Flowers
1/2 part of Yarrow Flowers
1/2 part of Rue

A simple journey incense used by my more shamanically inclined Witchcraft students. Its scent aids the process of journey and spirit flight, but can also work well in more traditional astral travel/remote viewing work. Rue in all forms should be avoided by pregnant women.

Journey Incense No. 2
1 Part Benzoin
1 Part Nutmeg
1/2 Part Angelica Root
1/2 Part Poke Root
1/4 Part Damiana Leaf

A more focused and potent journey incense, used for both upper word and lower world journeys.

Oracular Incense
3 Parts Bay Leaf
2 Parts Sandalwood
1 Part Angelica Root
1/2 Part Oak Bark
1/8 Part Hemp
3 Parts Red Wine to Bind

This incense can facilitate deeper oracular workings, from in-depth divinations to the invocation of spirits and gods to be expressed through the practitioner's physical body. Ideally the smoke is inhaled, though it can be quiet caustic to the throat over the long term. I've found it best to be used in a large, but closed, room letting the incense permeate the room before the ritual, rather than inhaling directly.

Pipe Ceremonies: The pipe is often considered a Native American tool, but more and more Witches, influenced by Native traditions, are using pipes in their ceremonies and magick. Pipe blends can be used to induce trance, as well as a form of smoking your "prayers" and sending them to the spirit world as whiffs of smoke. Pipes, like drums and rattles, are considered alive, and spiritual tools themselves, and must be awoken and "fed" regularly. For those maintaining their respiratory health, and the vigor to climb hills and valleys in our path of nature might forego pipe rituals and focus more on the more ambient incense and fire magick.

Modern Pipe Ceremony

While pipe ceremonies are specific to many North American tribes and cultures, and are not easily assimilated whole into modern Neopaganism, many tribal teachers are training non-native students and encouraging new traditions of pipe prayer ceremonies to develop. The basis of the ritual can be adapted to a Pagan perspective and used quite effectively by modern Witches, while still be culturally respectful of its original context. I see ritual as a "technology," a structure in which we make connection, much like the "technology" of all of these paths. The structure can be adapted to the belief system, culture and traditions of the users, but it carries some basic points. Generally a pipe ceremony is done in three "rounds" of prayers, and contains the following:

Opening Invocation: Performed by the leader of the ritual, acknowledging and inviting in the divine. In Witchcraft, this would be an evocation of the Goddess, God, and/or Great Spirit.

Opening to the Directions: The pipe is offered to the four directions, stem end pointed to each of the four direction, to invite the powers of the quarters to join you. In more shamanic traditions, the pipe stem is also offered to the realms above, below, and center, as well as to the genius loci, or spirit of the place, and the ancestors. Though a pipe ceremony really has nothing specifically to do with a magick circle ritual, if you are more comfortable creating sacred space in that manner, you could incorporate the pipe offerings in a more traditional circle casting. Only once the pipe has been "offered" to the spirits may incarnated people then smoke it.

First Round: In the First Round, the prayers are offered to invite other spiritual allies and to ask for blessing for the community, for the world, or for specific other people. Prayers may be done out loud or silently, but the pipe is then lit, the leader inhales and holds the smoke in the lungs while thinking of the prayer and focusing attention, and then exhales, to release the prayer. When done, the pipe is passed to the next person, who does the same. The pipe goes around the circle of participants, clockwise.

Second Round: The Second Round of pipe prayers is done much like the first, but these are specific prayers for yourself and your life. Witches might think of them specifically like a spell done via the pipe and smoke, but a spell that invokes not just personal power, but also the power of the deities and spirits to manifest it.

Third Round: The Third Round of prayers are done as prayers of gratitude for what you already have, and to offer thanks to the spirits gathered in the ceremony.

The third round closes the space and ceremony, but if you did any other rituals, such as a magick circle ritual to open the space, then close as you normally would in that tradition.

Pipe Blends

While the pipe herb of choice by most is tobacco, it is not the only herb of choice. Many smudging herbs such as sweet grass, cedar and sage can be used. Author Kristen Madden, in her book *Magick, Mystery and Medicine*, suggests angelica as a pipe herb. Other herbs can be blended, based on taste, smell, and magickal correspondences, though herbs only traditionally used for smoking should be used. Mints, sagebrushes, salvia sages, and other herbs such as lemon balm, lobelia, mullein, and coltsfoot are used as pipe herbs. Do not use incense recipes for pipe blends, as many of the materials are not conducive to deep breathing. Specific blends can be used for different intentions. Some are stimulating, some are prayerful, and others are more trance inducing. Any pipe blends should not be used by pregnant women or those with respiratory illness, and they should only be used in moderation, during ritual, by those in good health, as any smoke can be damaging to the lungs with extended use.

Pipe Blend Formula

1 Part Angelica Root
1/2 Part Coltsfoot Leaf
1/2 Part Mullein
1/3 Part Lemon Balm
1/4 Part Lobelia

Fire Magick: Smoke produced from fires is another effective way to walk this sub-path, assuming you have the space to build a fire. You can burn specific woods in the fire and letting both the flame and the scent of the smoke released induce trance, or throwing herbal blends into the fire, like the incense and pipe blends above.

Fires of Azrael

One of the most famous magickal fires, described in the novel *The Sea Priestess* by Dion Fortune, is the Fires of Azrael. A mixture of cedar, juniper, and sandalwood, it is said to induce a trance that will reveal your past lives to you. Let a fire burn, and as it begins to die put the cedar log, juniper twigs, and sandalwood chips on the coals. Gaze into the embers, using the technique of scrying, and let the embers reveal information about your past incarnations. The combination of these three woods can also be used as an incense to induce inner vision, or also as an incense of protection. Some say the formula revealed by Fortune is actually missing a few ingredients to truly make it effective, but I've had great results with the Fires of Azrael as an incense using only cedar, juniper, and sandalwood.

THE ESSENCE OF FLOWERS

One of the safest ways to work with toxic plants is through the essence. While many think essence refers to the essential oil, a very concentrated and complex chemical, the flower essence is actually a very dilute solution. By soaking the fresh flowers in water, you are imprinting the energy, the essence, of the flower's spiritual properties into the water, preserving it for future use. They are akin to homeopathic remedies, very dilute doses often with none of the original plant detectable in a dose, yet they work powerfully on the mind, emotions, and spirit. In magickal terms, essences work through the Law of Contagion. Once two substances touch, they are always touching. That water, even diluted, is now a touchstone for the power of that plant. Usually the preparation process is ritualized, calling upon the spirit of the plant, asking for its blessing and often an offering is made to the plant spirit. Essences are available commercially, though I think the ones you make yourself are the best. To make an essence, on a sunny day, place a clear glass bowl of spring water or distilled water beneath the plant you wish to make an essence. Sit and meditate with the plant, commune with its spirit. Ask its permission. Ask it how many flowers, if any, to pick to make the essence. Some plants prefer you not to pick, and will simply transfer their energy to the water. I like to touch the water to the living flower, and then put it back down on the ground. You can draw empowering symbols over the water, such as an invoking pentagram, spiral, triple knot, or Celtic cross. Then let the flowers and water soak in the Sun for at least three hours. If its cloudy, keep it out about five hours. Check in with the flower spirit and ask if it's done, and if you feel it is, take the bowl of water, and place it in a larger dark glass bottle with 1/4 −1/3 of a high proof alcohol such as a vodka, brandy, or rum in it. This mixture of bowl water and preservative alcohol is now your Mother Essence. Label and date it. When you buy a commercial essence, it is at the "stock level" of dilution. Shake up the Mother Essence, and place 1-5 drops into a dropper bottle that is filled with 1/4-1/3 of preservative and the rest with a pure spring/ distilled water. This is now your Stock Bottle. Several stock essences can be blended together for a dosage bottle. Simply repeat, placing 1-5 drops of each essence into a bottle containing 1/4-1/3 of preservative and the rest pure spring/distilled water. Take a few drops of the dosage bottle when you want to feel the effects of the essences. Some you take for an immediate shift, while others create long lasting healing and transformation for you.

Witch's Flying Essence
5 drops Datura Flower Essence
3 drops Monkshood Flower Essence
2 drops Mugwort Flower Essence
2 drops Cinquefoil Flower Essence
1 drop Rose Flower Essence

   Use this essence before doing any astral travel or shamanic journey. Take three drops directly, or in your chalice during ritual.

Meditation Essence
4 Drops of Horse Chestnut Flower Essence
4 Drops of Lavender Flower Essence
2 Drops of Lungwort Flower Essence
1 Drop of Monkshood Flower Essence

   If you have difficulty doing basic meditations, or focusing your mind, breath, and attention, use one to five drops directly a few minutes before your meditation practice.

Dream Essence
3 Drops of Mugwort Flower Essence
6 Drops of St. John's Wort Flower Essence
4 Drops of Lavender Essence
2 Drops of Scullcap Flower Essence
1 Drop of Datura Flower Essence
1 Drop of Blackberry Flower Essence

An excellent essence blend to experience dream journeys and improve your ability to remember them. Take a few drops before bed.

Psychic Power Essence

5 Drops of Vinca Flower Essence
5 Drops of Queen Anne's Lace Flower Essence
3 Drops of Spiderwort Flower Essence
1 Drop of Blueberry Flower Essence

This essence can be taken regularly, three drops three times a day, to improve psychic ability gradually, or as a boost before doing magick that requires psychic sight and intuition.

CHARMS

One of the safest ways to work with powerful and potentially toxic plants is to not ingest them at all, but to use their energy and call upon their spirit via charms. Just as animal magick practitioners craft fetishes from the animal they work with, or in the likeness of that animal, plant magicians can also do the same. The most famous of such charms is the *alraun*, or manakin, made from the true mandrake root, *Atropos mandragora* and its related species. This really awakens the spirit of the plant, and the root serves as a "home" for it. I know few Witches who have done it, as it is now difficult to obtain the roots, or grow them. A variety of other root charms can be made, such as those with valerian, angelica or Solomon's seal. Datura and belladonna both make excellent root allies, and meditation with them yields specific results on how to prepare and care for them. I've had amazing experiences with my datura root fetish. Often root charms are anointed with body fluids and oils, smoked in special incense and wrapped in thread or cloth strips and carried in a special bag.

A variation is a bottle charm, filled with a mixture of live and dry plants for visionary work, a form of herbal homunculus or servitor spirit, designed to aid your trance and journey work. Choose a variety of herbs for either exhibitory or inhibitory work, and include some of your own special power plant allies, even if they do not have specific trance associations. Make them into a tincture with a higher proof alcohol, but do not remove the herbs. Place the mixture in a decorative bottle. Adorn it with cords and markings. Empower it with a name and image, and give it specific instructions on how you want it to aid you – altering your brainwaves as if you consumed the herbs, opening the way, carrying you into the spirit world, or anything else you can imagine.

The simplest way to work with herbs is to simply carry a charm of dried herbs in a pouch, and hold it, put it under a pillow, or in your pocket when you want to feel its effects magickally.

Fig. 45: Mandrake Fetish

ENTHEOGEN RITUALS

No matter how you partner with green allies, it's important to use them in a ritual, rather than recreational, context. When you use such sacred plants in the context of ritual, they are not only more effective, but less is required to have an experience. Many report taking sub threshold doses of a plant substance, but have a better "trip" than those on larger doses. It all goes back to the relationship with the plant spirit, and ritual gives us a context in which to meet and know the plant spirits.

Mystical rituals, traditions, and structures give us a context to experience the unknown worlds of spirits. Those who perform such rites in the context of a tradition have the tradition's framework to anchor them. They have a context in which to interpret the experiences in a helpful way.

Those who explore entheogens outside of a mystical framework often take longer to induce trance, and the trance quality can be exciting and even profound, but also muddled, confusing, and not necessarily life changing or wise. The communication is unintelligible because the spirits, be they plant spirits or other spirits, don't have a common interface, a symbol system with which they can communicate. They lack a context for the journey, and are not able to clearly relay information in a way we can understand. When we look at the transcripts of drug trip experiences from the 1960s, lacking cultural or magickal context, we see strange and inspiring, but not all together clear, journeys. When we look at the visions of those in a magickal context, the experience can still be quite strange, but somehow more easily digested, both by the person experiencing it, and by those who receive the information from the otherworld.

I use trance inducing plants in the context of a ritual, with a sacred space set, be it in a circle (See **Chapter Fourteen**) or some other form, and invocations to not only my gods and allies, but to the plant spirit itself, asking its aid in opening the gates, and helping me learn its mysteries in the otherworld. I combine the plant magick in my traditional rites, using incense, an herbal formula in my chalice, and an oil or potion to anoint myself.

Some would argue that spirit contact in a magickal or religious context is less "pure" than unprepared context, because there is no religious coloring of the experience in the latter. While this might be true, those who practice the art of Witchcraft are practical at heart, and we care less for purity than for finding something transformative that can be integrated into our lives and shared with society. Those who do not have a spiritual context still have the context of their life, but also the clutter of their life, of their minds, different from that of a mystical initiate, reflected in their cluttered and incomprehensible journeys.

Plant trance magick is not the first path to travel, and those with experience in the other paths have much more success on this path due to the discipline, clarity, and healing the other paths bring. It is often combined with the isolation techniques of the previous chapters, particularly fasting, to both enhance the herbs' effect on your system, and to make sure it doesn't react with any other substances in your system. If you are on prescription medication, you might want to rethink the use of entheogens, at least in regard to ingesting them medicinally. Flower essences and incense can be a safer route.

Sickness and Addiction

The path of poison has at least two shadow manifestations. The first is illness. As a path of poison, literally or symbolically, we are poisoning ourselves, taking our body out of balance with foreign substances to induce a new awareness. Such experimentation can result in illness, ranging from a violent purgative effect of the digestive tract, to more serious issues. Dosages of all herbs, even seemingly benign ones, is important. There is a fine line between spiritual epiphany and nausea.

Sometimes sickness that is not induced by our own herbal making, but the sicknesses of life, and the sicknesses that mark the cleansing purge of energetic initiation can be quite liberating in terms of trance. Some of most profound mystical experiences occurred not during initiations, but the purges that followed them, in fevered dreams while I appeared to have the flu or pneumonia. Sickness opened the gates for me to commune with otherworldly beings, and receive inner world initiations and blessings. You can take the time you are sick and, with intention, possibly turn it into a time of spiritual growth and insight. Yet other times, an illness is just an illness, a time for your body to recuperate, not necessarily do more work.

The second shadow of this path is the potential for addiction. Many would-be magicians learn no other path of gnosis but the drug-induced way. They rely on the substances for all forms of magick and spirit contact, and soon find that former dose is not enough. They have built up a tolerance, be it physical, or psychological. They need more and more to go deeper, and lose what little equilibrium they had with their entheogenic substance. Without their herbal ally, they are powerless in doing even the simplest of magicks.

I've found the poison path a great supplement to the foundational traditions of meditation, breath, sound, and movement. Those are tools requiring nothing but yourself, usable anywhere. With those foundation stones in place, I have had more powerful experiences in the plant world than peers who have focused exclusively in working with trance inducing substances. They have great gifts and wisdom to offer, but I've found using them for major workings, and using other skills for daily workings, the best strategy for my own spiritual practice.

AIDS TO THE PATH OF POISON

This path of the green allies is a difficult one, and much thought and consideration should go into it before embarking. Keep the following in mind:

Be Healthy: If you do not have a healthy and strong constitution, the path of poison is *not* for you. If you are frail, sickly, or have a range of physical illnesses, injuries, or biochemical issues, then this path is not for you. If you are on constant prescription medication, or herbal medication, this path is not for you. There was a time in the Craft when potential initiates who were sickly, overweight, physically handicapped, or mentally ill would be declined admission, for the herbal path was a much bigger part of the Craft, and those with such disadvantages risked injury, illness or madness with the path of poison. While now all are welcome to walk the path, great care must be used when working with herbal preparations.

Pregnancy: If you are pregnant, avoid *all* formulas on the path of poison, and take only herbal health supplements recommended by your doctor or other qualified medical professionals. Many herbs used in the Witchcraft traditions, even some protective ones, can induce an abortion.

Just Say No: This path should only be taken by those who are willing and able. If it's not for you, you don't have to do it, much like the paths of isolation and pain. Don't let friends or covenmates pressure you into doing something that is not right for you. Be in alignment with you Will, for you are responsible for your own decisions and the consequences of such.

Discipline: While it may appear to be a free form path of drugs and hallucinations to the casual observer, those on the green path know it's a path of discipline. You must be in control, and know when to say yes, when to say no, and when to say enough. Take baby steps until you know more of what you are doing, and even then, only increase the seriousness of your herbal work incrementally. You must measure yourself, and not grow overconfident.

Mixed with Other Paths: The path of poison works best in conjunction with other paths, including restricted diets to work directly with the plant and not get sick. Read throughout this entire book before attempting to work with herbal allies, so you will best know how to work with them alongside the other gates.

Closing the Gates: Time your rituals to make sure you have enough time to detox and for the effects of the plants leave your body totally before entering the mundane world with its duties and responsibilities, including operating heavy machinery such as a vehicle. While wine, mead, beer, and herbal liquors are often used to open the gates, some grain alcohol, particularly scotch, can be used in a single shot-size dose, to help close the gates. Eating, grounding stones, and simply bed rest will also help you return to a normal, grounded state.

CHAPTER EIGHT: THE GREAT RITE

In all the tales of Witchcraft, nothing is more titillating than the idea of the Witch's Sabbat as a dark orgy, where all carnal desires are satisfied beyond the wildest imagination. If only that were true. Well, it is in many ways, but not in the ways such a description would suggest.

Witchcraft as a spiritual tradition does have a way of satisfying all desires. As we recite the words of the Goddess in our Charge, "I am that which is attained at the end of desire." I do enjoy my life to the fullest and experience things that, prior to my experience in Witchcraft, were beyond my wildest imagination. Yet I've still not experienced the carnal orgy ritual in the physical world so many people think of when they think of Witchcraft.

While I'd like to think that image is from the Inquisitors repressed minds during the Burning Times, giving vision to their own unvoiced deep desires, we do find a freer sexual ethos in the Pagans of the ancient world, and that philosophy is a part of modern Witchcraft. Modern Pagans are not restricted by the same moral code of the Jewish, Christian, and Islamic world. But it would be erroneous to think we have no moral code in regard to sexuality. Cora Anderson, co-founder of the Feri Tradition, wrote in *Fifty Years in the Feri Tradition,* "The Craft as we know it has a code of honor and sexual morality which is as tough and demanding as the Bushido of Japan and of Shinto…" For many of the Wiccan tradition, the guide is "harm none" in regard to all, in including sexuality. Everyone involved must be clear in their communication and direct about their feelings and the repercussions of their actions. Everyone must take responsibility.

One of the main aspects separating us from many other traditions is the view that sexuality is sacred by itself, with no ritual context. We do not look at it as primarily a source of procreation. It is a force of procreation, but so much more. It is the source of all creation. We do not ever look at it as a source of sin or guilt, as we do not have a theology of sin or guilt. It's simply that as Witches or Pagans we have a view of nature, the material world, and our bodies as sacred. How are bodies are created, through sex is sacred. We see sexuality as a core magickal principle, if not the core principle, for sex is the beginning of creation. Our mythos usually start with the division of the divine into Goddess and God, and their union, sexual union, as the start of all life. Through sacred sexuality, we can find that primal life force, and our own creative power. Through contact with another, we can see the spark of the divine looking back at us. It is through this kind of gnosis, through seeing the divine in both our partners and ourselves, that we find a sense of enlightenment through sexuality.

Many mystic traditions, in both the east and the west, have systems of sacred sexuality, and you find similar teachings in Witchcraft as well. For some of these traditions, the secrets of sex magick are simply symbols for higher plane forces, and have nothing to do with the physical body and real sexual arousal. For others, the higher spiritual descriptions are codes for very real physical actions and very real sexual contact, be it alone, with a partner or in a group. For some, the teachings of sex magick are not lofty, but practical. It's a method for casting spells. Others approach sex magick as the highest form of theurgy, worshipping the divine through the self and/ or other. You find all of these concepts in the sexual working of the modern Witch.

THE TABOO

Such traditions recognize that sexual energy is a powerful way to enter gnosis and direct energy. We are all capable of channeling sexual energy, and the pleasure of such contact is all the encouragement we need to explore sexual magick, or is it?

While sexual magick seems like such an easy method of reaching an altered state of consciousness, it poses some problems. For most of us, the idea of sexuality, religion, and power are, at least initially, incompatible. Most practitioners of Witchcraft today are not raised in a Pagan family or culture, and have societal expectations and ideas around sexuality. Most people do not explore the use of entheogens, isolation, yogic body posture, chanting, astral travel or meditation either. But sex holds a charge that seems particularly powerful.Exploring ritual sex is taboo in the truest sense of the word. For most of us, we think of something taboo as off limits, something that is restricted, and it is. The taboo is generally prohibited from "normal" or daily use. Not everybody can do it. It's something sacred. Something that "normal" people cannot do. It is set apart, and those who engage in the taboo are also set apart from the normal society.

Witches, by their very nature, explore the taboo. We explore what is forbidden. In going beyond the normal boundaries, walking past the edges where others fear to tread, we find power.

You might fully avoid all the other paths before this one, yet we all desire sexual pleasure, sexual contact. We all desire intimacy. And on one level, we know its normal. Yet we have all sorts of societal conditioning telling us what kind of sex we can or can't have, what we should want, and when we should want it, while simultaneously bombarding us with sexual advertisements, television, movies, and other media. We are stuck between a rock and a hard place, wanting sex and being overwhelmed by it, yet feeling we must restrict it to be "good" and "moral" in accord with some predetermined plan.

This inner conflict inherent in so many of us living in the modern world drains a lot of psychic energy. Consciously or not, we spend a lot of time thinking about sex, feeling guilty about sex, and worrying about sex, far more than we do having sex. That drains a tremendous amount of energy, yet we grow used to it. But in growing used to it, we lose potential energy we can be using for magick and our own healing and enlightenment process. Well, most "normal" people are not on a magickal path, nor are they seeking true healing or enlightenment, so they don't know what they are missing. As Witches, magicians and mystics, we need to free all the available energy possible towards our magickal pursuits.

Pursuing the taboo by breaking our social conditioning is, at first, extremely stressful. It's one of the ways to open the gates in itself, as it forces you to perceive yourself differently from what you always believed yourself to be. Yet the stress is directed through the energy channels of the body, and can create a greater sense of awareness and freedom. Through repeated breaking of restrictions, you no longer hold that same psychic tension, and can direct the free sexual energy in more creative and magickal pursuits.

There was a time in our modern Witchcraft culture where we had our own restrictions. Defining ourselves exclusively as a fertility cult, heterosexual themes were dominant, and many teachers of the Craft brought their Christian sexual mores and upbringing to their Pagan practices. While there is nothing wrong with more conservative views of sexuality, modern Witches realize it is one path among many in regard to orientation, gender identity, and practice. Today Witches are both monogamous and polyamorous. They are straight, bisexual, and homosexual. Witches are transsexual or simply unable to be labeled, going beyond traditional roles and identities already established. Such extremes are the minority, and, like much of the rest of society, more conservative heterosexuality is the majority, but it is not the only identity, and all are a part of the overall Pagan community. As Pagans do not have the same Christian restrictions against such practices, and various examples of such practices can be found in the ancient Pagan world, if not in quite the same manner as the modern world. They are a part of our reconstructed Pagan community.

THE GREAT RITE

While I'd like to illustrate an advanced and unbroken teaching of sacred sexuality as found in the eastern lore and tantric texts, modern Witchcraft's sacred sexuality is only beginning to blossoms as Witches explore old teachings in our new world. Our primarily sexual rite is actually a main part of many Wiccan rituals. Known as the Great Rite, it is a ritual sex act to embody the union of the Goddess and God in the act of creation.

The Great Rite is often performed at initiation rituals, as a method of transferring the current of initiation from initiator to initiate. In some traditions, it is when the secret names of the gods are whispered to the initiate. It is also a method of raising power for ritual and spellcraft. The Gardnerian Book of Shadows says:

The Great Rite is far the best. It releases enormous power, but the conditions and circumstances make it difficult for the mind to maintain control at first. It is again a matter of practice and the natural strength of the operator's will and, in a lesser degree, of those of his assistants. If, as of old, there were many trained assistants present and all wills properly attuned, wonders occurred.

As Witchcraft has changed through its transition from secret taboo mystery tradition to something more accepted by the mainstream with a wide variety of practitioners and traditions, the idea of having properly attuned "assistants" during ritual sex seems strange. Though many traditions of Craft identify as a fertility religion, physical sex between priestess and priest is not always required. The Great Rite has been adapted to ritual, in "token" through the chalice and blade, and the blessings of the cakes and wine. The athame blade or wand, as a symbol of the masculine, is plunged into the chalice or cauldron, the tool of the feminine, to ritually recreate the cosmic act of union between the Goddess and God that began the universe.

Sexual energy is the primary force of creation, be it the power of the physical land, or the power of the cosmic universe. By then blessing the wine and cakes, and partaking in consuming them in community as ritual sacrament, we take in the power of the Goddess and God. We awaken our own indwelling divinity, our own creative power and, like the Goddess and God, have authority to create, be it create our own life and own worlds.

The traditional instructions of Cakes and Wine follow:

Magus kneels, fills Cup, offers to Witch [she is seated on the altar, holding her athame; Priest kneels before her, holding up the cup].

Witch, holding Athame between palms, places point in cup.

Magus: "As the Athame is the Male, so the Cup is the female; so, conjoined, they bring blessedness."

Witch lays aside Athame, takes Cup in both hands, drinks and gives drink. Magus Holds Paten to Witch, who blesses with Athame, then eats and gives to eat. It is said that in olden days ale or mead was often used instead of wine. It is said that spirits or anything can be used so long as it has life.

Herbal wines and cakes, partaking of the magick from the path of poison in the previous chapter, can be used in this rite, adding to its power. Invocation rituals, such as the Drawing Down the Moon goddess invocation and Drawing Down the Sun god invocation are often merged with the Great Rite, both in token and in its sexual form.

In exploring the polarity issues found in Witchcraft, I find it fascinating that some traditions have the priestess hold the athame or wand, the male symbol, and the priest/magus holds the chalice, the female symbol. Such traditions believe the etheric polarities reverse on the higher planes, and that the feminine energy become active and projective, and the masculine energy becomes receptive and responsive. These ritual roles activate the reversal of polarity. Many modern and solitary traditions believe everyone has both polarities within, and can enact magick, including the Great Rite, solitary. The blade is held in one hand, and the cup in the other. My own ritual for the Great Rite is done solitary, but could be divided between two people.

Exercise: The Great Rite in Token

Hold the blade in the right hand (if right handed) and the chalice filled with water or wine in the left hand while in a magick circle (See **Appendix**).

Raise the blade up to the sky. If outdoors, point the blade at the Moon (or Sun) and try to catch the reflection of the Moon (or Sun) in the still liquid of the chalice. Say: "May the gods touch this blade with light."

As you inhale, drawn down the energies of the Moon/Sun and stars to touch the blade, filling it with power. Say: "As the Sword is to the Grail, the Blade is to the Chalice, Truth is to Love. May all paradoxes be resolved within me."

Plunge the blade into the chalice three times and project the energy into the liquid. Draw an invoking pentagram with the blade in the liquid, with three circles around it. Drink.

Take the blade and draw an invoking pentagram with three circles around it over the cakes/ bread resting on a peyton or other form of ritual dish. Eat a cake. Pass the cakes and chalice to other members of the circle if not alone.

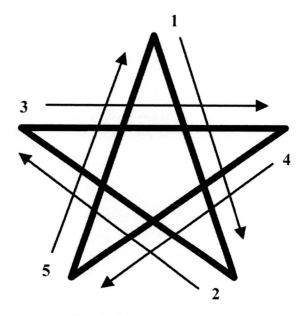

Fig. 46: Invoking Pentagram

The roots of our ritual sacrament and its link with sex might be found in the controversial text of *The Gospel of Aradia,* and specifically the Conjuration of Diana. Though the text that comes to us via Charles Leland has strange threats toward Diana until she grants the Witches request which most modern Pagans would never do, similarities to the cakes, wine and sexual union rituals are found. The threats might be a post-Christian influence found in the text, similar to threatening the saints to perform their "job" in forms of Christian "magick." Yet the cakes with salt and the wine with honey is equated with the body, blood and soul of the Goddess and consumed in a feast in her honor. There is singing, music, dancing, and leaping, followed by "freely love" in the dark.

I do not bake the bread, nor with it salt,
Nor do I cook the honey with the wine,
I bake the body and the blood and soul,
The soul of (great) Diana, that she shall

Know neither rest nor peace, and ever be
In cruel suffering till she will grant
What I request, what I do most desire,
I beg it of her from my very heart!
And if the grace be granted, O Diana!
In honour of thee I will hold this feast,
Feast and drain the goblet deep,
We, will dance and wildly leap,
And if thou grant'st the grace which I require,
Then when the dance is wildest, all the lamps
Shall be extinguished and we'll freely love!

And thus shall it be done: all shall sit down to the supper all naked, men and women, and, the feast over, they shall dance, sing, make music, and then love in the darkness, with all the lights extinguished: for it is the Spirit of Diana who extinguishes them, and so they will dance and make music in her praise.

The Conjuration of Diana includes elements from many paths, but it's interesting to note how the sexual element is the pinnacle of the ritual, showing its power and sacredness in the tradition.

EASTERN SEXUAL PRACTICES

Due to the repressive development of the western world regarding sexual energy and spirituality, much of our esoteric sexual lore is supplemented by eastern traditions. Yogic tantric practices and Taoist sexual alchemy have become more popular in the west as we are opening to the link between sexuality and spirit. Such practices have been adapted and grafted into western occultism and Witchcraft, expanding Paganism's natural association with sexuality, life force and fertility.

"Tantra" has become the buzz word for sexual spiritual practices, though the term tantra simply refers to a text. These sacred texts proposed instructions for a variety of life's lessons, and sacred sexuality was one of a number of topics, including diet, medicine, society, etiquette, and relationships. The Kama Sutra is one of the most famous of these Hindu texts in the west, and the true translations go far beyond what most assume is simply a manual of kinky sexual positions. There are also similar manuals from Asian and Arabian traditions of sacred sexuality that are less well known to westerners.

One of the key concepts found in eastern forms of sexual magick is the concept that sexual energy is usually wasted in the west. Most people in modern secular cultures keep the sexual energy only in the lowest energy centers, the root, belly, and possibly solar plexus chakras. The sexual energy is not circulated, and vital life force is loss through sex. The "goal" of orgasm is not emphasized, and some techniques even encourage the man not to ejaculate, while still experiencing an orgasm within the body and spirit. The experience itself is the only goal, whatever that experience may be.

Exercise: Energizing the Chakras with Sexual Energy

If you have no experience working with sexual energy in a magickal context, it's best to attempt this exercise alone at first, and then gradually build your technique until you are comfortable with a partner or group. Sexually stimulate yourself, and be aware of the energy growing in the lower body as sensation begins to build. At first you will feel it mostly in the root or belly chakras, at the base of the spine and/or at the naval area. The root concerns your survival and pleasure, and in modern chakra teachings, is visualized as red. The belly is the center of intimacy and trust, usually depicted as orange. Concentrate on drawing that energy up through your body. As you inhale, imagine inhaling the sensation of energy up to the yellow solar plexus, your center of personal power. Feel the sensation grow at the solar plexus. If the energy builds too much at the root or belly, overpowering the sensation in the solar plexus, continue to breathe the energy upward until the solar plexus is a more dominant sensation. Repeat this process, bringing the energy even further upward, to the green heart center. The heart is the chakra of love, compassion, and empathy. The sexual energy may change here, as strong emotions and repressed feelings can surface. If you are a man, do not allow yourself to ejaculate yet, though you might feel strong sensations during this process identical to orgasm without ejaculation. Continue this practice, drawing up the energy from the heart to the blue throat chakra for communications. Draw the energy up with your breath to the purple third eye chakra at the brow. Draw the energy up to the white or violet crown at the top of the head, and feel the energy spurting out like a shower. Many men allow themselves to ejaculate at this point, as they have raised the vibration of the sexual energy to charge all seven chakra points.

Once you are comfortable with this process, you can perform it with a partner, guiding each other in the process of raising the energy. You might feel energy exchange at points of touch, particularly at the root chakras, and share the refined energy exuding from the crown.

The Chinese Taoist forms of internal alchemy use an entirely different system of energy points and circuits in their exercises. One technique used to circulate energy, or chi, throughout the body, and a cornerstone of health in Qigong and more advanced form of sexual alchemy is known as the Microcosmic Orbit. It has been adopted into many forms of Reiki healing and some traditions of magick.

The pathway this orbit takes is like a figure eight around the outside of the body. The crossing midpoint of the "8" at the perineum, and one must contract the "hui yin" or perineum point, as done in Kegel exercises. The circuit goes up the spine and over the top of the head. Along with the Hui Yin, the tongue must touch the root of the mouth behind the teeth to complete the circuit, as the energy travels down the face, throat, chest and belly, to the perineum. It then travels down the back of the legs, beneath the feet, up over the top of the feet and up the front of the legs until it reaches to the perineum for another circuit.

Exercise: Microcosmic Orbit

While sitting or standing, bring your attention to the Tan t'ien energy center, located three finger widths below the naval. Contract the Hui Yin position and place your tongue in the proper position. Hold the Hui Yin and tongue in position during the entire exercises. Feel the energy build at this center, gathering up chi, or life force, like a ball. Many imagine it as golden healing light. Imagine dropping this ball into the figure eight circuit, down to the perineum, going down the back of the legs, up the front of the legs to the perineum, up the back, over the head, down the chest and back to where you began. Continue the flow. Generally the breath is coordinated with the orbit. On the inhale, one focuses on the "Governor Vessel" moving up the back along the spine and ending at the roof of the mouth, and on the exhale one focuses on the "Conception Vessel" moving down the front. Continue the orbit, completing several circuits and, when done, bring your focus back to the Tan T'ien, grounding yourself and the energy back in your center of gravity.

Taoists believe this orbit exercise aids many ailments and illnesses over the long term, and prevents new illnesses and injuries from taking root. In more advanced Taoist teachings, the sexual energy is shared with a partner through sexual contact of the genitals and kissing, linking the orbits of the two partners together. This exchange of sexual energy become a catalyst for higher forms of meditation and experiencing the "Cosmic Orgasm." *Taoist Secrets of Love* by Mantak Chia goes into a greater level of detail on these traditions and partnered teachings. The microcosmic orbit is of great benefit when done alone, and is quite sufficient to both build energy and alter consciousness of an individual, using life force and sexual energy rather than other meditative techniques.

In the Reiki traditions, the Microcosmic Orbit, or MCO, is transformed into the Violet Breath or Dragon Breath to transfer energy during the Reiki attunement. Universal life force is gathered and transformed into violet energy by drawing blue energy up from the Earth into the root, white energy from the heavens into the crown and red energy from the stars into the brow, mixing as violet energy that is then blown out of the mouth and into an initiate. I've found simply circulating violet energy in the body quite transformative, healing, and meditative.

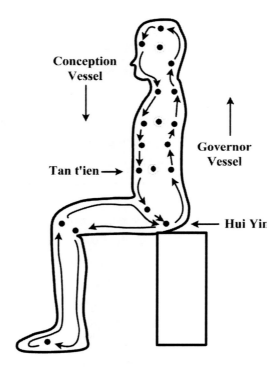

Fig. 47: Microcosmic Orbit

Sexual Apotheosis

One of the deepest forms of sexual gnosis and the Great Rite is the practice of sexual apotheosis. Apotheosis refers to the deification of another. Political, military, scholarly or religious leaders of antiquity were often deified after death, worshipped as gods. In terms of sexual rites, one is not simply worshipped like an intangible spirit after death, but the divinity of the individual is celebrated in flesh. The giving of pleasure to the partner is paramount in tantra teachings.

Such rituals of physical worship usually work in one of two ways. Both views are deeply entwined with the Great Rite as a sexual celebration, no matter how you perform the Great Rite. The inherent holiness of sexual union is a part of our great mystery. In the Charge of the Goddess we are taught, "Let My worship be in the heart that rejoices, for behold – all acts of love and pleasure are My rituals."

With the first, the divinity worshipped is essentially the soul, spirit, or Higher Self of the sexual partner. The divinity of the individual is an extension of the greater creative divinity. In this philosophy, we are all extensions of the divine. We see this philosophy in many of the Pagan rituals descended from The Church of All Worlds, with the blessing "Thou Art God" or "Thou Art Goddess." Many Pagans are theologically pantheistic or panentheistic, and both philosophies hold that the material world is divine. Pleasing another can be seen as akin to pleasing and pleasuring the divine, and in essence a form of worship. The ritualized act of devoting yourself sexually to another, and seeing the essence of the divine shine through them in the act, is immensely powerful. When both partners do it at the same time, an incredible experience of love, spirit, and sexual power can occur.

Exercise: Soul Gazing

Soul gazing is an exercise that can be done in or out of a sexual context, but I've found it particularly powerful to do in a sexual setting. It requires a partner. Also known as Face Scrying, you and your partner gaze into each other's eyes for an extended period of time. It's okay to blink if necessary, but it's not a staring contest. There is often the tendency to giggle or make jokes at first, but once your mind has settled, all manner of psychic impressions can occur. As if you are scrying into a crystal ball, images may be conjured in the eyes of your partner. Their face may shift, revealing past life images, animal allies, fears, joys, and eventually their true nature. You are seeking to gaze at their core self, their soul self, and reveal that part of yourself to them. In essence, you are seeking the divine within each of you, a direct experience of the eastern saying Namaste, meaning "the divine within me honors the divine within you."

The second manifestation of this form of magickal worship occurs through the act of ritual invocation, where a priestess or priest invokes a specific divinity. In some traditions the Goddess of the Moon is invoked into the priestess through a Drawing Down the Moon ritual, or a specific goddess is invoked, such as Diana, Arianrhod, or Isis. The same is true of God invocations, with a general invocation of the Sun god or Horned god, or a specific invocation of figures such as Lugh, Apollo, Pan or Cernunos. The worshiper is then sexually communing with the deity through the invoked priest/ess. The experience is different and more specifically attuned to an aspect of divine power, rather than the generalized worship of the first method. Sometimes a pair or group are all invoked with harmonious deities, and experience sexual union in the flesh.

One method of invocation that often has sexual connotations is the sacred kiss. A sign of blessing in Witchcraft, it is one of the "three passwords" to enter the magick circle, along with Perfect Love and Perfect Trust. In ritual blessings and invocations, the Five Fold Kiss is performed. The kiss is given on the feet, knees, pubic triangle, breasts/chest, and lips.

"Blessed be thy feet that have brought thee in these ways." (He kisses her feet.)

"Blessed be thy knees that shall kneel at the sacred altar." (He kisses her knees.)

"Blessed be thy womb, without which we would not be." (He kisses the top of the pubic triangle. For a man being invoked, womb would be replaced by phallus.)

"Blessed by thy breasts, formed in beauty and in strength." (He kisses her breasts.)

"Blessed be thy lips, which shall utter the sacred names." (He kisses her lips.)

In some traditions, a five pointed star is kissed in various ways, such as the left foot, brow, right foot, left breast, right breast and back down to the foot, or a more expansive seven fold kiss, on the seven chakra centers of the root, belly, solar plexus, heart, throat/lips, brow and crown. In such kisses, there is often energy exchanged, opening and awakening the chakras much like a tantric exercise.

Both techniques are profound for all parties involved, and are rewarding in and of themselves as consciousness expanding experiences. They can also be paired with other forms of sexual magick when performed by experienced Witches. Such traditions have been found in the eastern teachings, but are wholly appropriate to modern Witches.

SEXUAL SHAMANIC TRANCE

One rarely touched upon aspect of sexual magick is the shamanic element to repetitive motion and stimulation. While we often vary our touching and movement to bring unexpected pleasure, the repetitive motions of intercourse have a lot in common with the repetitive movements in shamanic dance, and the shamanic music using drums, rattles, and singing bowls. A fast paced regular rhythm is established, and that rhythm helps induce trance. The same can be said for sexual rhythms. One can enter an altered state of consciousness, and either experience the ecstasy marked by a sensation of leaving the body and going to another world or simply expanding awareness beyond the body, reaching a more "cosmic" point of view.

Many magickally oriented people report profound awareness that cannot easily be put into words during or after sex, and even spontaneous spirit contact. Visions during and after are not uncommon, but because few texts and traditions discuss such a topic, they can be alarming. Perhaps many of our legends of incubi and succubi, assaulting the unwary at night and taking sexual fluids are simply a spirit contact during erotic dreams. Putting such situations in a ritual context, with the specific intention to commune with spirits, journey to otherworlds, or expand consciousness can make it even more powerful.

SEXUAL SPELL CASTING

Sex has become a component to modern spellcasting, finding its way into the techniques favored by chaos magicians. It is a simple and profound way of "launching" a spell by someone who otherwise has little magickal training, yet is also effective for those who are more advanced in their understanding, techniques and experience.

Basically the desire is transformed into a sigil, a magickal symbol, using a simple alphabet technique. Your intention is reduced to as simple of a statement as possible, possibly even just one word. Duplicate letters are crossed out until only a small number of letters remain. Those letters are combined graphically into a pleasing image, which embodies the intention, yet gives your conscious mind a measure of distance from the intention. This technique is great for those who obsess over spells they cast. It allows you forget about it, as you are not focused on the intention, but the sigil created from the intention.

One focuses on the sigil, gazing upon it during orgasm. Orgasm can be reached with a partner, group, or solitary experience, but the important factor is that, at the moment of orgasm, and ideally through much of the ritual, you are focused on the sigil, not on your pleasure, your partner's pleasure, or any other sexual performance issues. The sigil can be hung on a wall or ceiling, put on the floor or even painted on a lovers chest or back in body paints. Put it anywhere, in any media, that allows you clear sight of it during orgasm. Imaging releasing the erotic power into the sigil, and then do something to destroy the sigil. Wash it off the body, burn the paper, or simply throw it away and forget about it. The intention is erotically charged, and amazing results can occur.

RAISE AND PROMOTION

R A I S E A N D P R O M O T I O N

S E D P M T

Fig. 48: Statement – Letters – Sigil

Sexual fluids can also be used in ritual. Some traditions use sexual fluids as sacraments. In a day of more awareness regarding the transmission of STDs and HIV, such practices should not engaged in lightly, yet they still have magickal significance and should not be rejected and discarded.

While some Witchcraft traditions use blood as an anointing fluid, to magickally align a tool with your body, others use sexual fluids for the same purpose. Both contain the powers of life and a genetic link to you. Sexual fluids can be charged with an intention via the sigilization method above, then used to anoint tools like the athame, wand, peyton, chalice, and cauldron. This technique should be reserved for your personal tools, not coven, group or public tools for a larger community.

OBSESSION

Obsession is the bane of sexual power. The Zodiac sign Scorpio is classically linked with sexual power, and is in fact known as the sign of sex and death, for the powers of life and death are conjoined in it. Scorpio is also known as the sign of secrets and obsession, for such powers are also deeply entwined with sexuality.

Desire is good. As Witches, we spend much of our time exploring our desire. The exploration helps us understand what is ego desire and what is divine desire, aiding us in fulfilling our True Will, our soul's purpose, in the world. Desire for a result can fuel some powerful magick. Putting all your thoughts, emotions, and intent toward a stated goal until it becomes like an obsession is quite a powerful bit of magick, yet so many of our traditions teach us to "let go" of our intention once set into motion, or to do magick without a "lust for results." They do so because it's a very fine line between such forces working for us, and us working for them. Sometimes obsession takes control, and our inability to let it go and let it manifest thwarts our efforts, making the obsession self perpetuating.

While desire and obsession can play a role in all forms of magick, when you actually add sexual contact into a magickal working, you are playing with potent forces that have the potential to lead to obsession. Some people confuse sexual energy with emotions, or defined relationships, and obsess over teachers, students, and covenmates, often resulting in an unhealthy and controlling situation. Others get obsessed with working with sexual energy because it is so powerful, and never learn other techniques of magick, or how direct it. They become stuck and stunted because they don't now other ways to open the gates. The charge from breaking "taboos" magickally and sexually diminishes over time. What once released stored energy because it was novel no longer releases the same forces, even though it can still be effective. An addictive component comes about, seeking more ways to stimulate the same response. Rather than integrate the taboo into their life and consciousness in a healthy way, new lines to cross are constantly sought out, without making peace with the old. Such cycles become difficult to break out of, and maintain a Witchcraft practice.

Moderating sexual mysteries, reserving them for specific occasions, rather than making them the focus of all magick work is the best advice to avoid this pitfall. It's also important to establish and maintain healthy secular forms of sexual expression and relationships. Though all sex has a spiritual element to it, not all sex needs to be focused on ritual, magick, and gnosis. Sex just for the pleasure of it, with no other goal, is just as holy, if not more so.

AIDS TO THE GREAT RITE

Sexual energy is powerful, primal and catalytic. It's easy to get swept away in not only the energy, but the emotions associated with it, and lose perspective. Keep the following in mind before seriously embarking upon this path.

Examine Your Sexual Ethics: Do you have sexual ethics? Have you thought about sex in terms of ethical conduct? What are the conditions you have around both your sexual behavior and your sexual nature? How much of that is inherited from parents, society, and previous religions, and how much do you really agree with and believe? Why do you agree or believe? Most people rarely take stock of what they think and believe around sex, and create conflicts internally between what they believe and what they desire.

Explore your Fantasies: If you can do so in a safe and responsible way, explore your sexual fantasies. There is a vast reservoir of repressed power there for most people to free. Your life, and magickal practices, can evolve and transform when you are in conscious relationship to that energy.

Start Slowly: If you have little experience in ritual sex, do not plan elaborate rituals. Things have a tendency to not always go as planned with sexual rituals, and it's good to learn to control your energy alone before engaging and joining it with another's. Smaller masturbatory rituals can be great building blocks to larger workings.

Great Rite in Token: While some never explore the Great Rite beyond the cup and blade and I think that's unfortunate, there is still great power in the token rituals. When done properly, they do stimulate and raise sexual life force, even if there is no bodily orgasm. Explore the ritual slowly, meditatively, and with your inner guidance. It can unlock many secrets.

Normal Sex Life: Maintain a "normal" sex life, whatever that might mean to you. Don't devote so much of your sexual energy exclusively to magick that your lover/partner/spouse feels lost and neglected. If possible, try to engage that person in your magickal sexual practice. If not, make sure you devote enough time to both. Don't lose your relationship while you seek the mysteries. Witches believe in a balance of both, for magick is found in ritual and in every moment of daily life.

Boundaries: If working with others sexually, establish clear boundaries and discuss the emotional ramification of your actions and your partners actions. Regardless what anyone says, you do not have to sleep with your High Priest/ess to become a Witch. Some traditions do work sexually, so you might not find your path on those traditions, but there are many paths to the power of the Witch and never let someone convince you to have sex when you don't want to do so. Covens that require sex as part of their initiatory process should make that clear near the start of your commitment to the training and tradition. It shouldn't be sprung on you in a moment of pressure. Magickal sex does not absolve you of previous vows and commitments, so decide well before taking action and talk to all those involved. Beware of those using positions of power and authority for their own sexual benefit rather than actually teaching the mysteries.

Herbal Supplements: Many of the exhibitory trance herbs used work well in sex magick and the Great Rite. Some herbs have a specific history with love and sex magick, either due to their herbal action for arousal and lust, such as damiana, used in teas and cordials, or rose, for it's loving magickal properties. Generally herbs with astrological influences of Venus and Mars are best in sex magick. Some elevate the heart rate, metabolism and respiration, so clear any use with your medical practitioner, particularly if you suffer from any ailments. Jasmine, particular jasmine oil, is said to raise the vibration of any act, aiding in raising sexual magick to a form of high magick as is generally considered safe to use, albeit expensive.

Safety: Act safely and responsibly, for you are responsible for the results of your actions. Just because it is magickal and spiritual doesn't mean there still isn't the chance of pregnancy, STD and HIV transmission. Use common sense and use precautions. Use good judgement and discernment even outside of the areas of immediate health and safety, and particularly around the breaking of taboos and exploring the darker side of sexuality. While its good to go beyond the norm, do so with support and caution, not haphazardly. Determine with prior deliberation what taboos you want to break and in what setting. Deciding such things in the moment leads to difficulties.

CHAPTER NINE:
THE WAY OF PAIN

The path least explored by modern Witches is the way of pain. It was the most difficult for me to teach and to write about, as it's an extremely sensitive topic, ripe for misunderstanding and misuse. Yet any manual on the ways of gnosis would be incomplete without discussing it at least somewhat.

Most of us see Witchcraft as a life affirming, ecstatic tradition and don't understand the path of pain. We seek the ways of pleasure. Yet any good Witch knows that everything casts a shadow. You cannot seek the wisdom of one side of the coin without holding the other. They are inseparable. You cannot know how to cure if you don't know how to curse. You don't appreciate the pleasure of life if you do not acknowledge the pain. Unlike other traditions that seek to renounce the material world and minimize both pleasure and pain, Witches find wisdom in both, for we find divinity in the flesh and blood, in the material world. Everything is of the gods. Some use pain as a test to transcend the material world, and pleasure as a temptation to our renouncement. We find nothing inherently wrong, or right, with either. Their virtue depends on the circumstances. What are your goals and intention? What is your True Will? Only then can you determine if pleasure or pain will be an aid to your magickal journey. While both are paths to the mysteries, and both have wisdom to offer, I, too, must admit the path of pleasures is much easier to embrace, at least at first.

Many of the techniques on the roads of ecstatic movement and isolation border the realms of pain. Physical exhaustion and struggling against restriction are not pleasurable roads, yet they are not quite the same as inducing sharp sensations to induce gnosis. Several techniques can be catalogued and specifically defined in a mystical context. Some are found in more traditional depictions of Wicca, while others hearken back to tribal societies, and our modern world's desire to capture some of the aesthetics of tribal culture in our "global village." Today Native American practitioners still make flesh and blood offerings of the self, and perform rites like the Sun Dance, most known for the painful piercing of the chest or back, tied to a rope and ritual Sun-pole

One of the reasons why modern Witches have such a hard time with pain and sacrifice is the strong association of religious sacrifice and suffering with Christianity. The crucifix embodies the tortured inspiration for the religion. The idea of sacrifice is linked with theological concepts such as sin and salvation, concepts that are antithetical to the Witch's spiritual worldview. We don't believe anyone should be sacrificed for us or require salvation. We don't believe anyone can do our spiritual work for us, or simple belief in a figure will open the gates of initiation. We also realize such pain and sacrifice, from another or from ourselves is not necessary for our spiritual growth and is one of many paths. As many Christian religions deny the spiritual essence of the physical world and its pleasures, we sometimes try to deny the spiritual essence found in the pains of the physical world. As Witches, our true theology is one of moderation, cycles, and seasons. All things have their purpose and path. Sacrifice, offerings, and pain are as much a part of Pagan history and nature based traditions as Christian, if not more so. By looking at some possible methods in this work, we can see how the way of pain can serve us today.

Flagellation: Flagellation is the act of whipping, either done by oneself or another. Generally it is thought of either as a punishment or an act of erotic stimulation. It has a history in mysticism, in both Pagan and Christian traditions, for a variety of purposes. In Witchcraft, the ritual whip is known as a scourge.

BDSM: Beyond simple flagellation found in a variety of ritual and sexual contexts, BDSM, an abbreviation for the terms "bondage and discipline/dominance and submission/sadism and masochism," includes a wide range of behaviors and actions.

Generally seen as a subset of sexual fetishes, many modern practitioners of BDSM find a spiritual dimension to the practice, and many mystics explore the role of BDSM as a magickal technique. The path itself includes elements of the previous discussed sexual paths and restriction/isolation paths, but also can include inflicting physical pain or humiliation in a strictly consensual context. The combination of restriction or control with erotic elements and pain can break old identity patterns and environmental awareness, akin to a magickal ritual. BDSM has developed into its own subculture, much like the GLBT and Pagan communities, and those seeking to explore this avenue of gnosis should seek more detailed resources and teachers from that community.

Piercing: The ritual act of piercing the flesh is found both in religious rites and secular society. The piercing of ears is now fashionable not only for women, but also men, and has become a rite of passage for many teens. Piercing of other body parts, in a neo-tribal esthetic has also become popular. The location of the piercing can have spiritual significance. I had one covenmate who pierced her tongue in order to watch her words, and always think before she spoke. Similar piercing, or piercings at similar times, can act as a bonding experience in a group. Before ear piercing was more fashionable for men, and still considered somewhat rebellious, it was a rite of passage when I was in a rock band. We each got our ears pierced at the same time, forging a bond between us. While some piercing can be done at home, and at one time home piercing of the ears was not uncommon, I highly suggest going to a trained professional with properly sterilized equipment if you choose this path.

Tattooing: Tattooing is a method of making a permanent mark in ink upon the skin. Like piercing it was once considered taboo, but has now its become quite fashionable. Those on a magickal path use tattooing to make magickal marks, to invoke specific forces into their bodies and lives, and to mark specific life passages. Some traditions of Witchcraft encourage tattooing as a mark of initiation. Many tribal traditions see tattooing as a spiritual art, and there are now modern tattoo artists who also evoke a spiritual component to their work.

Branding: Unlike piercing and tattooing, branding, burning a specific mark into the flesh, has not become fashionable, but it serves a similar purpose. This method evokes the powers of fire and metal, working differently than tattooing and piercing. Such scarring can be used in rites of passage and initiation rituals, marking a very specific time or event.

Cutting: Shedding blood to make magick is a long-standing tradition. Blood from cutting, or even blood from menstruation, is used to release power. The act of cutting, and the slight pain of a shallow cut, focuses the mind. Blood magick is a specific form of magick, not to be confused with self-abuse issues. One cuts only in specific ritual settings for a specific purpose, not to simply relieve stress, release emotions, or induce pleasure. Blood magick is linked to our word "blessings" coming from the Old English *blétsian*, originally meaning to consecrate, or make holy, with blood.

Offerings & Sacrifice: "Sacrifice" is a word that scares most people who are not deeply involved in magick. Sacrifice simply means to make sacred. Those who fear Witchcraft immediately hear the word and think of human or animal sacrifice. Though our Pagan ancestors might have practiced some form of human sacrifice, we do not. Most modern Witches do not perform any type of animal sacrifice. Traditions that have and still do usually did so in the context of making a food offering, not being separated from their food source. Killing animals for food was a regular part of life, unlike the lives of most of us today. But the sacrifice I'm talking about is one of making an offering of something that is sacred and important to you, to the spirits, gods or the magick itself. The act of giving up something important to us, or something hard to acquire, has tremendous energy to it. The ritual of offering, done under such conditions, can induce new perspectives, shifts in identity, and magickal gnosis different from other forms of trance. But the offering must have energy invested in it. Today many people try to emulate our Pagan ancestors, but make offerings of things that are worthless to them, or untouched by their own hands. The traditional offerings have always meant something to the people making the offering, or were something crafted by human hands not duplicated in nature, like various alcohols, breads, cheese, chocolate, hand-carved votive offerings, coins, or crafted jewelry.

Purging: Purging combines aspects of isolation and often the magick of plant allies. Through the use of a restricted diet with particular entheogen substances, the mystic seeks to purge, emotionally, mentally and, most notably, physically, vomiting prior to deeper trance. While one could argue it is not the same pain reaction as the other techniques on this path, such experiences are certainly not pleasurable and carry a similar form of psychological and magickal release.

Ordeal: The ordeal refers to any form of experience that feels like a severe test or trial. Ordeals are the experiences of life that threaten to destroy us, but if they do not kills us, literally or metaphorically, they serve to make us stronger. Ordeals are seen as initiatory experiences, be they controlled rituals, or the workings of our daily life.

Pain, in any of these forms, serves as a focus. The physical stimulation of the nerves can focus and sharpen the mind in ways that are just as profound, yet different, from drumming, dancing, and sensory deprivation. While all create a physiological reaction, the endorphins released by the path of pain are different from other paths. Often the fear of pain is just as stimulating as the pain itself. Distinguishing between the fear and anticipation of pain, and the actual sensation of pain becomes an invaluable part of a Witch or magician in the work of "know thyself." We often anticipate things to be worse than they are, and invest them with psychic power. Facing our fears unlocks that psychic power. By having focus through the pain, we can direct that power towards our magickal intentions.

THE SCOURGE

The scourge is one of the least used and most misunderstood of the modern Craft tools. Many of us have a distaste for the scourge. I know I did. I remember questioning one of my first teachers on the topic of the scourge, as it was in some of the reading she required. She distastefully answered, "We do not do such things today. I would never let a man whip me." And that was the understanding I had of the scourge for many years.

For those of us who trained in non-British Traditional lines, and had the influence of both American and tribal psychedelics, the scourge was thought of as an archaic tool. It is a short ritual whip with several ends, akin to a cat o' nine tails, usually made from leather.

Generally seen as a punishment device used to harm or torture, or a tool of self-mortification, many Witches now believe it is either a remnant from the ceremonial magicians working in a punishment oriented Judeo-Christian frame work, or the scourge is in our tradition due to the personal sexual fetishes of Gerald Gardner, naturalist and founder of the modern Craft movement.

As for the use of the scourge in antiquity, flagellation does have some history in ancient Pagan practices, though very few think Gardner received it as part of a Pagan lineage, still there are some similarities between his working tools and those of the Cult of Mithras.

In the artwork of Osiris, the Egyptian god of fertility and the dead, we have a depiction of a flail. Held along with the crook, in the crossed hands of Osiris at rest. Though it would be easy to see a scourge, this flail was most likely used to thresh wheat, marking his agricultural power as a god of the green, though it is possible it was also used in ancient Egypt to beat slaves. The crook is symbolic of Osiris' role, and that of the Pharaoh, to "shepherd" his people. Modern Witches emulate the depictions of Osiris in the "God Position" (**Chapter Five**) while holding the scourge and the wand for the flail and the crook.

One of the earliest references to ritual flagellation is the ritual of *diamastigosis*, performed in the sanctuary of Artemis Orthia in Sparta. The rituals originated in a Pre-Olympian religion, and the figure of Orthia was represented by a xoanon, an archaic wood-carved effigy. A group of scourgers, led by a priestess holding the xoanon, would flagellate a group of male youth trying to "steal" cheeses under the guard of the scourgers. Unlike our modern scourging rituals, blood would be drawn and stain the altar. This was possibly an agricultural ritual, with ritual dances, maidens, and the winning of a sickle. According to the philosopher Plutarch, in his *Life of Aristides,* the ritual was more of a commemoration of an event from the Greek-Persian Wars. Eventually in the Roman era the rituals devolved into a blood spectacle attracting the curious and bloodthirsty rather than a sacred rite to Artemis Orthia. The followers of Dionysus were depicted using flagellation in their rites. Other references to flagellation occur among the Roman philosophers, but not in such detail as religious rites. The Mithric Roman cult had similar tools to the modern Witch, with the wand, cup, blade, and platter, as well as a sword and "Sun's whip" which does sound like a scourge of some sort.

As for Gardner's use of the scourge, we are not sure how it came into our traditions, though one popular theory, certainly agreed upon by some of my earliest teachers, was that Gardner added it because he simply liked the sexual titillation. Many believe his rules regarding skyclad rites, young priestesses, the Great Rite, and scourging are based upon his affinity for nudism and sexual exploration, rather than any old craft tradition. It was an acceptable way to both be involved in, and involve others in his sexual explorations that would otherwise be condemned by those around him. But making it "spiritual" made it more acceptable for both him and those around him. Cloaking it in the mystery of tradition put him beyond judgment. And while there might be truth to such claims, Gerald Gardner has been a great influence on how Witches today operate. It might behoove us not to dismiss his thoughts and writings out of hand without examining them for value for us today.

Gardner felt the scourge was a powerful tool, second only to the Great Rite in terms of raising energy, for it "stimulates and excites both body and soul, yet one easily retains control." As a man with respiratory problems, he found the scourge a powerful but physically easier method to raise energy, compared to dancing and the smoke of incense.

While the salt, water, smoke, and fire were used to purify the space and body, the scourge is said to purify the soul. Upon its presentation in the first degree rituals, it is described as a tool of "power and domination. It is also to cause suffering and purification, for it's written, to learn you must suffer and be purified." And most importantly, the scourge plays a role in the initiation myth of the Descent of the Goddess.

Based upon the legends of Astarte and Inanna, Wicca has its own version of the Descent of the Goddess. Though there have been many versions written and rewritten, the essential myth, often acted out as a play in initiation ceremonies, is the same. Our Lady descends to the Underworld to solve the mysteries of death. She faces challengers at the portal gates, and is stripped of her jewels and garments. She is courted by the Lord of the Underworld and rejects his advances. Rejecting the kiss, she is faced with his scourge. Such scourging links him to Osiris as god of the underworld. The Goddess then accepts him, which is not just an acceptance of his advances, but an acceptance and even love of death, of endings, so all can be reborn, and she is taught "all the magicks" and finds joy and knowledge.

Legend of the Descent of the Goddess

Now our Lady the Goddess has never loved, but she would solve all the mysteries, even the mystery of Death: And so she journeyed to the Underworld.

The Guardian of the Portals challenged her: "Strip off thy garments, lay aside thy jewels; for naught mayest thou bring with thee into this land." So she laid down her garments and her jewels, and was bound as are all who enter the Realms of Death, the Mighty One.

Such was her beauty that Death himself knelt and kissed her feet, saying: Blessed by they feet, that have brought thee in these ways. Abide with me; but let me place my cold hand on thy heart.

She replied: "I love thee not. Why dost thou cause all things that I love and take delight in to fade and die?"

"Lady," replied Death, "tis age and fate, against which I am helpless. Age causes all things to wither, but when men die at the end of time, I give them rest and peace, and strength so that they may return. But thou! Thou art lovely. Return not; abide with me!"

But she answered: "I love thee not."

Then Death said: "An thou receivest not my hand on thy heart, thou must receive Death's scourge."

"'Tis fate – better so." She said. And she knelt and Death scourgest her tenderly. And she cried, "I feel the pangs of love."

And Death said, "Blessed be!" and gave her the Fivefold Kiss saying: "Thus only mayest thou attain to joy and knowledge," and he taught her all the mysteries, and they loved and were one, and he gave her all the magicks.

For there are three great events in the life of man: Love, Death, and Resurrection in the new body; and Magick controls them all. For to fulfill love you must return again at the same time and place as the loved one, and you must remember and love them again. But to be reborn you must die and be ready for a new body, and to die you must be born; and without love you may not be born; and that is all the Magicks."

The scourge is almost always linked with the kiss, and the pairing teaches us the two sides of life – pain and pleasure, discipline and freedom, cursing and curing, hexing and healing, death and life. We appreciate all that we love and take delight in because, in the material world, it is transitory. We see two sides of the same coin which is our lives. The great initiatory question involving the scourge is, "Are you willing to suffer to learn?" In many ways, the scourge is symbolic of the ordeal, the suffering we often undergo in life, but growing wiser from the experience. In Qabalistically inspired Wiccan circles the kiss is the "tool" of Mercy, the light pillar of the Tree of Life, the scourge is the tool of Severity, the dark pillar. In such traditions, the scourge, along with the sword, is the symbolic tool of the "higher" sphere of Geburah, the realm of consciousness denoting power and might. On the most traditional peytons, or ritual pentacles, the kiss is denoted with an "S" and the scourge with a "$" (not a depiction of the dollar sign, as many erroneously believe, for the British Traditional lines would have little use for the American dollar sign, using the British pound.)

Fig. 49: Traditional Pentacle

In initiation rites, the initiate is flogged to show the movement of energy and magick through the law of return and in the highest initiations, the initiate then scourges the initiator three times more, to show in ritual the power of three in the law of return. What you do returns to you threefold.

In terms of magickal operation, the scourge works through two principles beyond the use of pain as a focus. Some say it induces altered states of consciousness through shifting the flow of blood within the body. Almost all British Traditional Witches would not use it to break the skin and draw blood, but the shifting of blood to the stimulated area shifts the awareness in the brain to induce trance. This flow is part of the purification process.

The second theory is that it awakens sexual energy, either by the fact that such acts are sexually suggestive, opening up the repressed sexual energy, or by directly scourging the sacrum and perineum points, stimulating the energy of the root chakra, and causing it to awaken in something akin to a kundalini awakening experience, providing purification, power, and altered consciousness. This is why it is used so much in an initiatory setting, to raise an inner initiatory energy to compliment the current of energy you receive from your initiator, connecting you to the tradition's line.

The scourge itself often has symbolism in its crafting. Different groups craft their scourge differently, but generally the leather strands are three, five, or nine in number. Others use more strands, though three, five and nine are more traditional for a scourge. Each of these numbers is sacred to our traditions, for the Triple Goddess, the five points of the pentagram, and the nine of lunar associations and the number of months of human gestation. Sometimes they are single strands, while others are whips of three strands braided. Often they have knots, usually five, as five is the number of Geburah, the Qabalistic sphere of might and power. The handle is a wooden dowel, usually nine or twelve inches, twelve being the number of Zodiac signs. The leather whips are either affixed to the wood with iron nails, or tied to an eye hook. The handle can be painted or also wrapped in leather. Some scourges I've seen have handles made of animal horn.

The scourging rituals often use these numbers, primarily multiples of three, though more ecstatic scourging rituals do not bother to count the number of lashings. Many modern day, politically correct traditions make their scourges not of knotted leather, but of ribbon, and move so gently that, little physical effect occurs. Such practitioners believe it is the sensation, not pain, that induces trance and does the purification, but I'm not so sure myself. Others stray on the side of too stern of a use, causing welts or drawing blood. While it certainly alters consciousness, it might do so in ways that are not conducive to an overall ceremony. In the modern context, somewhere between the two extremes is best, not causing injury, but enough strength to be felt.

THE WITCH'S MARK

The historic origin of the Witch's Mark comes from the age of the European Witch trials. In their search for "Satanic" Witches, Inquisitors believed the Devil marked his initiate Witches with a specific mark, said to be insensitive to pain. It was caused by the Devil's claw, kiss, licking, or a red or blue mark caused by his magickal branding iron. Known by some as the Diablo Stigmata, the mark was said to be a visible symbol of the pact between the Devil and Witch, along with familiar spirit and magickal power. The mark could take a form of a mole, scar, birthmark, callus, blemish, or third nipple. Accused Witches would be stripped, often shaved, and searched for an unusual mark, in a "hidden" place such as the armpit or a body cavity. They would be "pricked" with a pin or other sharp device, giving rise to the term "pricking a Witch" to see if the mark bled or caused pain. If it didn't, then it was definitively considered a Witch's mark, though Inquisitors would generally find something they considered a Witch's mark upon an accused Witch, regardless of their completely natural and normal origin.

Sometimes in the records of the Inquisition's Witch trials we find interesting lore that could have origins in genuine Craft traditions, but most of what we find is the fanciful imaginings of the repressed Inquisitors. Does the Witch's mark have any magickal truth to it? Controversial anthropologist Margaret Murray thought so, believing the mark was an initiatory tattoo of the old Witchcraft cult. Most scholars have disregarded Murray's ideas, and the fact that so many different types of marks could pass for the Witch's mark, it does not appear to be a consistent tattoo or scarring pattern of an organized religion. Yet Murray's ideas have spiritually inspired much of the modern Witchcraft movement, tapping into spiritual truths if not completely literal truths.

Many Witchcraft traditions today talk about the Witch's mark. Some believe it is wholly a psychic phenomenon. The Witch's mark, or Mark of Cain, is a mark in the aura, often near the third eye, that grants Witch's sight. Other Witches recognize this mark in the aura, but it lies invisible to all others.

Some modern Witches believe those born to the Craft have some visible pronounced mark like that of the Inquisitor's search. It is not the mark of the Devil, but a mark to indicate one of Witch power, or of the old bloodlines and Witch families.

Lastly modern Witches use the concept of the Witch's mark for exactly the purpose Murray described, even if it has no proven historic use during the Burning Times. A few modern Witchcraft traditions use ritual tattooing as a mark of initiation. Blue Star Wicca and the Cabot Tradition of Witchcraft often use ritual tattooing as a sign of initiation. The practice of ritual tattooing might not be a sign of a dark ages European Witch cult, but many older Pagan and tribal traditions have used tattooing as a mark for rites of passage and initiation. They are also marks of office, magickal and religious symbols, permanent cosmetic adornments, creative expression, and sometime even punishments to outcasts and criminals. While the word tattoo comes from the Samoan *tatau*, practices of tattooing through various methods are found all across the world, dating back at least to the Neolithic time. Several Eurasian "mummies" have been found with tattoos. In the Pre-Christian European era, tattooing was common amongst the tribal Celts, Germans, and Scandinavians, and the practice only declined with the Christianization of Europe. While tattooing was known in the Mediterranean, it usually was only applied to slaves.

Fig. 50: Modern Witch's Tattoo Marks

My first tattoo was a very specific ritual marking. One teaching I hold is that one is not a "cosmic" adult until the completion of the first Saturn return, at the age of twenty-nine and a half. The mark was a ritual of personal initiation into the time of cosmic adulthood with a person sigil. I chose a very talented tattoo artist who is also a Gardnerian priestess and Reiki Master, with very intense and spiritual ideas about the tattoo marking both body and soul. While getting my mark, she commented on how I was getting marked on the lower back for initiation, similar to how in the Gardnerian Tradition, the lower back is scourged to give rise to the kundalini in the spine. She found the parallel interesting.

About a week after the tattoo was complete, I got severely ill with pneumonia, the likes of which I had never had before. It wasn't an allergic reaction to the ink as far as the medical profession could tell, but I believe it was an initiatory reaction, similar to, but even more intense than, the spiritual cleanses of Reiki initiation. Although I never specifically seek it, the pain and delirium of illness has always been a gate for me to grow and develop spiritually, and I received much information, healing, and transformation during fevered dreams. I was able to recover enough to travel to England for a business trip. While there, I met with a Witchcraft elder, and in discussing differences of tradition and my tattoo experience, he gave me a hand-crafted scourge with a deer antler handle. The traditions I've trained in don't use such a scourge, but when I got home, I put it in a place of honor on my altar for further contemplation. I immediately got sick again, but did not connect it to the scourge's presence on the altar. The altar is a microcosm for your life and being, and whatever you put on or take off has an effect on you. After another two weeks of illness, I had a dream where the Goddess came to me and said, "Have you learned enough for now? Have you suffered enough?" and gave me an image of taking the scourge off the altar. I did and completely recovered within a few days. This experience showed me the direct link between ritual marking and the power of the scourge.

Obviously ritual marking and all that is associated with it is not an act of everyday magick, but a very significant and permanent change. The gnosis entered into during such marking rituals and the subsequent results are for big acts of personal transformation, or permanent enchantments upon the self. Some Witches mark themselves with magickal signs of protection, good fortune, love and health. Though many today get tattoos for "fun" with no specific purpose, I believe it's a sacred act and should not be entered into lightly.

For a more common use of marking, though lacking the factor of pain, temporary tattoos of henna and other body paints can be used to mark the self with spell sigils, as well as marking to shift and change identity temporarily. You can mark yourself with images associated with the energy you wish to invoke, such as animal signs, runes, and sigils of power. Explore and experiment with ritual marking and see what effects they conjure for you. They you will have a better idea of the forces of body marking, and can enter into ritual tattooing with a slightly better understanding of its power.

BLOOD MAGICK

Blood magick is a controversial subject, one many well-meaning critics of this manuscript suggested I avoid entirely, but I don't think one can ethically talk about this path of gnosis without talking about blood magick. Most modern Witches shy away from blood magick, though it still has a hold of many tribal traditions and older forms of Craft teaching.

Blood is the water of life. It is the part of us that connects with the oceans of the planet. The iron of our blood makes it red, connecting us to the iron of the Earth itself. Traditions across the world see it as sacred, both revered and feared. The wine in our cup, as well the grail of Christianity, is symbolic of the blood. Many of our traditions of magick call upon the Sang Real, Royal Blood, a play on words of San Greal, or Holy Grail, connecting our mysteries of the cauldron or cup to that of the blood. To Witches, this is not the mystery of a messiah's theoretical bloodline, but the mystery held in our blood. Many older occult traditions speak of the Witch blood, faery blood, angel blood, god's blood, or blood from the stars running through our veins. It is in the blood our life force lives. We may take it in the breath, but we store and circulate it in the blood. We inherit it from our ancestors. And the shedding of it can make magick.

Such blood magick is the stuff of nightmares for more mainstream Witches seeking to teach everybody that we are normal, we are not so different, we simply pray in our own way. Then we have to explain things like trance dance, entheogens, sex magick, restriction, and now pain and blood, and we look a lot different from your average Sunday church-going Christian. And we are. We explore the edges. Our path is not for everyone, and even in our traditions, the way of blood magick is not for everyone. In an effort to de-sensationalize Witchcraft, and distance it from anything that could be remotely perceived as Satanic, we have suppressed almost all teachings regarding the blood.

Gerald Gardner both depicted the truth about blood magick and warned us on its uses in the section on Power in the Book of Shadows.

Sorcerers chiefly used the blood sacrifice; and while we hold this to be evil, we cannot deny that this method is very efficient. Power flashes forth from newly shed blood, instead of exuding slowly as by our method. The victim's terror and anguish add keenness, and even quite a small animal can yield enormous power. The great difficulty is in the human mind controlling the power of the lower animal mind. But sorcerers claim they have methods for effecting this and that the difficulty disappears the higher the animal used, and when the victim is human disappears entirely. (The practice is an abomination but it is so.)

This image of the "evil sorcerer" committing blood sacrifice of another, animal or human, is the nightmare image modern Witches seek to avoid. With various Satanic scares throughout the United States at the end of the twentieth century, Witches want to have a wholesome and pure image. Many people already think we are all about sacrifice. I know even when I began my journey, my own mother initially got training in the Craft because she felt it was a sacrificial cult, and tagged along to keep me safe, rather than try to force me out. Luckily we both found out the Craft we joined had nothing to do with animal or human sacrifice.

Modern Witchcraft is just that, modern. Though it explores the edges, it generally works within the agreed upon societal rules of law and culture. While various historic writers may talk about Sacred King practices of sacrificing the leader or a proxy to renew the land, it is not a part of our society today, and is not done by Witches today. Many believe such ancient sacrifices were voluntary, and other involuntary ritual executions were much like capitol punishment today for a religious society that had no real concept of penal institutions. We have other options and an entirely different secular society today. Our ancient traditions should rule the land no more than any other religion, for we do live in what is suppose to be a secular society.

Animal sacrifice, is another matter. Again, most modern Witches find the idea repulsive. In a modern culture, we are quite separate from our food sources. While many eat meat, they don't have a direct relationship with the animals consumed, or participate in their deaths in the way our fairly recent ancestors did, and many still do who live on farms. I only have to go back to my mother's generation to find such a relationship in my family. Though she lived in a city, family members raised chickens, and she participated in both gathering eggs and the killing and plucking of chickens. Some modern Witches choose vegetarian life styles to be in integrity in this area. Others seek more awareness and thankfulness regarding the source of their food and a select few seek direct participation in the cycles of life and death by experiencing a farming lifestyle, even for a short time.

Traditions today that still honor religious animal sacrifice are linked to their tribal roots, and the sources of their food. African diasporic traditions in particular use animal sacrifice as a part of their rituals. Ritual sacrifices are done in the most humane way possible. The animal is cooked and eaten with love, and a portion shared with the spirits upon an altar. Such practitioners, even living in a modern society now are not so disconnected from the source of their food, and see it as sacred, a way to commune with the divine.

While traditions like Voodou and Santeria are often maligned and mistaken for Satanism, they are truly more akin to Witchcraft, though many Witches have lost touch with the basic facts of life, death, and blood in their own lives. And the modern Satanic churches have nothing to do with animal or human sacrifice. Those who claim to be Satanist and perform such practices are simply emulating stereotypes portrayed in movies, television, and other media. They usually have no basis in spiritual or magickal practice.

Lastly, there is the often forgotten potential of using your own blood in magick. Sadly, Gardner's statement seems to disregard the possibilities of self-sacrifice of a small amount of blood, rather than sacrifice of another. Such blood rituals have quite a history, including blood oaths and the making of blood "brothers." This is the magick most modern practitioners find acceptable, within reason.

Modern magician Aleister Crowley was an advocate of certain forms of blood magick. While he surely used "blood" in some writings as a code for higher occult principles, in The Mass of the Phoenix, he advocates a daily rite, done by every magician at sunset, requiring the drawing of blood from the chest, to anoint a sacramental cake. Various interpretations occur around this ritual, though most assume he does mean to draw literal blood, but not necessarily to scar or injure yourself.

There are several drawbacks to blood magick. The first and foremost are issues of self-harm. Harming the self, often through cutting, to relieve emotional and mental stress, has become a more prevalent disorder in our society, particularly amongst teens. Sadly many might think this lesson is justification for self harm as something "spiritual" or "magickal." It is not. This magick is not a coping mechanism to be done often, but an act of magick rarely done, and only in cases where it is necessary.

The main magickal drawback to this technique is it can't be done often. You can only lose so much blood to be physically healthy, and even less to be magickally healthy. If blood is akin to life force, bleeding it away removes life force that isn't easily replenished with any other technique. Many other methods allow you to replenish energy by sleep, breath-work, and eating, and while they aid the regeneration of blood, it physically has to replenish from the marrow of your bones. Its more difficult than replenishing pure psychic energy, which can come and go more easily.

Blood magick is an act of diminishing returns in terms of power. The initial use can release a great deal of power, but subsequent uses of the technique without a long lag time, release less. The same amount of power requires more blood, creating a spiral of destruction that can be quite harmful. Because of this, I only really advocate blood magick under specific circumstances:

Oaths: Very important and very specific oaths to the Self, and/or to the gods, can be sealed with a blood offering. Such oaths are really setting spells into motion. You promise to the powers what will be through both your effort and their support.

Protection Magick: Only done when all other method of protection have failed, and only once in any given situation. The shedding of a drop of blood in protection magick, either added to a Witch's Bottle for protection, or to a candle spell of protection can be immensely powerful.

The iron in the blood along with the life force gives the magick added power in protecting you. Blood should not be shed in protecting others with this type of magick.

Hallowing: Some traditions advocate anointing rituals tools with a drop of blood when first consecrating them.

Bonding with the Land: You can connect your consciousness to the land itself where you life or work magick by shedding a few drops of blood on the land as an offering to the Spirits of the place. This "feeding" of life force can link you in deep and profound ways, and the land will often give you much more in return in terms of wisdom, power, and knowledge. Blood offerings are not the only way to link with the land, but one of the most profound and immediate. The drawback is that it is difficult to break the link if you then want to move or stop doing magick at that location.

Offerings: In very rare cases and relationships with patron deities, the deity may ask for a blood offering from you. It won't be done all the time, and only on special rites and occasions, but it is not unheard of to be asked. Once should use discernment in the situation, asking the entity what this offering means and what repercussions it will have for both of you. If you feel the situation is not for your highest good, politely decline and offer something else. Rusted water, water that has had iron or iron powder rusting in it, is often a substitute for blood.

Initiation: Some traditions require blood shedding in initiation, either as an offering to the gods of the tradition, or a rite similar to adoption via the "blood brother/sister" technique of mixing blood. In this day where we have knowledge of blood-born illness transferred via such methods, an alternative is to have both initiate and initiator shed blood onto the same thing, usually a ritual object, stone, or part of the sacred land. Using the magickal principle of contagion, once two things have touched, they have always touched, once your blood has touched, you are bonded, even if that drop is no longer in your body. There is connection and an energy transferred.

Blood loss can certainly induce gnosis, but a gnosis that is difficult to recover from and potentially deadly. To ritually lose enough blood to cause lightheadedness or dizziness is quite harmful, opening you up to serious infection and damage. The amount of blood required for the magick listed above is just a few drops, easily available with a pin prick or small shallow cut. All instruments should be sterilized and all wounds thoroughly washed and dressed, ideally with an herbal healing salve. Comfrey salves and oils are ideal for knitting wounds, even minor ones. If in doubt, don't do it.

One aspect of blood magick that is open to priestesses of the Craft is the use of menstrual blood in ritual. Such actions contain the power of blood without the same dangers associated with wounding oneself.

THE ORDEAL PATH

Ordeals are trials. They are tests. They are the hammers of life that crash down upon us and cause us to react, respond, or reevaluate how we operate both physically and spiritually. They are a source of pain, but are different from the pain we have been describing thus far in the chapter. They are the pains of life. Not all of the pain of this path is induced through controlled ritual. Much of it comes via life's lessons, as the pain can be psychic, mental, and emotional as well as physical. How we work with that pain and the new perceptions it creates is a measure of who we are and who we will be.

Originally it was a tribal form of justice. Someone accused of wrongdoing was subjected to an ordeal, a life-threatening situation or task, believing divine justice would be meted out. If the accused survived, then innocence was declared. If death was the result, guilt. The divine was assumed to play a part in the testing, and to make a pronouncement on the worth of the individual. It's possible many who survived were guilty, but from this viewpoint, judged repentant and encouraged to live new lives, being reborn through the trial and determined not to make the same mistake. Others who died may have been innocent, but when presented with a test of skill, wits, courage, or power, they could not meet the challenge, and were deemed unworthy to continue by the results of their actions.

For modern Witches, ordeals are the initiatory experiences. For some of us, they are ritual initiations, such as the standard British Wicca three degrees, with sword-pointed threats and ritual scourging. For others, they are initiations by the gods and spirits. Lastly, they can be the life initiations, the trials and challenges of health, family, career, and society. Any initiation has much in common with divine judgment. Not all who petition for initiation are deemed suitable and accepted. Even when a teacher has no criteria to reject a student, the energies of a tradition may not "take" and sometimes the "cleansing" process of initiation drives people mad or makes them sick, creating a further test beyond the boundaries of the ritual circle of initiation. The magick is often in how the pain, madness, or illness is handled, rather than a judgment on its occurrence.

Trials of life create new perceptions. Our oldest mythologies on initiation have both magickal and mundane meaning for us today. One of my favorites ordeal myths is that of Odin, the Norse All-Father who hangs from the World Tree Yggdrasil for nine days and nine nights to procure the magickal wisdom of the runes. Many read this myth and see a similar picture to the Tarot card of the Hanged Man. One of the meanings of this card on a personal level is feeling stuck, like life has a hold on you and you can't move forward or back. The spiritual lesson of the card is knowing to surrender to the new situation, to immerse yourself in it, to allow yourself to be hung, and no longer struggle, till you see the world from a new perspective. Imagine being hung upside down. You would see everything completely differently. When you are energetically hung, you perceive things differently as well. The ordeal represented by pulling the Hanged Man card is an opportunity to enter a new state of awareness, to see things differently, and to find new connections and opportunities not readily apparent. The trials come to test us, but also to point us in new directions and force us to explore new options.

Fig. 51: Hanged Man Card

Shock and fright are a part of the ordeal process, be it in life or through a ritual process. Rituals are designed to jar the consciousness, and nothing alters your consciousness quite like fear – fear of pain, fear of death, or simply fear of the unknown. Many of the isolation rituals, such as vision quests, can bring up painful fears, making the ritual an ordeal. I've heard of initiation rituals in the Egyptian Mysteries that required the initiate to jump into a pitch black abyss and trust there is a rope to grab, and lower themselves down until they reach an unseen floor. One Pagan initiation ritual mimics death by putting you in a box and shoveling earth over you for a short time. Even the British Traditional ritual of initiation, where one is blindfolded, bound, and put to the point of a sword, fear arises. We question, "What have I gotten myself into?" "Can I trust?" "Will it hurt?" Life often brings us situations like this, where we question. Far better to first face these questions and test our mettle in ritual, to know we are able to handle the initiations of life.

Psychic pain reveals places of disturbance in the psyche. Experiences that disturb one individual and not another can reveal places of repression and trauma that lock away psychic power. Exploration of those pains in ritual, or facing them in life, open the gates and melt that frozen power, making it available to us and helping us integrate it into the overall whole. The work many practitioners label "Shadow Work," facing their repressed fears, angers, jealousies, resentments, and loathing, is painful, but ultimately illuminating, healing, and magickal. Such shadow work, as outlined in *The Temple of Shamanic Witchcraft,* is a ritual induced form of ordeal. Informal shadow workings, induced by life, can be just as potent when applied with the right intention.

Intense periods of difficulty in life, of pain and trauma, are calls to keep your spiritual discipline while perceiving new opportunities and options in handling those difficulties. We think of spirituality as a luxury and, when life gets tough, the first thing that goes out the window is our spiritual practice and viewpoint. We think we have to get "real" but when we are truly practitioners, there is nothing more real and grounded. It is from our spiritual awareness, we handle our problems and make life decisions, even in the face of hardship, illness, family crisis, employment difficulties, financial catastrophes, and societal emergencies. Even when we can't take action, the consciousness the situation generates is an opportunity for spiritual growth, awareness, and the direct revelation of spirit. Truly that is what gnosis is, our direct revelation, direct knowledge from the divine to be applied in our life.

INJURY

While the controlled use of these techniques are found in many traditions, it is important to note this path to the mysteries is not one of total masochism. It does not call for you to senselessly injury yourself, or use it as your sole method of gnosis, to the detriment of your health and well being, physically or psychologically. Senseless and permanent injury are the shadows of the path of pain.

Many of these techniques are used in initiatory settings, for they literally and figuratively mark major life changes. Acts of piercing, tattooing, and branding are not to be undertaken lightly. Many who see such traditions as spiritual as well as artistic believe they mark your soul as much as your body, altering your energetic vibration. You do not undergo a permanent mark to do a simple ritual.

While traditions of ages past might have been acceptable or necessary in an ancient society, we exist in a modern society and must work in that society, with its rules, custom, and standards. At one time the priests of Cybele were said to castrate themselves in honor of the Goddess, in emulation of the god Attis. The castration would be done voluntarily and in an ecstatic rite, yet today most see it as a gruesome ritual. The Goddess does not require that of any of us today. We need not maim ourselves to truly worship and work our magick. This same ancient society had any number of customs, offerings, and rites we would not find acceptable today, as our own culture has changed and evolved over time. Do not fool yourself into thinking physical sacrifice involving injury is necessary. These castrated followers and priests, known as the Galli, proved more mythic role model for those experiencing a transgendered path in our society, than a model for self mutilation outside of the context of medical treatment.

One undergoes the path of pain only when necessary. One of the precepts of the Witch is caring for the health and well being of the material world, and of our own bodies. If you continue to injure yourself, you will mostly likely not be strong enough to handle the psychic and physical work of a priest or priestess of the Mysteries. Your body will be too frail and you will ultimately fail at your quest, regardless of your threshold for pain. Like any path, too much is a detriment, and never more so than too much of these pain techniques. They are unforgiving in their results and there is little margin for error.

AIDS TO THE PATH OF PAIN

The following points should definitely be kept in mind when walking the path of pain:

Addiction: The stimulation of pain can be biologically and psychologically addictive. Practitioners of this path should be ever vigilant by asking themselves if their actions are necessary for the given situation. If the techniques spill into what might be labeled "recreational" use, or ritualistic settings are used as an excuse for potential recreational use, look into the possibilities of addiction. Some method of pain that do no lasting harm, such as scourging, can be a part of sexual recreation, though the more they are used recreationally, the less magickal effect they will have.

Experienced Help: Many of the rituals of pain or any ordeal should be overseen by an experienced practitioner whenever possible. Having someone who knows your limits, physically and psychologically, and in a position to offer or procure help is immensely important. Finding experienced help can be difficult, and may require looking beyond the Neopagan community. Many in the BDSM community are opening to profound spiritual experiences as the Pagan community is opening to the spirituality of BDSM.

Self-Harm Issues: If you have any concerns that the path of pain has lead you into the psychological arena of self-harm—physically harming yourself, usually but not always through cutting, to handle your thoughts, emotions and life—then seek professional help. Just as we can get physically addicted to strong sensations, we can use them in inappropriate ways to handle psychological issues, and end up doing more harm, quite literally, than good. If you have any self-harm issues in your past, than I highly discourage you from this path of gnosis.

Harm from Others: While the potential for self-harm can be there, another aspect, less talked about, is the potential for a teacher, mentor, or covenmate to harm or injure you, intentionally or unintentionally. Some have gotten overzealous with the scourge, drawing blood, which is not the point of Wiccan scourging technique. For those who work on the path of pain and are unsure where the boundaries are in this technique, having a "safety word" such as those used in BDSM, can be helpful. A safety word is an unusual word that is not likely to come up in any role play conversations in a BDSM scenario. When it is spoken, usually by the submissive, it indicates the desire to stop, have a break or reevaluate the boundary being crossed. So if at anytime you feel someone has crossed a line and you feel unsafe, you have final control, and your own will shall be recognized by the group or teacher. While you can push past limits, only you can truly determine where the line is for you.

Elastic Band Method: A simple method of using the path of pain in everyday life with no chance of injury to the self involves an elastic band. If you have a thought pattern or habit you wish to transform, but have thus far been unsuccessful, you can use the path of pain to reprogram your consciousness. Wear a rubber band on your wrist and, every time you start the unwanted process – thinking harmful thoughts about yourself, complaining, using curse words, over eating, rationalization, etc. – snap the band. Don't snap it so hard to raise a blister, but do it to make a reaction in your body and mind. That breaks the pattern and gives you the opportunity to alter your consciousness and choose a different action, more in alignment with your stated goals.

Not for Everyone: This path is not for every Witch, and like the others that walk the edge, you must determine what works best for you. Since I haven't studied in a tradition that emphasizes the scourge, friends of mine from British Traditional Wicca like to tease me about my flogging abilities. It's not a path that opens many doors for me, giving or receiving, when compared to working with plant allies, dance, breath and sexual energy. I've explored it, to not be afraid of it, and to find what gifts it has to offer, but it's not a priority in my own ritual workings. Likewise it may or may not be the path for you.

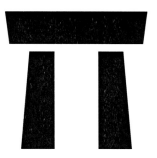

Chapter Ten:
The Power of the Land

One of the most forgotten paths of gnosis in a tradition that considers itself "Earth-based spirituality," is the path of the land. Our relationship with the land is a path to power, healing and enlightenment. Sadly many Pagans today do not get outside often enough to discover this truth. I understand. I, too, trained in a more temple oriented tradition, with many indoor rites. And while I still practice a lot of magick indoors, I've had other teachers and friends stress the importance of meditating outside, doing ritual amid nature, and simply being under the open sky or the canopy of the forest. Through this exploration of my relationship with the land where I live, and the lands I visit, my magick has grown. I feel so strongly about this relationship opening the gates of magick, I felt the need to include it amongst the paths of power, even though its is not one of the traditional eight, and simply assumed as an underlying part of our magick. In these modern times, with our modern lifestyles, it is not always apparent. Including it as a path emphasizes the importance of the land, and its spirit, in all our workings. No matter your path to gnosis, where you practice it effects your outcome.

Sacred Sites

When people first think of the power of the land and the concept of sacred sites, they assume one must visit historical sites traditionally held sacred by ancient peoples. Sacred sites conjure the image of Stonehenge, the pyramids at Giza, the buttes of Sedona, or the temples of Greece and Rome. Yet there are sacred sites throughout the landscape, sometimes in our own backyard, literally or figuratively. You don't need to go far to find such spots if you have the eyes to see them and the ears to hear them. They open up to sincere seekers and share their wisdom when approached with respect.

Ancient people chose particular locations as sacred sites due perhaps to their inherent properties, and some cultures enhanced those properties with man-made structures, from simple mounds to more elaborate temples. Sacred sites have one thing in common: they aid in the induction of trance. This trance state is perceived as a sense of awe, wonder, or divinity in the place, and that perception opens us to other levels of consciousness.

One factor that helps induce such altered perception is liminality. A site is liminal if its on the border, a place between. Liminal places and liminal times do wonders in inducing trance. Sacred sites are often at the thresholds, transitional places between two different states, typically two different terrains representative of different spiritual worlds. One of the reasons the Witch is associated with the hedge is it is the boundary between the clearing and the forest, between civilization and untamed nature. It is a transitional place, filled with both fruits and poisons. There is both risk and blessing to be found in such a place. The image of the hedge later became synonymous for the veil. A shamanically inclined worker would jump the hedge or pass through the veil, effectively doing the same thing with different symbolism and techniques. Sites that mimic this spiritual truth, places with actual hedges or veiled canopies, aid in the transition.

Liminal sites are gateways between different levels of consciousness, and different worlds. Though each is unique, here are some common thoughts about sacred spaces to help you in your own survey of the land around you.

Landscape: The major features of the physical landscape mimic the major features of the spiritual landscape, and such points can be used as entryways. Anything that catches your attention and brings your focus to the power of nature can be a sacred spot. Places of transition in nature, or the center of such regions, can be sacred spots. Mountains reach up to the heavens, connecting earth and sky. Islands, be they in an ocean or the center of a lake, connect land and water. Rivers mark the flow of not only water, but energy, and major points along the river can be sacred space. The forest in general is a magickal place, as the transition point is entering the forest, but places of power can be found in the forest, such as a hill, valley, or clearing. The center of a great plain or desert can be a sacred site as well. Each of these locations can also carry the added mystery of isolation, as they are often far from other people, and such isolation in nature can induce trance consciousness.

Earth, Sky, and Sea: While transitional spaces between two areas are sacred, the joining of the holy trinity of landscape features—earth, sea and sky—marks a major place of sacredness and power. The three features are also indicative of the three worlds, found prominently in both Greco-Roman and Celtic world-views. The sky is the stellar world, while the earth is obviously the terrestrial world. The sea is representative of the deep world, the underworld or land of the dead, as many perceive the underworld as a land in the far western ocean, not a realm beneath. Seashore cliffs and coves make excellent places for magickal workings, as to the deltas of rivers emptying into the sea.

Caves: Caves, as well as cracks and crevices into the earth, are considered portals to the world below. They have been used as shelters, temples, and initiatory chambers since the dawn of humanity. Their structure mimics both the womb of the Goddess, and the tomb in resurrection mysteries. Some note the womb and tomb are actually the same place metaphysically, for to be born in one world is to die in the other. In terms of structure, the cave walls and ceilings become a "screen" on which we can project our internal images, much like scrying into a crystal. Illuminated by a fire, the play of light and shadows upon a cave wall can be mesmerizing. The use of cave paintings can direct the inner world narrative, making certain caves decorated in specific symbols chambers for particular kinds of rituals. Some magickal practitioners speculate cave drawings were codes for both the ancient people, and those modern people who know how to use these sites to awaken ancestral memories and land based power. The oracle at Delphi was said to be influenced by subterranean gases released into her chamber from a crevice, to induce trance. While most caves don't have such a feature, subterranean chambers have the tendency to both alter perception and the energy body, inducing new patterns of consciousness and ways of thinking. One only has to spend a short amount of time in a cave, large or small, to feels its influence upon the psyche.

Wells: Like cracks and crevices, sacred wells are places where the terrestrial realm and chthonic realms meet. Rather than descend to the depths, wells are the uprising of blessings and power from the underworld. Traditionally they are sources of healing, blessing, longevity, and magickal insight. Offerings are made at wells, often in the form of tying a prayer cloth to a nearby tree, or leaving out bread. Some throw coins or other votive offerings into the well, but today, care must be made not to contaminate wells with material unfriendly to the environment or that may toxify the well water. Water can be drawn from the well and saved for future use, bringing the power of that sacred site to other regions. I've had amazing results using the well waters of Bridget's Well in Ireland and the Red Chalice Well of Glastonbury, despite using them on another continent in my healing practice in the United States.

Gateways: Gateways simply refer to natural formations that mimic the form of a gate, a doorway. It can be two prominent trees together like the vertical parts of a doorframe, particularly when those trees are oak and/or ash. Sometimes trees and roots grow in such a matter to create an opening, like a loop one can crawl through. In folk magick and medicine, rituals to leave the sickness behind in the gateway can be done, curing individuals of both minor and major maladies. If the area hasn't been used for such curing, it can be used for a gateway into the otherworld. They can also be places where stones form a natural gateway into a wild area, or an opening in the rock formation one can walk or crawl through. Such gates form natural temples, recognized by those who have the eyes to see them, and use them for what they are.

Geomantic Vortexes: Sacred sites, particularly those renowned today for being convergence points of geomantic energies. Called ley lines in the western traditions, these lines of earth energy connect and converge, creating vortexes of energy that link the heavens and earth. Many of the major sites of historic interests are also sites where such lines connect. Though most well known in the British Isles, according to the theory of these power lines, they run throughout the planet, including in areas near you. One of the most powerful lines I've ever felt ran through a public park in Ohio, not far from some Native American mounds.

Constructed Sites: While many constructed temples are in locations chosen for the qualities discussed previously, other times a site is chosen by people, ancient or modern, and the site is imbued with a quality or power. Many times this is intention, such as in the building of a church in the modern world, where the practice of placing such churches on Native or Pagan holy sites has not continued, yet the church builds a solemn power regardless. Other times it is unintentional, but based on the conditions of life in a particular area or building. Playgrounds can take on a particular quality, indicative of the joyful children playing, while mental insinuations can take on a sinister quality based on the lives and experiences of those living within its walls.

Exercise: Finding Your Own Sacred Sites

Go scouting in the area around your home or place of work for a sacred site. Often such places are wild and places because the best places are away from prying eyes, but for many of us who live in an urban environment, your place might be a public park. Get outside and see where you can find liminal places, gateways, and geomantic vortexes.

GEOMANTIC ENERGY

One of the major trance-inducing components to many sacred sites is the geomantic energy present there. Different sites have different energy, and that effects human consciousness differently. The planet Earth is a living entity, and is said to have many of the same structures as found in humans. The rivers are her blood. The stones and mountains are her bones. The forests are her lungs. And in the teachings of both modern holistic medicine and ancient medical models such as traditional Chinese medicine and Indian Ayurveda, humans are said to have invisible pathways of energy, meridians in Chinese systems or nadis in Ayurveda. The life force is carried along these lines like the blood is carried along the blood vessels. The Earth is also said to be covered in invisible lines of force, guiding her own life energy. These lines are known as ley lines.

Ley lines were originally considered ancient straight walking paths marked by stones and other natural formations, as outlined by Alfred Watkins in his breakthrough work, *The Old Straight Track*. Dion Fortune was the first to put forward, through her novel, *The Goat Foot God*, the concept of such lines actually being paths of magickal power. While the use of ley lines as such magick paths is new, they do have cognates to older magick folklore which mentions paths spirits traverse more easily, being the roads of ghosts and ancestors, faeries, Witches, and the Wild Hunt. In Eastern Feng Shui traditions, lines of power are associated with dragons, and perhaps in the West they have also been associated with the dragons or serpents of the Earth. Many sacred sites from the Pagan era were claimed by the Christian Church, and dedicated to St. Michael, the slayer of demons, devils and dragons. Perhaps Dion Fortune was putting forth secret knowledge from her esoteric training, or simply rediscovering something the folk Witches always knew. The image of St. Michael has been claimed by those of the New Age as one of the major lines of masculine energy, similar to the pingla channel of the chakra system. This Michael line runs through several sacred sites in England, both Pagan and Christian, including Glastonbury Tor.

These lines crisscross the world like a lattice or web, linking sacred sites known and unknown, creating a grid. Like our own meridians, there are places of particular interest on the paths, places were power wells up, or where several lines cross, creating a vortex of power connecting the Earth with the sky and stars above. Though the energy is often described as straight lines, at these power points, it can spiral in or out from the center. Ritual done at such places can be incredibly powerful, for any intention will be carried across the energy grid system to the entire planet. Powerful geomantic zones allow us to tap into the consciousness of the planet itself, and affect everyone and everything. Likewise, the flow works in reverse, as such places encourage the consciousness of the planet to reach out and commune with us, increasing our sense of spiritual connection to the Earth and all her children.

Exercise: Dowsing

Dowsing rods come in many from, from the hazel "Y" branch of water Witches divining for water to dual copper wire "L" shapes. They can be purchased or made quite easily. For the purposes of finding ley lines, I prefer copper or wire dowsing rods. They can even be made from metal coat hangers, with access to wire cutters. Fashion two L shapes, with a short handle and a longer end. Place something cylindrical around the short handle to allow the wire itself to rotate and move as it senses energy. You can use the cardboard tube found on many coat hangers, or a hollow pen casing or other plastic tube. Cleanse and consecrate them as you would any other tool (See **Chapter Fourteen**) and, with the intention of finding ley lines, walk around outside. Where the rods cross is a line. By walking a grid in the area you are mapping, you can find the lines and where they flow. Where two or more lines intersect is a powerful spot for ritual and meditation.

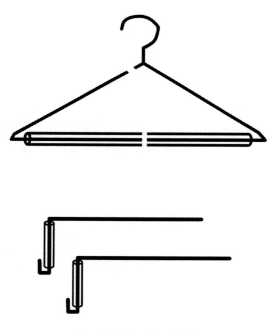

Fig. 52: Dowsing Rods

Geomantic energy is associated with underground water flows, and some practitioners believe that while some water flow is benign, others form geopathic stress zones, energy fields that induce illness in those who spend prolonged time in them. With magickal intention, these fields can also be doused for and, when necessary, neutralized. Toxic lines can be broken by burying a length of copper tubing perpendicular to the line itself, outside of the dwelling. This breaks up the flow of energy and dissipates it. Larger fields can be dissolved by magickally charging a crystal or other talisman for the reduction and removal of toxic energy, and burying it in the energy field. More information on resolving geopathic stress issues can be found in my book *Ascension Magick.*

GENUS LOCI

Originally a term from Roman lore, the genus loci is a protective spirit of a place. More broadly, in modern occultism it refers to the spirit of a place, protective or not. It was adopted into architecture and design as a metaphor for the sense of a location, not an actual spirit, but modern Witches see it quite literally as a non-human intelligence intimately tied with the land and a particular place.

While nature spirits are the animating force of a particular plant, tree, stone or stream, the genus loci is a collective spirit for a location. A home, forest, mountain, business, building, park, town, even an entire city can have a genus loci. Depending on the scope defined by a particular occultist, larger genus loci can cover mountain ranges, countries, and entire continents. Another term associated with it is the anima loci, the animating force of a location. For the purposes of this work, a genus loci or anima loci is the spirit of an area where we seek to do magickal work. Learning to commune with the spirit of place can be helpful in safely and effectively unlocking the power of the land to facilitate your magickal work.

A variety of nature-based spirits are associated with the genus loci. Elementals are equated with nature spirits, but technically their nature is solely of one of the four classical elements – earth, air, fire, or water. They are the intelligences of these four powers, and nature spirits and genus loci are more complex than the average elemental spirit.

Faeries are popularly equated with spirits of place. While many people equate faeries and nature spirits, to traditional Witches, most fey folk are an elder race intimately tied to both nature and the ancestors, yet are different from both, fulfilling the role of both guardians of the land and tutors to particular humans. Household spirits such as brownies or house elves are akin to the original meaning of the genus loci.

The term deva, from the Hindu traditions, has been used for both faery and nature spirits. Originally meaning "bright and shining god" referring to the "little" god of nature in comparison with the cosmic Hindu deities, it was adopted into Theosophical thought, and disseminated into New Age traditions. From those traditions, the deva is usually defined as the overarching spirit of a species of plant, animal, or mineral, or the overarching spirit of a location, guiding and directing individual nature spirits who actually construct and dwell within the physical body of nature. The large devas are known as overlighting devas. In that sense, a deva can be synonymous with the genus loci of a place. You can call upon the overlighting deva of a forest, park, or city for example

In modern northern traditions of Paganism, drawing from Teutonic mythos, the term "land wight" has grown more popular. In fact, in many ways these traditions have some of the best understanding of land spirits, with more complete terminology than other Neopagan traditions. The term "wight" usually meant "being" and referred to supernatural beings. Adopted into the poetic mythos of J.R.R. Tolkien in the tale of the barrow wights, it later got adopted as a term for undead creatures akin to zombies or vampires and popularized in role playing games and fantasy fiction. The original meaning is more like the Icelandic *landvaettir*, the protective spirits of the land and country. It generally translates to "land wight" and is used by northern tradition Pagans, modern Heathens, and traditional Witches. They share similarities, but are distinctively different from the elves and dwarves, giants and trolls. In east Anglian traditions, the term *hyter-sprite* could denote a similar spirit, of a more faery-like and playful protective nature, often in the form of the sand martin bird. The term *alfreka* refers to desecrated lands by human action, where the spirit of the land has been injured, driven away, or destroyed. Hostile land spirits are known as sometimes known as *meinvaettir*.

While they are non-human spirits, in a different order of evolution and intelligence than humanity, land spirits are all individual, and each one, regardless of the term used, behaves differently, and develops different relationships with particular individuals. You might make a connection with a land spirit that does not resonate with me, and vice versa, much like friendships in the human world.

Exercise: Communing with the Genus Loci

Choose a site where you want to commune with its genus loci. Come to the site with an offering. Different traditions have different offerings, and different locations resonate with different offerings. In the Celtic Isles, offerings of bread, cheese, butter, cream, honey, and beer are appropriate. In native New World traditions, cornmeal and tobacco are more traditional. Modern offerings with traditional history include hand-baked cakes, wine, beer, alcohol, honey, chocolate, candy, and other sweets. Go to the threshold of the site, the opening before you enter into the spirit's body. Make a heartfelt prayer and offering there. Ask to be friends and build a relationship. Meditate there and use your intuition. Was the offering accepted? You should feel a shift of energy, and feel welcomed by the land. Ask for permission to enter. Do you receive it? Then do so. Explore the site, and while in psychic communion with the land spirit, ask permission to do ritual. If you do not have clear psychic communication from the land, you can use a pendulum to determine yes/no answers, asking the land to communicate with you through the pendulum. (For those unfamiliar with pendulum working, detailed instructions are found in *The Inner Temple of Witchcraft*.) The land will open you to power spots and gateways when you are ready to experience them.

If it feels right after developing a relationship with the land, ask the genus loci for a token of your connection, a stone, stick or other natural item from the land. It is appropriate to make another offering at this time, to exchange energy, or to leave a safe, non-toxic token of your own, such as a coin, to link you to the land. Such exchanges should only be done when you are ready to form a bond with the land. Deeper partnerships to specific locations and land spirits can be forged through simple and safe blood offerings, but I do not recommend that unless you are certain you plan on living nearby and working magickally in the area for a long time.

FIXEDNESS

The drawback to finding a place of power that facilitates your ability to enter trance and commune with the powers of the otherworld is the lack of ability you seem to have in other places. When you are continually going to a location of ideal conditions, your natural talents may atrophy when in less than ideal circumstances. Like an athlete conditioned to play on a particular home field, when you lose the "home field advantage," you are stretched beyond your comfort zone. Finding a natural place of power is not a substitute for continual practice and experimentation. While it is important to build a relationship with the place where you live and work, a good Witch knows magick exists everywhere, and should be able to do magick outside of her natural environment and home territory. Business trips, vacations, and other travel should not force one into a relinquishing magickal practice. Those who rely too much on one place run the danger of becoming fixed in that spot, unable to do magick elsewhere. Bring magick and trance into other areas of your life, and learn to do ritual and meditation in a variety of places.

AIDS TO THE PATH OF SACRED SPACE

The following points should be remembered when working with sacred sites:

Places are Alive: From the Witch's perspective, places are living entities, and should be treated as such. Though they are non-human intelligences, you should treat them with the same respect you would treat another person. Make sure you make appropriate requests, offerings, and build a true reciprocal relationship with the land.

Times Change: Sacred sites are intimately linked to both the Earth and the stars. They can change at different times of day, season, and astrological cycles. So the energy you find at one moment might not remain consistent. Look to the following lesson to understand cycles in conjunction with sacred places.

Urban Sites: Just because an area is developed does not mean it doesn't have energy and power. Cities are often built upon vortexes, with the genus loci calling to it those appropriate for its energy. You'll find many power spots in an urban environment, though often their energy has an overlay of the human community built up around and upon it. You must work to reach the deep power of the land. My first book, *City Magick*, is a guide to exploring the power of the urban settings.

Malign Power: Not all places of power indicate benign power. There are many places of palpable power that might initially draw our attention but, upon further inspection, the power is not well disposed to benign magickal purposes, or welcoming to humanity. Many Native traditions recognize regions of nature not meant for human contact. They are not necessarily evil in a human context, but they are not predisposed to work with us constructively, as many other sites are. A bear is not evil, but one doesn't camp out in its cave to do ritual and expect all will go well. Such sites should be treated much like a slumbering bear, and avoided.

CHAPTER ELEVEN:
THE TIME BEYOND

While the location of magick influences the working and can be a gate to trance, the time when the magick done is also an opportunity to add to the trance state. Much as been written on magickal timing for spell craft, including the tides of the Moon, planetary days and hours, and astrological aspects, little has been written about the influences of such times beyond spell craft and upon the trance state.

Just as particular places induce trance by their very nature, particular times can induce trance. But most of us simply zone out through these opportunities. If we looked to them as potential times for magickal working, we could induce an alerted state much easier. By simply going with the flow of universal tides, gateways open and the brave can step through to the other side.

LIMINAL TIMES

While most who train in Witchcraft are familiar with the traditional timing of the Moon, Sun, and stars, just as traditional, for those who look to folklore, is the use of liminal times. Anything liminal stands between, being neither "this" or "that" but something other. When a time is liminal, it opens a doorway into new perceptions. Many of our more complicated astrological alignments are based upon liminality, such as the equinoxes and solstices, the points between the changing of the seasons.

Easier liminal points to observe occur daily, and their power has been found in faery folk lore, magick, and shamanic traditions across the world. The four liminal times of every day are sunrise, noon, sunset, and midnight.

Sunrise is the time between the darkness and the light, before the new day starts. Many eastern traditions advocate beginning meditation or yogic practice just before sunrise, to "catch" this energy to infuse the day. Many solar oriented traditions, including some ceremonial influenced Witchcraft traditions, begin ritual in the east, the place of the rising Sun.

Noon is when the Sun is highest, between morning and afternoon. It is another point of power for solar oriented traditions. The direction associated with the South, (when in the Northern Hemisphere.)

Sunset is a magickal time of twilight, most often associated with the faery faith traditions. It relates to the underworld or otherworld shamanic practices of Europe, where the mystery lands are seen in the west, where the sun sets. Avalon, Tir Na Nog, the Blessed Isles are all said to be located in the West. It's a time of power, but also of danger, for things are not always as they appear to the eye.

Midnight is "the witching hour." Associated with the time between the death of one day and the birth of another, and the highest point of the full Moon, it is the most feminine and dark of the four liminal times. It is a point of power, of Witchcraft and of the underworld and ancestors. Its direction is North, aligning with both the magnetic North pole and the North Star, each guiding points for magick.

Both shamanic and ceremonial traditions perform rituals to observe and mark these four liminal points of the day. In a ritual of ceremonial magick known as the Four Adorations, the Sun is observed as the passing of Ra. Written by Aleister Crowley, and can be found in Aleister Crowley's *Liber Resh vel Helios*, it has become a staple amongst many different Khemetic (Egyptian) influenced traditions. I first learned it as a part of ceremonial training through *Modern Magick* by Donald Michael Kraig.

Exercise: Four Adorations

At Sunrise face East. – AIR. Stand with your arms upright, as if you were supporting a heavy pole above your head. Sign of the Theoricus Grade. Say, "Hail to Thee who art Ra in Thy rising, even unto Thee who art Ra in Thy strength. Who travellest over the heavens in Thy bark at the uprising of the Sun. Tahuti standeth in his splendor at the prow, and Ra-Hoor abideth at the helm. Hail unto Thee from the abodes of the night." Make the Sign of Silence.

At Noon face South. – FIRE. Make the Sign of the Philosophus Grade or Triangle of Manifestation above your head. "Hail unto Thee who art Hathoor in Thy triumphing, even unto Thee who art Hathoor in Thy beauty, who travelest over the heavens in Thy bark at the mid-

Course of the Sun. Tahuti standeth in His splendor at the prow and Ra-hoor abideth at the helm. Hail unto Thee from the abodes of the morning." Make the Sign of Silence.

At Sunset face West – WATER. Make the triangle over your belly, point down, the Sign of the Practicus Grade. "Hail to Thee who are Tum in Thy setting, even unto Thee who art Tum in Thy Joy. Who travellest over the heavens in Thy bark at the down going of the Sun. Tahuti standeth in His splendor at the prow and Ra-Hoor abideth at the helm. Hail unto Thee from the abodes of the day." Make the Sign of Silence.

At midnight face North – EARTH. Step forward with left foot. Raise right hand up over your head, palm facing forward like a greeting, known as the Sign of the Zelator Grade. "Hail unto Thee who are Khephera in Thy hiding, Even unto Three who art Khephera in Thy silence. Who travellest over the heavens in Thy bark at the midnight hour of the Sun. Tahuti standeth in his splendor at the prow and Ra-Hoor abideth at the helm. Hail unto Thee from the abodes of the evening. Make the Sign of Silence.

Simpler shamanic traditions go to the four directions at the appropriate times, and pray to the spirits of the direction. What they lack in precise poetry as found in the Four Adorations is more than made up for in heartfelt prayer and personal poetry. Honoring the four liminal times alters consciousness and keeps you in flow with the tides of the day. Doing magick at these times, from simple to complex rituals and meditations, can be more profound than doing them in the more "solid" times of day.

CELESTIAL TIMING

The timing of the planets and stars is the tradition most familiar to modern Witches and magicians. Corresponding our spellcraft to the tide of the planets and stars has become popular in modern Witchcraft, yet how their movement affects consciousness is less explored. One only needs to keep a detailed journal to track the alignments between planets, and celestial phenomenon such as Moon Void of Course or Mercury Retrograde, to see how astrological alignments not only affect our craft, but our consciousness. They can open windows into new worlds of both magickal consciousness and personal development. Other times they open whole doorways and, when the brave step through, they are utterly transformed.

Rather than looking for points of "good luck" in the alignments, and waiting out the more difficult times, each alignment can be seen as an opportunity to grow into new level of awareness. When these moments coincide with rituals to induce trance, the opportunities are even greater.

Moon: The Moon is a power in all magickal operations, and most Witches know spells on the waxing Moon are to manifest blessings in your life, while spells on the waning Moon are to banish or curse things from your life. The full Moon is the peak of waxing power, while the dark Moon, just before the new, is the strongest time for waning power. Witches tend to celebrate the Full Moon, for it was outlined in the Aradia material and adopted into the Charge of the Goddess and the Gardnerian Book of Shadows.

Whenever you have need of anything, once in the month and better it be when the moon is full, you shall assemble in some secret place and adore the spirit of Me Who is Queen of all the Wise.

For consciousness exploration, the waxing Moon brings heightened emotions, illuminating what we feel quite clearly. The half Moon, or start of the second quarter, where the right side of the Moon is illuminated, marks a transition point, where we might be in conflict, yet the conflict brings greater awareness. The waning Moon is a time of greater rest and reflection. The dark Moon is a time of regeneration and preparing for new beginnings. It is a time to gather power. Because of its dark nature, it can also be a time when fear rises, and an opportunity to face repressed emotions and work with the shadow and underworld forces. The waning half Moon, with the left half illuminated as the fourth quarter begins, is also a time of stress, though successfully moving through it can lead to the regeneration and power of the darkness.

The Moon can be "in" any of the twelve Zodiac signs. It moves through the whole Zodiac in less than a month, making it the fastest of the planetary bodies. While the Sun and Moon are technically luminaries, most astrologers refer to them as planets. For astrological purposes, they behave much like the other planets. Each sign colors the power of the Moon, flavoring it with a particular style. The sign's energy can be used when opening the gates as much as spellcraft. By timing your other techniques to the Moon phase, you can enhance their overall effectiveness.

Aries – Warrior magick, physical exercise, blood magick

Taurus – Sacred pilgrimage, song and music, gnosis induced by sensuality

Gemini – Trickster magick, sacred dance, shapeshifting, meditation, astral travel

Cancer – Feminine consciousness, food magick, sex magick, Goddess visions

Leo – Masculine consciousness, sacred vestments, body marking, art magick

Virgo – Sacramental plants, sacrifice, ordeals, abstinence

Libra – Yogic exercise, breathwork, spoken word, art magick

Scorpio – Sex magick, exploring taboo concepts, underworld journeys, sacramental plants

Sagittarius – Meditation, breathwork, seeking inner plane teachers
Capricorn – Horned God visions, control, binding and isolation techniques
Aquarius – Group workings, community consciousness, experimentation
Pisces – Sacred dance, dream magick, healing, artistic inspiration

The last point of Moon magick to remember is the Void of Course. The Moon goes Void of Course when it has completed any of the major alignments, called aspects, with other planets while occupying a Zodiac sign. Its energy is said to be un-tethered, or ungrounded to the Earth, until it switches signs and prepares to make new aspects in this new sign. Magicians and Witches say to do no magick while the Moon is void, for it will bear no fruit and the energy will simply dissipate. While that is quite true, it's a great time for rest and reflection, but also idle speculation. Fantasy based magick, where you want to explore an idea, but not necessarily manifest it, is best at this time. Witches are known to be responsible for their thoughts as well as their actions and words, but sometimes you want to explore certain thoughts, and are unsure of their effect upon your life. This is the time to explore the taboo when you don't yet want to manifest it. It's a great time to explore whatever fantasies are suppressed, to understand them, before you decide to manifest them or disregard them.

Sun: Just as the Moon is an important heavenly body in our magick, the Sun also plays an important role. Most think of the Sun as the physical source of light, and the marker of our Wheel of the Year mythos, not necessarily the bestower of magickal power, but the movement of the Sun opens gates of consciousness as well. Astrologically, the Sun represents the Self, and our own personal energy is the most important factor in changing our consciousness. It represents the development of the ego, of the personal self in this lifetime, and its alignments can greatly influence how we see ourselves and our relationship with the physical and spiritual worlds.

The Sun's cycles wax and wane just like the Moon's, but not in a manner obvious to most. The daily cycle of the Sun waxes with the rising of the Sun until noon, indicating a time of growing energy, while its power wanes from noon to sunset. From sunset to dawn its influence is still felt in the reflecting Moon, but its presence is not apparent because it is below the horizon. Here we have the four liminal points of the day, explored with the Four Adorations. But the cycle is also seen in the year. The yearly cycle begins with the Winter Solstice, or Yule, and waxes through the Witch's Wheel of the Year with Imbolc (Feb 2), Ostara (Vernal Equinox), Beltane (May 1) and peaks at Litha, or Midsummer (Summer Solstice). From then wanes, moving through Lammas (Aug 1), Mabon (Autumnal Equinox) and Samhain (Oct 31) until starting over again.

While the fire festivals are technically not solar holidays, but agricultural holidays, the Sun is approximately at the midpoint between its flanking equinox and solstice.

Each of these days are liminal points of power. The Winter Solstice is the day of longest night, yet the light starts growing from this point forward. The Summer Solstice is the day of shortest night, but the night starts growing from this point forward. Both equinoxes are times of balance, of equal light and dark, but the balance soon tips one way or another. The four remaining holidays, the Celtic fire festivals, are ideally between the solar holidays, occurring in the fixed signs of Aquarius, Taurus, Leo, and Scorpio, even though we tend to observe the calendar dates, rather than the astrological degree. They are all days between, outside of time, best used in meditation or in journey to the otherworld. Journeys at this time reflect the theme of the year, and the Sun's placement in the Zodiac. Many books have been written about these holidays, and those who can open the gates can go deeper. Rather than simply celebrating the journey of the Sun god, one who can easily enter trance can journey *to* the Sun god and follow him on his yearly journey, gaining greater insight and personal power.

While these eight points are particularly important, like the Moon, the Sun is also in one of the twelve signs of the Zodiac at each time. The sign flavors the energy of the Sun, which also goes through alignments with other planets, like the Moon. While it never goes Void of Course like the Moon, its relationship with the other planets can open particular gates of awareness, joining together the Sun's energy with that planet's, either in an smooth or challenging manner. While the study of planetary aspects in detail is beyond the scope of this book (and can be found in more detailed astrological texts,) one obvious aspect occurs during eclipses.

Eclipses are special alignments with the Sun, Moon, Earth, and a part of the Moon's orbit known as the nodes of the Moon. Also called the Dragon's Head and Dragon's Tail, as it appears when they align a great serpent is "eating" the Sun or the Moon. During a solar eclipse, the Moon comes between the Sun and Earth at the dark Moon, blocking our view of the Sun. During a lunar eclipse, the Earth's shadow falls upon the Moon at the Full Moon, blocking the light of the Sun. What do eclipses mean? Over the centuries, they are considered moments of extreme power and good fortune or, more traditionally periods of ill omen and misfortune, for the light is blocked. Modern Witches are not clear in their own teachings on eclipses. They can be treated as particularly powerful dark/new and full Moons. Generally I see them as powerful times to explore what you really feel in relationship to who you are in this world. Solar eclipses explore more of your public identity, while lunar eclipses explore more of your inner magickal side, and possibly open you to past life experiences that can help you understand your current incarnation. Many choose to only meditate and explore consciousness on these dates, rather than perform spellcraft, since the energies are so intense.

The last obvious solar alignment is what is known in astrology as your solar return. In everyday terms, it is your birthday, when the Sun returns to the point in the Zodiac where it was when you were born. The time leading up to your birthday can be difficult, not because you are a year older, but because it is the end of a cycle, the solar cycle, and can feel like a mini-death and rebirth. The return itself aligns you with the Sun, and gives an influx of life force and creative energy, usually used for outer world pursuits, but could be applied to more magickal endeavors through a birthday ritual. Using techniques in harmony with your Zodiac sign (see the Moon's list previously) can be very effective.

Planets: The planets are the remaining forces governing our celestial clock. Our days of the week are named after the seven magickal planets of the classical world, each day permeated with the energy of that planet and its archetypal force.

☉	Sun	Sunday	Child	Health, Success, Inspiration, Joy
☽	Moon	Monday	Priestess	Past Lives, Psychic Powers, Magick, Emotion
☿	Mercury	Wednesday	Magician	Memory, Spoken Words, Travel
♀	Venus	Friday	Enchantress	Love, Sexuality, Attraction, Luxury
♂	Mars	Tuesday	Warrior	Battle, Physical Actions, Courage
♃	Jupiter	Thursday	King	Royalty, Riches, Benevolence
♄	Saturn	Saturday	Elder	Limitations, Control, Protection

Likewise, each hour of the day is said to be ruled by a planet, creating combinations of the two, hour and day, to link the particular planets together. Those who wish to harness the energy of the planet can perform ritual on that day, or to combine the energy of two planets, perform ritual in the proper planetary hour that combines the right day and time.

	Sun.	Mon.	Tues.	Wed.	Thurs.	Fri.	Sat.
Day							
Hour 1	☉	☽	♂	☿	♃	♀	♄
Hour 2	♀	♄	☉	☽	♂	☿	♃
Hour 3	☿	♃	♀	♄	☉	☽	♂
Hour 4	☽	♂	☿	♃	♀	♄	☉
Hour 5	♄	☉	☽	♂	☿	♃	♀
Hour 6	♃	♀	♄	☉	☽	♂	☿
Hour 7	♂	☿	♃	♀	♄	☉	☽
Hour 8	☉	☽	♂	☿	♃	♀	♄
Hour 9	♀	♄	☉	☽	♂	☿	♃
Hour 10	☿	♃	♀	♄	☉	☽	♂
Hour 11	☽	♂	☿	♃	♀	♄	☉
Hour 12	♄	☉	☽	♂	☿	♃	♀
Night							
Hour 1	♃	♀	♄	☉	☽	♂	☿
Hour 2	♂	☿	♃	♀	♄	☉	☽
Hour 3	☉	☽	♂	☿	♃	♀	♄
Hour 4	♀	♄	☉	☽	♂	☿	♃
Hour 5	☿	♃	♀	♄	☉	☽	♂
Hour 6	☽	♂	☿	♃	♀	♄	☉
Hour 7	♄	☉	☽	♂	☿	♃	♀
Hour 8	♃	♀	♄	☉	☽	♂	☿
Hour 9	♂	☿	♃	♀	♄	☉	☽
Hour 10	☉	☽	♂	☿	♃	♀	♄
Hour 11	♀	♄	☉	☽	♂	☿	♃
Hour 12	☿	♃	♀	♄	☉	☽	♂

Fig. 53: Planetary Hours

For example, if you want to do magick combining the sensual aspects of Venus with the more aggressive nature of Mars, you can do the ritual in the day of Venus, on the hour of Mars, or the day of Mars in the hour of Venus. If you want the balance of the Sun and Moon, the powers of the child of light and the priestess of night, you can do it on Sunday, in the hour of the Moon, or Monday in the hour of the Sun, depending on which power is more prevalent in your magick.

There is no one universally accepted method of calculating the hours. There are two standard methods, one considered the easy method, but less accurate, and the other more difficult, but more worthwhile for the technique.

The easy method simply calculates the hours in sixty-minute blocks, like the modern hour, and starts the day hours at midnight. The first hour of the day is 12 A.M. to 1 A.M. Hour two is 1 A.M. to 2 A.M., and so forth.

The second method uses the periods of light and darkness for day and night, and requires you to calculate the number of minutes from dawn to sunset, divide by twelve, and use that number as your planetary "hour" for the day. To find the night time hours, measure the minutes from sunset to the following sunrise, divide by twelve and use that number for your planetary hour for the night. Only near the equinoxes are the hours of day and night equal, and near the solstices they are the most uneven.

For example on a Thursday evening of the Full Moon some November in Boston, the Sun sets at 4:24 P.M. and sunrise the following morning is 6:32 A.M. From sunset to sunrise, there are 14 hours and 8 minutes of darkness. Fourteen hours is really 840 minutes (14 x 60 = 840) plus the 8 minutes leaves us with 848 minutes of darkness. On this evening, a planetary hour (848/12) is 70.666 minutes, which I would round up to 71 minutes. So our planetary hours would look like:

Evening Hour 1	4:24 P.M. – 5:35 P.M.	Moon
Evening Hour 2	5:35 P.M. – 6:46 P.M.	Saturn
Evening Hour 3	6:46 P.M. – 7:57 P.M.	Jupiter
Evening Hour 4	7:57 P.M. – 9:08 P.M.	Mars
Evening Hour 5	9:08 P.M. – 10:19 P.M.	Sun
Evening Hour 6	10:19 P.M. – 11:30 P.M.	Venus
Evening Hour 7	11:30 P.M. – 12:41 A.M.	Mercury
Evening Hour 8	12:41 A.M. – 1:52 A.M.	Moon
Evening Hour 9	1:52 A.M. – 3:03 A.M.	Saturn
Evening Hour 10	3:03 A.M. – 4:14 A.M.	Jupiter
Evening Hour 11	4:14 A.M. – 5:25 A.M.	Mars
Evening Hour 12	5:25 A.M. – 6:36 A.M.	Sun

Rounding our numbers gives some slightly imprecise calculations. 6:36 A.M. is four minutes beyond our 6:32 A.M. sunrise, but works well enough for our purposes. I tend to start my working well after my calculated hour has begun, to make sure I'm within the proper hour, regardless of minor math issues. If we did not round to 71 minutes per planetary hour, our calculations would have ended the twelfth hour at 6:24 A.M., 8 minutes short of sunrise.

If you want to work a trance to commune with the darkness of the underworld on the Full Moon, while having the blessings of Jupiter's good fortune and benevolence, you might choose a Saturn hour, Hour 2 or Hour 9. I would probably choose Hour 9, as it would be darker and more still between the hours of 1:52 A.M. and 3:03 A.M. than earlier in the evening.

TERRESTRIAL TIMING

While celestial timing is more prevalent, we should not forget the earthly clocks all around us. The land itself tells us about magickal times of power, if we only look and listen. The difference being that such times of power are regional, linking magickal times to magickal landscapes, and promoting our connection to both time and space, forging a holistic relationship with our environment.

Terrestrial timing usually deals with the firsts and the lasts of a season. Each marks a special shift in the energy of the land and its relationship with the heavens and, in particular, the Sun and Moon. Though our ancient Pagan ancestors in the temple traditions might have had complex knowledge of celestial events, rural people went by what the land was doing as much as anything else.

Usually such terrestrial markers are found through measuring the "first" of something for the season, which causes one to be vigilant in paying attention to the land. The days that bring environmental shifts have power.

First Flower: The blooming of the first spring flower in your area marks the rise of life force. The first of particular flowers can mark a time for magick specifically related to that flower. The first elder or hawthorn might mark a time for faery magick for example. The first datura flower can mark a time for underworld magick. The blooming of the first witch hazel marks a time for the ancestors, particularly our Witchcraft ancestors.

First Rain: The first rain of a season can carry us into the underworld journey, connect us to the rain gods in the heavens, or enhance cleansing and purification rituals. Rain brings life, and in most parts of the world is seen as a blessing of prosperity, good luck, fertility, and love. While most westerners see rain as a bad sign on a wedding day, in the east is a mark of good fortune.

First Ripening: When the first grains or fruits ripen, it is a time of abundance and manifestation. It is a time for vision work and magick to bring into manifestation what you want and plant seeds for the next year.

First/Last Leaf to Fall: The falling of the leaves marks the start of the season of death. It is a time to release, to let go, and to compost old energies, thoughts, and feelings so they might be transformed.

First Frost: If the falling of leaves is a sign of the time to let go, the first frost is the time to say good-bye as the land starts to wither for the winter season.

First Snow: First snow marks times for peace, for clarity and reflection, like the reflected light off of the snow. There is nothing quite like the first snowfall and the hush that envelops the world. It can also be a time of kindling the consciousness of the child within, and the desire to play.

Lightning: Lightning and thunder storms, first of the season, or anytime, are times of power. Storm rainwater is particularly potent for potions and remedies, and performing ritual during such storms magnifies any intention. Such weather creates a clear connection from the heavens to the earth and underworld beyond, and almost anything can be accomplished by those daring enough to explore the other realms at such a time. Journeys to merge with the storm itself can be quite fruitful as well. Where lightning strikes can indicate a sacred place, particularly a sacred tree, and soot from such a lightning strike makes a powerful additive to potions, oils, and ointments.

Obviously this list is for those in a climate more traditional to the Wheel of the Year mythos. You might find you can adapt the list of firsts and lasts to include local seasonal variations for your climate. It might be the first locust or ladybug, the first flooding of the river, the first butterfly seen, or the first tree to fall. Watch the clock and calendar of the landscape and see what makes the most magickal sense to you.

Gregorian Calendar Days

Some Witches, either holding dual faith in mainstream and/or esoteric Christian traditions, or seeking to use the cultural momentum, focus not on Pagan traditions of timing with celestial or terrestrial events, but use calendar days, often Catholic holidays, as times of power. Others look to the uniqueness of the Blue Moon, the second full Moon in a calendar month, or the last day of February on a leap year. All of these times can be seen as magickal, and appropriate times to do workings, though I must admit they are not an important part of my own magickal practice.

BETWEENNESS

The shadows to sacred time are two-fold, but both deal with the theme of stepping outside of time, beyond the cycles and seasons of the human condition. Though Witches are said to stand "between the worlds" in a "time that is not a time," we still live in the world, and must be actively engaged in it. Ours is not a traditional of complete detachment or withdrawal from society.

On one end of the spectrum, we can become obsessive with magickal timing. We step out of the time frames of normal society, because it doesn't match our magickal models of time keeping. We start to time not only major workings to astrological alignments and calculations, but minor aspects of our lives. It is near impossible to observe all the alignments at their exact times and hold a normal job and family schedule. While modern society tends to work by a nine to five, five-day work week, astrological activities do not. You can't always take time off of work or family obligations to do specifically magickal actions at the right moment. For big events, you can certainly schedule. I tend to make time for all the Wheel of the Year holidays, and the full and dark Moons. But sometimes you have to fudge, and work the time closest to the alignment, particularly when leading public ritual, where you need to schedule events to suit modern schedules, or else you will have few participants.

When you become so obsessive with "proper" timing that you can't function well, you truly get stuck in a place between, having little contact with the outside world. If you continue down that path, you become paralyzed, unable to take action if the alignments are not right, or take foolish risks because the alignments appeared to be correct for such actions.

The second manifestation of betweenness is far less linear, and more intuitive. Rather than obsessively calculating and observing to follow predicted patterns, you get into a very magickal flow of timing, without retaining your human sense of timing. Much like being ungrounded from your place and body, your consciousness becomes ungrounded from this time. You begin to see the fluid and non-linear nature of time. It's an amazing insight and can help greatly at divination and magickal evolution, for one time is all time in spirit, but not observing human schedules can cause problems for employers, family, and friends. Since they cannot see the same patterns of magickal time, they will not be in synch with you. People who step beyond time in this way become somewhat detached from the human experience. While this is encouraged as a skill, to turn on and off, it should not be the default state of reality. The more you become immersed in a magickal life, particularly if your vocation is not in ordinary society, the more you are at risk for living between times.

The secret overcoming both of these pitfalls is to maintain human obligations in society, as well as magickal timing and seasonal rituals. Making magickal timing a part of your regular life, and inviting friends and family to participate in seasonal or lunar rituals, can be a great benefit. Having regularly scheduled events during the week can help keep one foot firmly in traditional society, yet give you freedom to observe your magickal seasons and astrological tides.

AIDS TO SACRED TIMING

The following points should be kept in mind when working with sacred timing:

Purchase an Astrological Calendar: An astrological calendar, and the knowledge of its use, is essential to work with astrological tides of energy in an appropriate manner. They can look intimidating, but with a little practice you will be able to read one like a professional. Many are available as applications for your computer or phone, and more complex applications for generating full astrological charts and various permutations are now easily available to consumers.

Get Outside: Observe the cycles and seasons, for there will be many tides of power not measured by your books and calendars. Watch for them and remember them.

Observe Sacred Times Regularly: Repeat rituals at times of power, and your experience will deepen and grow, and there will be subtle shifts. Don't simply do a full Moon ritual, but keep the lunar cycle, celebrating each full Moon. Celebrate the entire Wheel of the Year.

CHAPTER TWELVE: SACRED GARMENTS

Another path to gnosis in traditional occult circles often disregarded as archaic in modern groups is the use of special ritual garb, vestments, jewelry and other ritual tools. At one time the ritual robe or cloak was a mandatory part of the Witch's tools, as much as the athame, wand, and chalice. As magick has become more integrated with mundane life, the concept of ritual garb has literally fallen out of fashion in certain circles. A potent tool to induce a change in consciousness is lost, and the very idea is not even passed on to newer students of the Craft. While I applaud the union of the otherworldly and everyday, I believe that union best comes through some deeper magickal work.

The initial division between magickal and mundane is purposeful in the early stages of magickal training. Most importantly to keep inexperienced and naturally talented magicians from loosing sight of the boundary between physical and spiritual realities. In that confusion can come a lot of magickal, emotional, and even physical harm. Students are encouraged to develop either a general sense of the magickal self, or a full magickal persona.

To create this sense of the magickal self, we use several techniques. Traditionally we take Craft names used only in circle, or in magickal gatherings. Though as our mundane garb becomes our magickal garb in modern traditions, likewise our magickal names often become used in our mundane life, and the technique becomes less effective. Names evoke a power and personality. To go with that name, we wear certain clothing only in ritual. Those robes, cloaks, or other items become signals to our mind that we are entering a magickal space, and assuming a certain magickal authority. When we are having a bad day, or don't feel "in the mood" yet there is magickal work to be done, the very act of putting on ritual clothing can put us in the correct mood and mindset for magick. By using the clothing, you create a mental trigger. You associate that clothing with a particular frame of mind and your past successes with ritual, trance, and spell craft. When you put it on, you are now in the same space as those past times. Your mind recreates that framework, including altering your consciousness to a magickal mindset. Just as scent can be used to program the mind, evoking the past awareness when the scent was used, clothing can be used in the same way. Perhaps it's a combination of sight and feel, of the color and the texture on the skin, but regardless of how it works, magickal and religious traditions have known that it does work for centuries.

As the adornment of the body with clothes and jewels are used to create a magickal persona and the trance state associated with it, the removal of the same articles helps return you to an ordinary level of consciousness, and a more fully "human" way of looking at the world. Some have difficulty grounding back into the ordinary, and enter delusion when they take their magickal persona and awareness into personal and work relationships. The wearing and removal of garments is an effective way to create a boundary and barrier to such unfortunate behavior.

As your spiritual awareness grows, we learn to recognize the division between spiritual and ordinary as artificial. While the division serves a purpose, once we are grounded and disciplined, it becomes less and less necessary. We know we can do magick wearing anything, yet if we trained in such technique, there is a bit of an extra emphasis, extra power, that comes with wearing ritual garments. It still serves a purpose, even though it is less serious than when we began.

The use of ritual tools and jewelry is well known throughout the ancient Pagan world. For those who follow the mysteries of the Descent of the Goddess, the oldest form of the myth, the Legend of Inanna, states that she had seven powers to relinquish at seven gates – a crown, a necklace (or earrings), a double strand necklace, a breastplate, a bracelet (or ring), a measuring line with a rod, and her robe. Though the wearing, loss and, eventually, return of the seven tools, she learns about her path and power, altering her awareness as she faces her underworld sister, Ereshkigal.

Modern Witches still use tools similar to Inanna, a well as quite a few others.

Ritual Robes and Cloaks: The standard vestment for the modern Witch is a ritual robe and/or cloak. When donned, they bring an air of magick. As an actor can shift into a role when donning a costume, a Witch can more easily shift into the magickal persona when dawning a robe. Technically a robe is more like a gown, having arms, often sew in a "T" shape and might have a hood. A cloak is more worn for outdoor rituals, almost always with a hood, and without arms, though some cloaks have slits through which the arms can pass, making ritual easier. Ideally the materials are all natural, with cotton being favored for robes, while cloaks are cotton or even wool for those of us in colder climates. Silk is also a highly sought material for robes, as silk is said to be a "living" cloth and holds a higher magickal vibration. While synthetics can be used for practical purposes, they contribute very little to the magick. Most Witches wear black robes and cloaks, though the cloaks may have colored linings, often of the Witch's "power" color, or a color to denote their rank or office within a formal group. Magickal symbols can be stitched into the robe/cloak, binding specific spells and blessings into it.

Fig. 54: Robe Pattern

Skyclad: While many modern Witches tend to favor the robed approach, those descending from a British Traditional Wicca line tend to work skyclad, meaning clothed in the sky, or naked. While technically not wearing a sacred vestment, the divestment of all mundane clothing has a similar effect, altering consciousness and perception, because it's a mode of operating that is not part of the "normal" world. Being skyclad is an act of equality amongst circle-mates, and an act of returning to a state of child-like awareness before the gods, pure and unspoiled by society. While practical considerations have to be taken into account when working outdoor rituals in colder seasons, some traditions will use a natural oil or grease for protection from the cold it is still a powerful ritual act capable of transforming the psyche.

Magickal Jewelry: For some, it is not the robe (or lack there of,) but the jewelry that signifies the magickal persona. Rings, necklaces, and bracelets are all common part of the magickal persona. Wearing them signifies a time for magick. Many of these tools are symbols of rank in a coven, with a pentacle pendant being part of the first degree, a ring for the second degree, and a bracelet or another necklace for the third degree. Some Witches wear them all the time, but often covertly, wearing them out only for ritual and magickal workings. Other items are used only for magickal operations, and not worn during daily life. The metals, jewels, and shape all contribute to the magick being done. Silver enhances psychic ability. Gold brings energy and power. Copper tends to evoke the powers of love and attraction.

Head Coverings: Head coverings are a part of many religious traditions vestments. We have examples in the Jewish *yarmulke*, the nun's habit and the brother's skullcap. Many shamanic traditions encourage covering of the head, particularly when you don't want to be possessed by the spirits or gods. In some Native Traditions, there is the ritual feathered headdress. In Voudou traditions, one wears white on the head, such as a kerchief, to signal the desire not to be "ridden" or possessed by the lwa spirits. Though not as prevalent in Witchcraft, we do have some traditions of head coverings. The archetypal image of the medieval Witch or wizard is one with a pointed conical hat. Some have conjectured that it is symbolic of the "Cone of Power" Witches raise, though it was simply part of the fashion of the time. Some modern Witches have adopted it, in jest or in all seriousness. More traditional are the crowns of the High Priest or High Priestess. Many Witchcraft traditions focus on the concept of sovereignty, and name their ministers "Lord" and "Lady" in emulation of the God and Goddess. The crown is a symbol of this. The Ladies often wear crescent crowns, while the Lords wear either solar or horned crowns.

Footwear: Ritual attire also includes footwear. While most Witches tend to prefer going barefoot, having nothing disconnect them from the ground, particularly when outside, this, in itself, is a means of gnosis. If your daily default dress is to have footwear, then removing shoes and socks can be a gateway to awareness, putting you directly in touch with the Earth. In some ceremonial traditions, sandals, gilded with gold or silver or simply gold or silver paint, are used. Footwear should be taken into account depending on where the ritual is, the terrain and if dance will be involved, as the type of shoe, or lack thereof, will affect you.

Ritual Tools: Though technically not clothing, many ritual tools become a part of our "outfit" in magick, including all manner of sticks. Ranging from the wand, walking stick, rod, and staff, they become a part of our magickal identity and persona, an extension of our will. The same can be said about magickal blades, such as the athame, boline, and sword. Other magickal talismans, such as jewelry, pouches and cords also become part of the magickal self-identity.

Masks: Masks are a very shamanic form of ritual vestment often neglected in classical occultism, but reclaimed by those traditions with a more shamanic bent. Strange to think Witches have sometimes shied away from the use of masks, considering the holiday of Halloween is associated both with masks and the with Witches' high holy day of Samhain. There is some evidence to suggest the otherworldly or supernatural appearance we associate with the modern Halloween stereotype of the Witch, green-skinned and monstrous, could come from ritual garb and masks, similar to more tribal shamans. In a Swedish document from the twelfth century, *The Law of Västgötaland*, there is a passage that possibly refers to the more shamanic nature of the Witch, or "hedge rider."

"Woman, I saw you riding on a fence switch with loose hair and belt, in the troll skin, at the time when day and night are equal."

The reference to the "troll skin" could be a ceremonial skin, pelt, or mask worn by the Witch on this rite that occurred at a liminal boundary (the fence), at a liminal time (the equinox). The ritualist assumes the characteristics of the being the mask emulates. Perhaps these Swedish Witches assumed the form of a troll. Animal forms are most popular, either wearing masks of a specific animal, or an animal influenced deity, such as a horned god. The mask lends to the art of shapeshifting, through moving and "dancing" like your animal.

Exercise: Mask Making

As with any other form of magick, start your mask making with a clear intention. What purpose does the mask serve? What persona or entity will it help you embody to alter your consciousness? Establish your intention and the basic idea for your mask. Gather the following materials available at most art and craft supply stores:

Plaster gauze, about one roll per mask (varies by roll)
A lightweight air-drying clay such as Creative Paper Clay
A large bowl of warm water
Two towels you won't mind damaging
Scissors
Rolling pin
Power drill
Two 2 ft. x 3 ft. squares of canvas
Some basic clay modeling tools, or a butter knife
Embellishments: Paints, feathers, beads, shells, stones and whatever else you desire
Glue

Paint

Sealant – clear gloss or a matte spray enamel

Ribbon or string to tie the mask

Small felt square

Plastic mask base – if making masks solitary. If you are working with others, you can use your own face

Petroleum jelly or other ointment – If making masks based on human faces

Ritualized mask makers can cleanse all the objects used in the construction of the masks in sacred smoke, and begin the process with a prayer, candle lighting, or other ceremony of intention. Making masks can be quite messy, so make sure you have a nice flat work area, and cover your work area with paper, cloth or plastic to keep the mess to a minimum.

Part I – Creating the Basic Mask Form

First create the form for your mask, the base for its construction. The base is made from strips of plaster gauze, either on a plain white unfinished plastic mask (found at craft supply stores,) or upon the face of the person who will be using the mask. If working with a plastic base mask, wet the strips of plaster gauze in the bowl of water, and place them over the mask. If working on a person, make sure the person's face has a thick layer of petroleum jelly, including the eyebrows, hairline, and facial hair, to prevent the plaster from sticking to the hair and skin. The mask model can lay down comfortably on a pillow to stay still while the mask is being made. And with proper music and ritual mood, can trance during this process to connect to the spirit the mask will embody. My friend Matthew Venus, who taught me this process of mask making, suggests the use of a Witch's Ointment instead of petroleum jelly, to help the trance process. He also suggests adding herbal magick to the warm water used to wet the gauze, making a light infusion of magickal herbs that correspond with the mask's intention. Just make sure you choose herbs that are non-toxic and will not cause the skin to react, and that your subject is not allergic to the herbs. A light infusion of mugwort is an excellent choice for most masks.

What shape shall your mask be? It could be full face, half face with a nose, half face without a nose, or another creative design. Start with small strips around the boundary of the mask at the outside of the face or base mask. If working with a plastic base mask, leave a quarter of an inch of space between the outer rim of the base mask and the edge of the gauze, to make sure you can easily remove the base mask from the plaster when the gauze is dry and hardened. Work your way inward with the strips, leaving space for eyes, mouth and nostrils if you want the mask to be functional. Make sure to cover the entire area of the mask at least three times with the gauze strips, as evenly as possible. This makes your mask sturdy and durable enough for the later steps.

Let the mask harden. If working with a partner, let it stay on the face for fifteen to forty minutes, depending on temperature and humidity. A space heater or hair dryer can quicken the process. Make sure the mask is hard enough to not collapse when you remove it. Loosen it around the edges and slowly work it free from your partner's face without damaging it. If working with a plastic mask base, leave it on for an hour or two and then pull the plastic mask away from the plaster by the edge that you left.

Hold the mask up to the light o find any translucent areas. If there are any places where the light shines through, add more gauze to strengthen it. Then let it dry for another hour or two. Now is the best time to make holes for stringing the mask. Mark a spot about a half inch from the outer edge, near the temple of the mask on each side. Use a power drill to drill holes at these marks. Make sure you use all proper caution when handling a power tool.

Part II – Sculpting your Mask

Once your mask is dry and the structure is complete, you can choose to paint and decorate it as it is, or give it further character by sculpting it with added clay. The benefit of a sculpted mask is one with greater character, definition and shape. Use a light-weight air drying clay such as Creative Paperclay or LaDoll clay. Both are non-toxic and easy to work with, and Creative Paperclay is all natural. While they are durable, they are not indestructible, and too rough handling of your mask can result in damage. You can also empower the clay with herbal magick by adding a finely ground herbal powder to it as you sculpt your mask. While the mortal and pestle is more romantic, for this work, you might find a coffee grinder and sieve serves better. The powdered herbs can be kneaded into the clay easily.

Put your clay on the canvas square on your flat surface. Put another piece of canvas on top and use your rolling pin to flatten the clay between the sheets of canvas. The canvas helps keep the clay from sticking to the rolling pin and gives it a more uniform flatness. Roll both vertically and horizontally until the clay is an inch thick and large enough to lay on top of your mask.

Peel off the top canvas layer. Use warm water to dampen the surface of the plaster mask form slightly, and lay your flattened sheet of clay over the mask form by flipping the bottom canvas sheet over the top of the mask so the clay is on top of the mask form. Carefully peel the canvas away from the clay on the mask. Flatten the clay onto the mask, avoiding any air pockets between the clay and mask. Use your clay tools or butter knife to clear excess clay from the edges, eyes, nose, mouth, and string holes of the mask. Use water, your hands, and your tools to sculpt the mask. Smooth the clay and build up the mask with extra clay, forming eyebrows, cheeks, lips, nose, horns, ears, fins, or anything else you desire. Make sure the extra clay is firmly attached and will not easily break off as the clay dries. Give the mask life and personality.

When done, let it air dry for one to three days, depending on the thickness of the clay. You might find the mask cracks upon drying. You can add more clay and allow it to dry again and any lumpy parts can be smoothed with a fine grit sand paper.

Part III – Embellishing the Mask

Once the mask shape is complete, you can embellish the mask. Start by painting it. Acrylic paints are ideal for masks. You can paint it in whatever colors and patterns are appropriate for the mask's intention. Once the paint is dry, seal it in some way to both protect and strengthen it. Clear gloss or a matte spray enamel is best to seal the mask. Use three coats, letting each one dry before applying the next coat.

Further embellish the mask with any other appropriate decorations. Glue stones, shells, feathers, sequins, glitter, or anything else that suits the intention of the mask. For comfort when wearing, you might want to add a square of felt inside of the mask, where the bridge of the nose will sit. The felt helps cushion your nose from the weight of the mask. Attach a strong string or ribbon into the side holes, long enough to tie the mask with some excess string, so you can use it for ritual.

Part IV – Empowering the mask

Ritually consecrate you mask in a manner appropriate for its intention. Use some of the other paths of trance described in this book, including chanting, sacred smoke, and consecration with herbal mixtures and bodily fluids to help empower your mask. The mask will then serve you as a tool for trance, metamorphosis, and spiritual gnosis.

Plaster and clay masks are not the only types available to you. Masks can be made from paper, leather, cloth, wood, and a variety of synthetics found in costume kits and theater design. Though I prefer more natural masks for magick, use what works for you. An excellent resource for mask making and masked dance in the context of Witchcraft is *Sacred Mask Sacred Dance* by Evan John Jones and Chas S. Clifton. I highly recommend it if you are interested in working more with masked trance.

Some masks are worn in spirit only, envisioned by the practitioners. William Gray shares the Leaf Mask meditation, found in his book *Western Inner Workings* (p. 150), but most likely from the work of Robert Cochrane. With it, the practitioner touches specific parts of the face, envisioning the leaves of the Green Man upon the face, evoking the power of the Plant Lord.

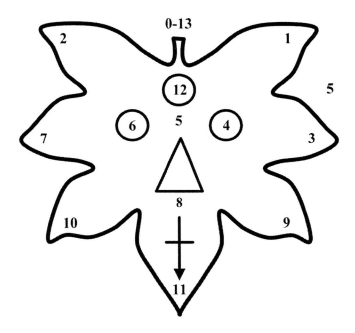

Fig. 55: Leaf Mask

Leaf Mask Prayer

O goddess, (Overhead)

Thou who created heaven (1, Right Temple)

and Earth (2, Left Temple)

Order (2, Left Temple)

From Chaos, (1, Right Temple)

Time (2 Left Temple)

From Eternity (1, Right Temple)

I pray to thee. (Cross arms and bow)

Thou that listens (3, Right ear)

To our deepest voices, who shinest forth the pleasing Light, (4, Right eye)

Who inspires (5, Between the eyes)

Our inherited wisdom (12, Forehead)

And who protecteth us from the baleful might of the Destroyer, (6, Left Eye)

I pray three grant us the inner voices (7, Left Ear)

Speaking of spiritual things, and let Love (8, Between the nose and lips)

be our guiding light.

In the name of the Father, (9, Right Jaw)

The Mother, (10, Left Jaw)

And the spirit that moveth all. (11, chin, then to 12 at forehead, and 13 overhead. Cross arms again)

This face touching prayer combines sacred movement and visualization with the concept of the spirit mask, making it a simple, yet effective working. The ritual movement is not unlike the movement of the Goblin Cross, a Pagan variation on the "Sign of the Cross" or Qabalistic Cross, using the lines and vision of a banishing pentagram, moving breast to brow, shoulder to opposing shoulder, and back where you started. You envision the star as almost a face mask or shield.

CONSECRATION OF VESTMENTS

Like any other ritual tool, sacred vestments should be cleansed and consecrated toward the purpose of magick. Ideally if you can purchase handcrafted goods created by another Witch, so much the better.

Cleanse your ritual clothing and jewelry as you would any other ritual tools. For those unfamiliar with purification and consecrating techniques, explore The Five Essentials in **Chapter Fourteen**.

Exercise: Creating the Magick Outfit

Create a magickal outfit for ritual purposes, make one that suits your own practice and traditions. You can hand-craft your outfit, sewing robes yourself, or purchase and gather materials that establish your own magick personality. Cleanse and consecrate the outfit and use it for ritual. Note the differences when you wear the outfit, as opposed to when you don't wear magickal garments. Which do you prefer?

Vanity & Attachment

Vanity and attachment are the shadow sides to this path of power. For some, the clothing and tools become more important than the magick itself. The tools of the gate become confused with the gate itself. The tools are invested with magickal significance to the point of diminishing the personal power of the Witch or magician. People become attached to their tools and costumes, believing the magick comes from the tools rather than themselves and, without those tools, they cannot perform magick. They become crippled, disconnected from their own personal power.

Others get caught up in having the newest and most lavish outfits. They are on continual buying sprees for the things that make them look good or afford them status in a group, yet never develop a deep relationship with their tools or a specific magickal persona cultivated by a robe, cloak or crown. They become collectors, but not practitioners, of magick.

This has become such a problem that many modern traditions of magick do away with the benefits of this path completely, advocating no special tools, ritual outfits, or other accoutrements. Their belief is that magick is an everyday occurrence, and our everyday wear is totally appropriate for magick. While I do agree that magick should be a part of our everyday lives, and is for most practitioners, having a separation between magickal and mundane life, at least initially, prevents many a borderline student from having a break with functional consensus reality.

Ritual clothing can also punctuate the experience of a well-seasoned magician. Indigenous sorcerers and shamans today still use ceremonial garb. Our Pagan ancestors all had ceremonial garb when involved in religious services. There is a reason for it, from the most tribal shaman to the highest official of the Catholic Church. There is a technology at work when we don a garment, and that technology transcends religions and cultures. The power of this technology, generated from vestments, is what we seek to harness. But like all power, it must be used in balance, and not be our sole method to approach magick and mystery.

Aids to the Sacred Vestments

The following points should be kept in mind when working with sacred vestments:

What You Wear, You Become: You become what you wear. Whatever magickal persona you craft, beware of the archetype's full power, strengths, and weaknesses. You evoke both when you strongly identify with a magickal archetype, even for a short time. It doesn't mean you shouldn't don such dress, but the actual act of putting it on in ritual, and taking it off, can help you separate from the shortcomings of the archetype. The elderly Merlin-esque wizard figure has to be on guard for his trapping Nimue. The Hunter-Hunted god has to beware of the personal sacrifice. The priestess always donning the dress of Persephone has to beware of seasonal depression while the priestess of Isis must be on guard for tragic love. Work with the magickal personas towards specific aims, but do not let one figure write your life story. Identify with many divine aspects, so you can choose your own fate.

Be Creative: Ritual garb doesn't have to conform to any one standard unless you are joining a tradition with certain requirements. Ritual garb can be a modern pair of vinyl pants as much as a Renaissance dress. While it might not be traditional, or have traditional power associations with it, such as natural fibers do, if it makes you feel magickal, use it. Craft your own archetypal images that suit your own inner sense of a magickal self.

Don't Skimp, but Don't Overspend: We are told by tradition not to haggle for our Craft tools, but to pay what is asked. Yet we don't have to spend our life savings on everything we think we need. Search for the right items for you, including items with the right prices. Get good tools and clothing, but don't feel you won't be able to make magick because you got the $50 robe, not the $200 one. And remember, the best ones are those you make yourself, or have another Witch make especially for you.

CHAPTER THIRTEEN: THE DOOR OF DREAMS

One of the most popular gates of power and gnosis is the gateway through dreams. Whenever I teach a workshop on dreams, it better attended than almost any other kind of workshop, with the possible exception of a love magick workshop. Dream magick is so popular because it is a common thread linking all people, even people who otherwise don't think of themselves as psychic or magickal. Everybody needs sleep, and everybody dreams, even those who don't remember their dreams clearly. It's a defining part of the human condition. When people find their dreams can actually be a doorway to healing, self-knowledge, spiritual development, and even manifesting their desires, they want to know more.

THE WORLD OF DREAMS

The magickal and spiritual perspective on dreams has been all but lost in the west. People hunger for it, but most of our lore ranges from dismissing dreams as figments of the unconscious brain to potential therapeutic techniques to understand the mind. Mainstream literature consists mostly of dream dictionaries, simple guides to help you interpret your dreams and what they mean to you, though they never turn out to be as simple, or as helpful, as they promise on the back cover. They usually don't explore beyond basic symbol psychology.

Cultures and time periods more in tune with spiritual realities have retained lore on dreams, and if we look to our own Pagan roots and folk wisdom, we can find the importance of the dream state. From the shamanic point of view, all dreams are real. The world we live in now is a dream, a collective dream, dreamed by everybody. It's popular today in modern metaphysical thought to cite catch phrases as the Law of Attraction and the Power of Intention, in effect saying, "you create your own reality." That's exactly the shamanic point of view of reality, it is a dream you create, and collectively, we dream together the world in which we live. When we sleep, we can focus on other worlds, often individualized, or only shared with a few. We have more direct control over these worlds because fewer people have access to them, but essentially, all the worlds —the seemingly "real" physical world and the worlds we enter when we sleep—are created by the same principles.

Our personal dreams, our own micro worlds, can also open up to the dreams of others, and planes of reality beyond human consciousness. We can experience psychic phenomenon such as astral travel and remote viewing, or have more subjective experiences akin to shamanic journey or Qabalistic pathworking. As dreams open us to others realms, at times, beings from these realms can interact with us while we are in the dream state. Because we don't share the responsibility of creating our personal dreams with the rest of the world, we create worlds more specifically attuned to us, and can experience otherworldly beings specifically attuned to our spiritual vibration. While in the waking world we are so focused on not only our own creations, but the collective creation around us, we tend to block out contact from other worlds. In the dream state, we have, theoretically, fewer distractions, and can become more easily aware of these visitors. In dreams we can enter other worlds, or bring spirits from other worlds into our personal dreamworld, having a level of experience and communication not often possible in the waking world. It's not uncommon, while in a dream, to experience contact from a deceased love one, a spirit guide, deity, or angel. Altered consciousness is a necessary component to such contact and, for many people, the dream state is the only focused time in such an altered state.

DREAMING TECHNIQUES

Going to sleep and dreaming is a ritual. Like the other rituals of this book, it represents a technology of consciousness, a proven method to alter brainwaves. Like any technology, there is an art to its application, to draw out its more powerful and profound uses. While we all use this particular ritual technology, some of us have better technique with it than others. Understanding the process, and how to deepen and control it, gives you an advantage if you truly want to put the doorway of dreams to work for you.

During the dream state, we enter similar states of brainwave activity as we do during meditation, shamanic journey, and ritual. The only difference is we enter these states unconsciously. We fall asleep. Because the focus is different from meditation, we don't struggle with the random thoughts of the conscious mind, constantly distracting us from entering a new level of consciousness. But because the conscious mind is rendered inactive through sleeping, there is no conscious direction to these deeper states of awareness. It becomes a difficult dilemma for the new practitioner. Many have difficulty meditating, because their mind distract them, so their brainwaves cannot be lowered. When we sleep, our brainwaves automatically lower, but we can't take advantage of this meditative state, because we're asleep. The key to this dilemma is to awaken in our dreams, without ending the dream. Such dreams are called "lucid dreams," and they are the golden keys to developing your dream magick.

Before we can learn dream lucidly, we must learn some preliminary techniques to prepare for the work. The first and foremost is the skill of remembering dreams. If you can't remember even your ordinary dreams, having a lucid dream is not going to help you much if you can't remember it. We might be having lucid dreams all the time already, but losing the memory of such dreams upon waking!

Dream Recall

Remembering your dreams is an exercise in discipline. Though I've encountered many people who say they can't remember their dreams, it's more of a matter that they haven't yet learned how to bring information from one state of consciousness back to another. It's a skill that can be developed like any other, though some people have a greater natural affinity for it, just like other talents.

The first step in remembering your dreams is to train the mind to recall what just occurred prior to waking. To do this, keep a notebook and pen, or a simple recording device, next to your bed. When you wake, before you get out of bed or do anything else, write down the first thing you think of or remember. If you don't remember anything, write down, "I don't remember my dreams this morning." But write something. Don't simply think it was an aborted attempt and not write anything down. The very fact of writing conditions your consciousness to know that something important is going on, so after a while of writing, even if it is only "I don't remember my dreams this morning" you begin to remember them in greater and greater detail.

Another method to remember your dreams is to set your alarm clock to snooze a good half hour before you have to get up for your day. Allow the alarm to wake you partially and hit the snooze button. In the period between snooze rings, you will have more vivid dreams and be able to recall them more easily upon waking. Write them down first thing, as instructed in the previous technique.

Dream Clarity

You can make your dreams clearer and deeper, weeding out the day-to-day stresses and phobias that can occur in dreams, through a technique known as the Dream Circle. As you are laying down in bed, before going to sleep, go backwards through your day, mentally listing everything that occurred. If you easily fall to sleep, it will be a broad overview of your day. If you have difficultly falling asleep, particularly if your mind is worried about the details of the day, or about the coming day, make a more detailed list. Start out with the last thing you did before getting into bed, perhaps brushing your teeth. What did you do before that? Go backwards until you fall asleep or reach your waking of the day, when you began the day by writing down your dreams of the previous night.

The purpose of this exercise is to clear the top layer of your consciousness of the daily thoughts and feelings that influence you. Imagine the dream world is like a vast body of water. The daily trials of life are like a pond scum floating on the surface. When you dive deep into the dream world, you pass through that layer of scum and bring it with you into the dream, and when you come back out, you are covered in it, and your dream is colored with your daily worries and interactions, even if the dream itself had a magickal or profound meaning that had little to do with your daily life. The dream circle literally "circles" back through your day, clearing out what might interfere with you finding clarity and meaning in your dreams.

Intentional Dreaming

Once you have some recall of your dreams, you can set a specific intention, and have your mind and spirit do things while your physical body is asleep. One of the classic reasons for intentional dreaming is to answer a question or solve a problem your conscious mind can't seem to resolve. Write out your question or problem on a piece of paper, with a clear intention to solve it in your dream tonight, and to remember that solution. Your intention might be something like a petition spell, worded thusly:

I, (name) ask in the name of the Goddess, God and Great Spirit, to find the answer to (articulate your question or problem) while I sleep and dream tonight, in a manner that is for the highest good, harming none. I ask to remember this solution upon waking, clearly and with all the details necessary to execute it. So mote it be.

Follow your dreaming techniques normally, doing the dream circle and having a notebook or recording device on your nightstand. When you awaken, you will have your answer, though the answer you receive, just as in divination, is often not the one you want, but the one you need. One of the reasons why it can be difficult to solve consciously is the conscious mind doesn't want to see the real solution to the problem, so the sleeping mind acts as a dark mirror, reflecting what is needed, but not necessarily what is wanted. Integrating both the waking and dreaming minds, and the wisdom they contain, is an important step in the magickal progress.

Lucid Dreaming

Lucid dreaming simply means "clear dreaming" but really refers to being in a clear consciousness, awake, while the body still slumbers and dreams. You become aware that you are dreaming in a lucid dream. This waking consciousness is a key to going deeper magickally in your dream work. While some people have spontaneous lucid dreams, dreams that vividly engage all the senses, almost indistinguishable from reality, except for the subject matter, most of us do not. We can learn to trigger such dreams.

The traditional way to trigger lucid dreams is to determine a symbol that will "wake" you in the dream, and intend to dream that symbol when you want to dream. In the teachings of Carlos Castaneda, author of the infamous *The Teachings of Don Juan,* the lucid trigger was to look down at your hands and in seeing your hands, you will remember you are dreaming. Other triggers can be just as simple, looking down at your feet, looking at the Sun or Moon, or anything at all. Some practitioners, myself included, like to use something nonsensical as a trigger. I tend to dream of primordial forests, so I choose a tropical palm tree with coconuts as my trigger. I know another who uses pink elephants and another who uses the image of the Easter Bunny.

Before going to bed, simply visualize your trigger. State that you will dream of this trigger symbol. State this trigger will induce a lucid dream when you see it. In the dream, you will see your trigger, and your lucid dream, or waking dream, will be induced. For some, the lucid dream is only an awareness of dreaming. For others, it is dream control.

Dream Control

Beyond simply being aware of your dreams while dreaming comes control over such dreams. Once you have a lucid dream, you can learn to use your will and imagination to guide and eventually control the dream. You can change the tone and direction of the dream. You can create objects, settings, and characters. You can do anything you can imagine doing in the dream. It becomes great practice for learning the arts of manifestation, of linking thought, emotion, creativity, and manifestation together. While manifestation on the dream-plane is much quicker than anything on the physical world, it gives you practice over the same power in your spellcraft.

Dream control also helps you go deeper in your personal development, as fantasies can be explored and nightmares tamed. Creatures found in nightmares can be bound, questions and issues with them resolved before they overtly creep into your physical life or trigger issues with the shadow self, the repressed part of us that often sabotages our efforts when we are not in healthy relationship with it.

There is no simple "how to" for controlling dreams. Each practitioner does it differently with different levels of success. It involves the same techniques of pathworking and visualization, but applied in the dream state of consciousness, rather than waking meditation. Like other forms of magick, you are directing your will upon the world. This is simply a different, and more pliable, world. Only effort and practice can unlock this secret for you.

Continuing Dreams

Dreams that end abruptly can also be continued, to resolve unresolved themes and issues. Dreams can be continued in two ways – awake or asleep. Both have benefits and drawbacks, and you might find one technique more helpful than the other. I tend to favor waking dreams for dream continuation. Those with good meditation skills tend to favor the waking technique. Those who are more adept in dream magick tend to favor the sleeping continuation.

Waking dreams are the easiest to continue, though those unfamiliar with the practice often feel like they are not valid, or that they are making it up. If you awaken from a dream and want to continue it while awake, lay back down without writing about it. Count yourself down into a meditative state (**Chapter One**) and envision the last thing you remember from the dream. Imagine you are still asleep and dreaming. What happens next in the dream? Let the waking dream unfold like a shamanic journey or other visual meditation, and see how it resolves. When done, count yourself up and journal about the experience.

For a sleeping continuation, those with strong will and memory can simply go back to sleep with the intention of continuing the dream, and they will. If time is a factor and you need to get up, write down your dream as you normally would and begin your day. That evening review your dream, and use the Dream Intention technique to intend not to solve a problem or question, but to go back to the dream. With it fresh in your mind, you will go back to the dream, either repeating it and continuing further, or picking up where you left off.

DREAMING GATEWAYS

While we most often perceive dreaming as a gateway to the inner world, from our magickal perspective the worlds "within" are located in the same place as the worlds beyond our bodies. In and out reach the same destination. Dreams can be gateways to enter other dimensions of consciousness, just as much as shamanic trance or astral travel. While we can unintentionally and unexpectedly open gates to these levels of consciousness in our dreams, these openings tend to benefit us most when we acquire the ability to clearly recall and control our dreams. Then, in a lucid state, we can intentionally open a gateway to another realm. There is a wide range of possibilities for dream gateways, but some of the most prevalent are:

To Another Physical Space: Dream gateways can be used much the same way as remove viewing exercise, to travel in your dream body to someplace in the physical world, where you gather details about that place. Be careful, as you are even more likely to shift in time when doing remote viewing via dreaming, so explicitly state your intention of when as well as where you wish to visit.

To the Land of Ancestors: One common connection in dreamwork is to the dead, most often someone related to you or someone with whom you feel an emotional connection. Many times the spirit of the deceased will gate into your dream, but it is possible to seek out the spirit you desire to communicate with as well.

To Another's Dream: You can gate into the dream of another living person. Sometimes we do this unconsciously, sharing a dream with a loved one or magickal partner. It can be done consciously, and should only be done with that partner's conscious permission. Gating into someone's dream without permission is often considered a form of psychic attack. It is most effective when the recipient is also asleep. If the target is also a magickal practitioner and has functional protection magick and wards, your dream ritual might be ineffective, or trigger the defensive wards if you don't have their conscious permission.

To a Joint or Group Dream: Another method used to dream with another is to open a gate into their dream, but rather than go through it into another's dream, use it to bring them to your dream, or go on a journey beyond either of your personal dreams. When someone is skilled at dream work, they can be an effective group leader, gathering several people into one journey.

To a Shared Astral Space: By yourself, with another, or even a small group, you can use a dream gate to connect to a constructed place on the astral. Covens often create astral temples shared by the group, or you might create a personal sacred space in the astral while in meditation and ritual, and have access to it via dreaming.

To Higher Planes of Conscious: These dream gateways include what we think of shamanically as the upper and lower worlds, the higher astral, emotional, and mental planes as well as the sephira of the Qabalah.

Exercise: Dream Travel

Before attempting any work with dream gateways, focus on a door or gateway in the physical world. It can be any gateway you can walk through, a doorframe in your home, a door in your office, or an ornate fence gate at a public park. Gaze at it, memorizing the details until you can vividly recall it whenever you want.

Determine what kind of gateway you want to create. Where do you want your journey to bring you? Do your own cleansing rituals before bed, be it a cleansing bath or smudging. While in bed, hold the intention for the destination of your gate. Envision the physical gateway you have chosen, and it, or something similar, will appear in your dream for you to enter. Go to sleep and allow the journey, and the gate, to occur in your dream. When you awake in the morning, record your experience to the best of your ability. Often dream gateways tend to be very lucid and clear, but at other times they can seem like distant memories.

An excellent book to deepen your understanding of Dreaming Gateways and further psychic phenomenon around dreaming is *Psychic Dreamwalking* by Michelle Belanger.

UNCONSCIOUSNESS

The unconscious is the dark side of dream magick. Dreams put us in touch with our unconscious mind, and the collective unconsciousness of our species. This deeper connection gives rise to three problems for the dreaming Witch: unconsciousness itself, escapism and nightmares.

The critical point in working effective dream magick is keeping awareness, and its often all too tempting to slip back into a sense of unconsciousness, for that is our natural default state when sleeping. Just as a student is on the verge of truly going deeper and mastering our dreaming state, there is a series of evenings where no dreams can be recalled with any clarity. Just as the issue was going to manifest, the inner dreaming mirror grows dark and cloudy. In this case, as the unconscious comes to light, it appears too much for the conscious self, which retreats back to the unknown.

Rather than simple forgetting, sometimes the unconscious mind seeks to be elusive, and provides entertainment. We have fun dreams which are wonderful, but in an effort to fulfill our fantasies, the magickal work stops. The dreams do not go deep. They float along the surface of desire. Since it is easy to indulge in fantasy, be it mythic or heroic portrayals of the self, or an exploration of things that can never be in the physical, we do indulge. Occasionally it is quite helpful, but some Witches fool themselves into thinking they are doing deep work, when in fact, they are simply playing in the dream worked. In terms of psychological work, if guided, it can be productive, but most often it is not guided, and results in nothing of substance.

Lastly, and perhaps most disturbing but ultimately most rewarding, is the possibility that what resides in the unconscious is too terrible to face, at least at first, and manifests as nightmares, revealing its form bit by bit to the dreamer while conveying an emotional charge. This can discourage even the hardiest of dreamers to stop delving deeper with dream magick. Yet if such disturbing things are conjured by the psyche, it is worthwhile to examine them, to understand and not run from them. If understood and released, the energy goes towards work in other areas of life. One can mitigate the effects of nightmares with other forms of magick, including this charm against nightmares.

Charm Against Nightmares

Bowl of water on the nightstand
St. John's Wort
Mugwort
Angelica Root

Fill a clear glass or crystal bowl with water and place it beside or beneath your bed. If you are sleeping with a partner, make sure its on your side, unless you want to protect both of you against nightmares, though it would be more effective for you both to have separate bowl charms. Sprinkle a pinch of St. John's Wort herb, Mugwort herb, and the root of Angelica into the bowl and ask the spirits of the herbs to banish all nightmares.

St. John of the Light, banish all phantasms
Mugwort of the Moon, banish all ill
Angelica of the Angels, bring blessed guidance and protection
Three Allies, act as one. Bring me a restful night sleep.

You can use a pinch of Mistletoe as a substitute for any of these herbs, or in addition, making it a four herb charm. Make sure the bowl is out of reach of children and animals while you slumber.

Ultimately, the very qualities that give dream magick its strength and versatility can become its drawbacks as well. Finding the balance between these two points is the key to successfully navigating the sea of dreams.

AID TO THE PATH OF DREAMS

The following points should be kept in mind when working with dream magick:

No Stimulants: Dream magick tends to work best with a relaxed mind. Avoid the use of caffeine, television, computer, and really all electronic media a few hours prior to your dream work. Relaxation music or light reading is fine. Learn to relax. Do simple exercises, like an evening yoga routine or Tai-Chi. Take a warm bath. Do not over stimulate yourself and your consciousness prior to the work, or you'll find your dreams rushed and lacking clear focus and energy.

Sleeping Positions: Particular positions when sleeping are said to facilitate the dreaming experience, and have parallels in many different culture and traditions. Sleeping on the left side is universally seen as superior in most people. It stresses breath through the right nostril, stimulating the right side, the creative side, of the brain. Sleeping on the right side can be more restful, and conducive to when you want to dull your dreaming experiences. Sleeping on your back is more akin to a meditative or shamanic position. If you can fall asleep on your back, it can be helpful for this work. Sleeping on your stomach or in a curled up fetal position can be restful and even promote dreams, but they are often harder to remember.

Dream Temples: You can create your own dream sacred space, ritualizing the process of dream magick. Keep electronics to a minimum in your sleeping chamber. If you cannot remove them all, unplug as many as you can. Cover television screens or computer monitors with cotton or silk coverings. Match the color of your sheets to your dreaming intention based upon the correspondences of color magick. You can light a candle before bed, using intention and light to set the magick of your dream. I suggest snuffing the candle before going to bed, unless you have an absolutely safe area to leave it, such as a fireplace, or a sturdy cauldron. You can also light incense (see **Herbal Allies** below).

Herbal Allies: Review the herbs of dreaming in **Chapter Seven** to find herbal supplements to aid your dream work. You can make a dream pillow by combing the following in a small sachet to place on the pillow as you sleep: lavender, mugwort, oatstraw and marigold.

Stones: The following crystals are said to promote powerful dreaming, and can be used as talisman on the nightstand, beneath the bed, or under your pillow: Herkimer diamond, rhodochrosite, amethyst, moonstone and moldavite.

Dream Interpretation: Interpreting dreams for personal messages or prophetic meanings is beyond the scope of this work. But if this interests you, invest in several good dreaming dictionaries, including those within from a Pagan point of view. While one dream dictionary might fail you, having several to compare can give you new insights. Also talk about your dreams to someone you trust who knows you, such as a magickal mentor or teacher, when something significant arises in your dreams.

CHAPTER FOURTEEN:
WALKING THE SPIRAL

Having been through twelve gates of power, how do you best put this knowledge to use? You've been presented with a wide range of techniques and tools, and it is up to you, as a magickal practitioner, to determine which tools from your ever expanding toolbox, are appropriate for the intention you have.

In my initial training with my own teachers, I learned that Witchcraft is triune in nature, being a religion, a science or philosophy, and an art. In fact older books and teachers call the study of magick the Ars Magica, or the Art of Magick. Like any other artistic endeavor, it requires creativity. Sadly many people, particularly those swayed by the images of magick in movies and popular culture, think magick is solely a science. If you say the right words or mix the right ingredients, poof, you have magick. But it is an art form, as you have an endless variety of choices, of combinations to try.

The previous chapters are much more in-line with the science. They give you theory and mechanical technique. Now you must determine how to apply these techniques, alone, or together, to effectively perform your magick. Though it can be applied to almost any magickal intention, for most magick requires some form of altered consciousness, the magick best performed by the techniques in this book is the inner experiential work of communing with spirits. It is the magick of traveling to other planes of consciousness, or bringing the inhabitants of those planes in contact with us. It is for putting the forces of the other world into motion to effect change in our reality. The Gates of the Witch are truly for communion with the otherworld.

THE FIVE ESSENTIALS

There are no hard and fast rules in the way Witches apply these paths to their magick. The Gardnerian Book of Shadows simply tells us, "You may combine many of them into the one experiment, the more the better." It then specifically relates to the "Five Essentials" or five necessary ingredients for magick, and gives a little guidance in combining the Eight Way of Power with the Five Essentials. Though often omitted from popular Wicca, or adapted. The Five Essentials do contain important wisdom. In the Temple of Witchcraft tradition, the three requirements for magick are Clear Intention, Will, and A Method to Direct Energy. The Gardnerian essentials focus more specifically on the techniques of Gardnerian circle magick, purifications and tools. I'm included the Five Essentials here, along with the wisdom on combining them, placing the name of the technique as described in the Book of Shadows next to it's number, to avoid any confusion, as the order of the techniques in the Gardnerian Book of Shadows (**Chapter One**) is different from the order explored in this text.

The Five Essentials:

1. *The most important is "Intention": you must know that you can and will succeed; it is essential in every operation.*
2. *Preparation. (You must be properly prepared according to the rules of the Art; otherwise you will never succeed.)*
3. *The Circle must be properly formed and purified.*
4. *You all must be properly purified, several times if necessary, and this purification should be repeated several times during the rite.*
5. *You must have properly consecrated tools.*

These five essentials and Eight Paths or Ways cannot all be combined in one rite. Meditation and dancing do not combine well, but forming the mental image and the dance may be well combined with Chants, Spells, etc., combined with scourging and No. 6 (Blood Control/Breath Control), followed by No. 8 (The Great Rite), form a splendid combination. Meditation, following scourging, combined with Nos. 3 (Rites, Chants, Spells, Runes, Charms, etc.) and 4 (Incense, Drugs, Wine, etc.) and 5 (The Dance), are also very Good. For short cuts concentration, Nos. 5(The Dance), 6 (Blood Control/Breath Control), 7 (The Scourge), and 8 (The Great Rite) are excellent.

By looking at the five essentials, we do get a working model for constructing our rites.

Intention

First is intention. What do you wish to accomplish with your magick, either in terms of terrestrial results, as in traditional spell casting to alter your physical life, or in terms of communion with the otherworld. Many explore mind altering techniques to just "see what happens." Though I think we should be open to the unexpected and able to adapt, I'm not a big fan of free-for-all techniques. I have a lot of friends involved in a variety of psychedelic pursuits, and they most often advocate not having any intention, not trying to control it, to be casual, and just let it happen. They are not Witches. We walk the fine line, balancing our intention with surrender as to how that intention manifests. My untrained friends have some interesting experiences using entheogens, but rarely do they receive anything that gives direct knowledge, wisdom, guidance, or change. Such explorations without intention are much like walking in nature to simply see nature. That's wonderful, but Witches walk through the forest to commune with nature. They use their magickal skills to open the lines of communications with trees, plants, and animals. They have intention, but are open to exactly how that intention manifests. I think all of the techniques outlined in the book should be coupled with intention. Even if your intention is simply exploration, setting the intention gives your energy direction, and makes it clear to the denizens of the otherworld why you are here.

Preparation

Preparation is the second essential. This includes both inner and outer preparation. For the outer world, do you have all the tools that you need? Depending on the techniques chosen, the tools can be few or many. For a Gardnerian style coven proper preparation includes being skyclad, though sandals can be worn and, if being initiated, being bound in the traditional manner. It can also include a cleansing or "lustral" bath for purification. For inward preparation, are you clear in your intention, the first essential, and prepared to accept the consequences of the forces you put into motion? Are you prepared magickally, making all the necessary internal changes for this working? For traditionalists, this includes proper initiation into the tradition by a qualified High Priest/ess.

I feel one of the biggest aspects of "properly prepared" is being prepared for not only the potential failure of your magick, but the success. If using these techniques to alter consciousness to encounter the otherworld, are you prepared for such contact? Who is in the spirit world? Why are you encountering them? These questions have been left largely unasked and unanswered in this book focusing on technique, not theology, cosmology, or a specific tradition. Sadly there are some branches of British Traditional Wicca, particularly in America, that use these techniques only for spells, and discourage communion with otherworldly beings, yet when you use these techniques, you are opening yourself up to such "ultra-terrestrial" contact. What exactly is out there, and why would you seek to contact them?

Witches generally believe there is more than one world in existence. We are all familiar with the physical world where we dwell, what some refer to as the "real" world. But beyond an invisible barrier, described as a veil, curtain, mirror, or even hedge, there exists a world of spirit, intangible and unseen, yet just as "real" as the physical. In fact, many believe there is not just two worlds, but that the veil covers a multitude of spiritual worlds, each with its own qualities, character, and inhabitants.

Two general models of the spirit world tend to dominate, one describing a vertical hierarchy, and one describing a horizontal one. In reality neither is truly vertical or horizontal. Both exist in directions we cannot physically point to, outside of space and time. The vertical reality is most often a tree, but sometimes a ladder, mountain, or valley. I prefer the model of the World Tree to help understand the spirit worlds. In the branches is a heavenly overworld. Here is a realm of sky, storm, Sun, and star gods. Here is the realm of angels and enlightened ones. In the roots there is a chthonic underworld. In the underworld dwell the ancestors, the gods of the dead and darkness, along with primal telluric beings, often known as the Fey. Between at the trunk is the middle world, the realm of the physical world. Everything in the physical world has its own spirit − not just every human and animal, but every plant, every tree, every rock, river, and hill. And the middle world has many that are intangible and invisible spirits: elementals, nature spirits, hungry ghosts, and spirits of blessings and misfortune.

Fig. 56: World Tree

In the horizontal reality, the general classifications are the same, but arranged as concentric rings. In the center is the primordial world, like a cauldron, from which all things bubble up. This is the "underworld." The next ring is the realm of space, time and the physical world. Beyond the physical is the heavenly "upperworld" of the gods and surrounding them all is the realm of pure spirit. The advantage of the horizontal model is that it explains why psychics can see ghosts, spirits and gods right next to us, rather than above or below. They are simply looking across the veil.

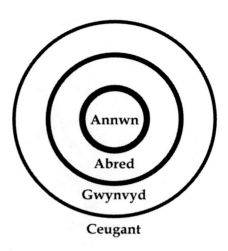

Fig. 57: Rings

Today, those who can see beyond the veil of this world, and get information from non-physical sources, are called seers or psychics. Those who can travel through the veil to these worlds, and come back at will are known as shamans, or more correctly shamanic practitioners. The word "shaman" most accurately refers to the magickal and religious practitioners of the Siberian tribes of Tungus, but for good or ill has grown in its use through the term "Core Shamanism," coined by anthropologist and practitioner Michael Harner. Core Shamanism refers to set of techniques that are fairly universal in nature, found in many different cultures and time periods. The techniques of Core Shamanism are not so surprisingly similar to the Eight Ways of Power. It is the belief of many modern Witches, myself included, that the Witches of old Europe fulfilled the function of the shaman, being able to see and travel beyond the physical to these spirit worlds.

Now prepared with the cosmology of the spirit worlds, you must be prepared to have some sort of contact from its inhabitants. Spirits can include:

Angels: Non-human entities that are embodiments of divine will, force and power. Each has domain over a different task or power.

Animal Spirits: You can encounter the spirit of various animals in the other worlds, completely independent from encountering them in the physical. Animal spirits that ally with you repeatedly are often considered your totem or power animal.

Deities: Entities classified as gods because each embodies a divine power of nature or certain abstract concepts.

Dead: The spirits of humans who are no longer living. They can be earthbound as ghosts, or residing in a place of rest and regeneration. Ancestors are those who are related to you by blood, or those related to your spiritual tradition.

Demons: While Witches do not subscribe to a Christian concept of hell with a hierarchy of demons and devils tempting us into sin, most indigenous teachings recognize that not all spirits are benign. Some are spirits of sickness and misfortune, causing blight upon people, animals and the land. Spirits are like people. Most don't care that much about you personally. Some are predisposed to be helpful and beneficent due to their nature, just as some people are naturally helpful. Some are mischievous. Others are malicious, just like people. Use a similar criteria to judge spirits as you would people. Following the five essentials will generally protect you from harmful spirits.

Elementals: the spirits of earth, air, fire, and water, embodying the concepts of physicality, the mind, the will, and emotion, respectively.

Fey: Members of an elder race predating humanity. They are deeply tied to the power of the land and nature and sometimes mistaken for nature spirits.

Masters: Enlightened humans who have passed from the world of the living into a world of pure consciousness. Each tradition has a different name for such trans-human spirits, such as saints, bodhisattvas, or demigods. In the Witchcraft tradition, they are known as the Mighty Dead or the Hidden Company.

Nature Spirits: The consciousness of various forms of nature, from a single plant to the overarching spirit of a forest or mountain.

While by no means a complete list of what you might encounter, this provides a good starting place in understanding the inhabitants of the spirit world. Such contact is the most difficult thing to prepare for, as it occurs differently for everybody, and it is real. We tend to either be surprised and unprepared for how real it is, or believe a real experience is simply our imagination and holds no importance, even though the message was deeply significant. When not prepared for it, and able to ground, balance, and center, spirit contact can have you doubting your sanity and scare you from magickal world. Spending time on the less advanced techniques, such as basic meditation, can help you prepare for more profound spirit contact.

For a more extensive information on the spirit world, and preparation for contact in a shamanic Witchcraft context, I recommend my book, *The Temple of Shamanic Witchcraft*. It outlines an entire course for spirit contact and personal development.

The Circle

The Circle is the third of our five essentials, and in recent years, the center of great debate. The Witch's circle is the basic ritual found in modern Witchcraft. Known as the Moon circle, magick circle and even magician's circle, it is really the core "liturgy" structure of the modern Craft both for religious rituals and practical magickal operations. There was a time in our Craft community, not that long ago, that doing magick outside of a circle was unthinkable, unless it was a bit of very simple folk magick, or an emergency. We were taught everything is enhanced in the circle. It protect us. It amplifies our magick. It is necessary for success.

While I do agree that a magick circle is quite wonderful for most applications of magick, I don't think it's essential. What I do think is essential, and what should be expressed in our Five Essentials, is the need for ritual and a format to bring one into a state of otherworldliness, to direct the powers generated safely towards the goal, and to then come back out of the otherworld, safe and sane. The magick circle provides a structure to accomplish all of those things. In a world where Wicca has gone from a secret initiatory tradition to one where you can find the details of our Craft in many books in a store, library, or copied on the internet, its great that this tool has been included for those who are following written instructions without a teacher. The magick circle provides a safe and highly effective framework that is not found in a lot of other traditions, making the haphazard practice of such traditions more dangerous. I truly believe the inner world masters of the Craft who guided its reconstruction put such a piece of ritual technology into our tradition to make it safer, more effective, and accessible to all seekers.

Almost all of the techniques outlined in this book can be used effectively within the magick circle. For those not familiar with this ritual structure, here is an outline of the circle ritual I use with basic instructions. The Gardnerian circle style is quite different and those interested in it can easily find version in print and online.

The Magick Circle Ritual

Casting the Circle: With your wand, athame, staff, or sword, trace the boundary of the circle in the air around you, the altar, and the working group. Imagine it in blue flame. Trace the circle three times. The circle is traditionally nine feet in diameter, unless working with a much larger group or space. Sometimes the additional second and third circles are drawn larger than the inner circle, six inches apart, making the entire space eleven feet in diameter. Most traditions start the circle in the east or in the north. Words spoken to cast the circle can be:

I cast this circle to protect me from all forces that may come to do me harm.

I cast this circle to draw the most balanced and powerful forces for my magick and block out all forces that are not in harmony with my intentions.

I create a space beyond space and a time beyond time, a temple of perfect love and perfect trust where the highest will is sovereign. So mote it be.

Calling the Quarters: The four directions are not only recognized, but associated with the four elements of the four primal powers of creation. Different traditions correspond the elements with different directions. Most British Wicca starts in the east, with air in the east, fire in the south, water in the west, and earth in the north. My own tradition starts in the north with earth in the north, fire in the east, air in the south and water in the west. Often, a guardian spirit, such as a totem, an elemental, an angel, or deity is called as well, to mediate the energy of that element. My basic quarters are:

To the North, I call upon the element of Earth and the Great Stag. Guide and protect me. Hail and welcome.

To the East, I call upon the element of Fire and the Wild Horse. Guide and protect me. Hail and welcome.

To the South, I call upon the element of Air and the Wise Crow. Guide and protect me. Hail and welcome.

To the West, I call upon the element of Water and the Swimming Salmon. Guide and protect me. Hail and welcome.

Evocation of the Powers: Call upon any entities, spirits and divinities you want to join you in the ritual. My evocation is:

I call upon the Two who move as one within the Love of the Great Spirit, the Goddess and the God. I call upon the ancestors of my blood and spirit. I call upon the guides in the realms above, below, and beyond. Hail and welcome.

Anointing: Anoint the wrist, third eye, and/or back of the neck with a potion made from protective and cleansing herbs or simply a combination of water and salt.

Great Rite: Perform the Great Rite in token and drink from the chalice. Cakes may also be blessed and consumed during the ritual, or at the end of the ritual, to aid in grounding.

The Work: Perform the work, be it spell casting, celebration, or trance pathworking. Energy can be raised for the work through the various paths of power. The energy can be used for momentum in trance work, to not only open the gate, but propel the journeys through the gate and into the otherworld.

Raising the Cone of Power: If energy has been raised and contained in the circle, it must be released, and ideally released with intention if there is a spell involved. This release is usually visualized and directed as a "cone" rising up and out from the circle, sending for the the spells and magick. If there is not a specific spell involved, it can simply be released with a blessing to the Earth for her own healing and balance. The energy can be gathered by the practitioners and used in journeywork. Such uses don't require a Cone of Power. To gather the power, the technique, such as dancing, singing, or scourging, is built up to an intensity, and abruptly stopped. If in a group, the leader of the group uses a prearranged signal, such as the dropping of a wand, to mark the end of the technique. At the abrupt stop, the energy propels the practitioner into the otherworld towards the intention of the journey.

Grounding: The energy of the Cone of Power is usually directed through two ritual forms postures. The Goddess Position (**Chapter Five**) is used to project the energy with a sweeping motion of the arms raised up. The God Position (also **Chapter Five**) is used to fully release the spell return to center. In the Goddess Position, the feet are apart and the arms raised as the cone is raised, imitating a Stone Age Goddess statue. When the cone is released the feet are brought close together, the forearms crossed over the heart, and the head slightly bowed, imitating an Egyptian sarcophagus. Then the remaining energy is released into the ground, usually by placing your hands or even your third eye/crown on the ground. For those unable to get onto the floor, the energy can be grounded through tools such as the altar, a staff, cane, or sword, or simply through intent alone, directing it to the ground.

Devocation: All the powers evoked are thanked and released.

I thank and release the Two who move as one within the Love of the Great Spirit, the Goddess and God. I thank the ancestors of my blood and spirit. I thank the guides of all three realms. I thank any and all spirits who have come in Perfect Love and Perfect Trust. Stay if you will, go if you must. Hail and farewell.

Releasing the Quarters: All the quarters are released, starting where you began the calls, and moving counterclockwise.

To the North, I thank and release the element of Earth and the Great Stag. Hail and farewell.
To the West, I thank and release the element of Water and the Swimming Salmon. Hail and farewell.

To the South, I thank and release the element of Air and the Wise Crow. Hail and farewell.
To the East, I thank and release the element of Fire and the Wild Horse. Hail and farewell.

Release of the Circle: Starting where you began the circle, move counterclockwise, visualizing either the circle dissipating, expanding or the light of the circle being drawn back into the wand or blade.

I cast this circle out to the universe as a sign of my work. The circle is undone, but never broken. So mote it be.

While the magick circle is the format found in modern Witchcraft, it holds the basic concepts found in all good magickal ritual. The basic elements I consider important to all ritual, beyond the other four "essentials" listed are:

Setting the Space: Where will the ritual take place? You do not necessarily have to cast a circle to set space, but your purification of the space (See next section) should clearly mark out where you will be working, inside and out, and what area is not a part of your ritual.

Recognizing the Space: Most magickal traditions recognize the space in relationship to the directions, either the four directions of the compass, or the three worlds of above, below and between. Some recognize all of these directions. Guardians are called to protect that direction and mediate its energy in the ritual.

Evocation of the Powers: Call the spiritual entities you wish to have join you in the ritual.

Altering Consciousness: Use one or more of the gateway paths to enter an altered state with your clear intention.

Raising Energy and/or Opening the Gates: If energy is raised for a specific intention, or as a product of your path to gnosis, use it for your work.

The Work: Fulfill the actual intention of the ritual, be it otherworldly or material spell crafting.

The Return: Return your focus from other worldly realities to the physical reality. Ground excess energy that prevents you from focusing on the physical reality.

The Release: Release all powers and entities gathered to you and return the space to "normal."

With this guidance, you can create your own effective ritual, within a magick circle, or innovate a new ritual form. The drawback of creating your own rituals outside the format of the magick circle is your rite might not have the inherent protections and safeguards built into the magick circle ritual, so I always suggest novices start with the circle ritual before experimenting too much. For those wanting more detailed instructions on the magick circle, ritual, and spellcraft, I recommend my book, *The Outer Temple of Witchcraft*.

Purification

Our fourth essential is purification. Scourging, one of our techniques, is said to purify the spirit, but usually ritual purification refers to purification of the self and the ritual space. All four of the elements can be used in purification of the self or space. Usually the body is cleansed with a ritual bath, and then dressed with proper ritual vestments, such as a black robe, or simply left skyclad. Part of being "properly prepared" can include being anointed with oils, ointments, or other potions attuned to the nature of the ritual and intention. A simple cleansing bath is:

3 Tablespoons of Sea Salt
1 Tablespoon of Hyssop Herb or 7 drops of Hyssop Essential Oil
1/2 Tablespoon of Lemon Verbena or Lemon Peel or 3 drops of Lemon Essential Oil
1/2 Tablespoon of Lavender or 3 drops of Lavender Oil

Put into a muslin bag and soak in hot bathwater before bathing. Sit in the bath for at least seven minutes, and let the water drain out completely before getting out or rinsing off. If you don't have the ingredients or time for a magickal bath, a simple shower or bath is better than nothing. Being physically clean helps you become psychically clean.

Floral waters—including the oils or hydrosols of sage, frankincense, rose, lavender, orange, lemon, lemongrass, and cinnamon—are also purifying and can be added to the bath, or used as an anointing fluid. Be cautious with cinnamon, as the essential oil is caustic.

Similar mixes of water, salt, and herbs, or simply water and salt, can be sprinkled around the ritual site to help purify it from unwanted influences. The liquid is "asperged" by dipping your fingers or a small branch of an evergreen into the liquid, and then dispersing the drops with a quick movement.

A technique to cleanse both people and the space is known as smudging. The person or area is fumed in the smoke of incense, particularly incense known for its cleansing properties. Just as the salt and water combines the element of earth and water to purify, the charcoal and incense smoke combine the elements of fire and air to purify. Herbs such as frankincense and myrrh, sage, lavender, rose, copal, cinnamon, clove, pine and dragon's blood,

These herbs can be used as a smudge, burned on self-igniting charcoal in a flame proof container, in stick form or in a bundle of herbs. Many metaphysical stores carry smudge bundles, particularly of sage, to be used in cleansing rituals. Often the smoke is wafted with a feather or fan, to immerse the space or person in its fumes.

Lastly, a ritual broom or besom, can be used to cleanse a space. Traditionally besoms are made from ash, willow, and birch, for power, protection and purification. The handle is from ash or rowan (mountain ash), the bristles are birch twigs, and the binding is willow. Though these are the traditional materials, I have used brooms made from other woods and still effectively "swept" the space clear. One takes the broom and either literally sweeps the space, or sweeps just above it, intending to sweep out and away all psychic harm and unwanted forces.

Consecrated Tools

Properly constructed and consecrated tools are our last essential in the art of magick. The modern Witch's altar usually has the following tools upon it:

Wand: Wands are tools of elemental fire, used to direct energy and power, casting the circle or used in healing or cursing. Traditionally they are made from wood, though modern wands can be glass, crystal, or metal. They are usually the length of the owner's middle finger to elbow.

Athame: the athame is a black handled, double-edged blade. It is a tool of elemental air and, like the wand, is used to direct energy. It is double-edged to remind us of the double-edged power of our thoughts, words, and deeds.

Cup: The cup or chalice is a tool of elemental water, traditionally constructed of silver, but can be made from crystal, glass, or copper. It is used to hold wine or water in ritual.

Stone/Peyton: The stone or ritual pentacle, the peyton, is a tool of elemental earth, though some use the peyton for all five elements. The peyton (or stone if the stone is flat) can be used as a ritual dish, to hold cakes or other offerings. Objects can be placed on the stone/peyton to bless and consecrate them with power.

Cauldron: The cauldron can be associated with water, fire, or earth, or more with the creative and destructive element of spirit. The cauldron is the womb of creation and the tomb of death. Ritually it is used to burn offerings, hold liquids, or contain offerings.

Candles & Candle Holders: Candles are used both functionally for natural light and to represent the Goddess and God. My tradition puts a black candle for the Goddess on the left side of the altar, and a white candle for the God on the right side of the altar. A central candle of varying color can be used for the androgynous Great Spirit or Divine Mind.

Miscellaneous: Functional tools including matches, candle snuffer, crystals, herbs, potion bottles, etc.

The first time the tools are used, they must first be cleansed just as the practitioner and space is cleansed. Along with smudging and sprinkling of water, you can purify a tool by placing it over (not in) a candle flame or exposing them to direct sunlight for a few hours (fire cleansing), leave them out in the open air on a windy day (air cleansing), passing through running water (water cleansing), sprinkling with dry salt if water will damage it, or burying the object in salt or the earth for a short period time (earth cleansing). If you have no access to any of the elements, or simply prefer your own inner technology, you can hold the tool, imagine it filling with a violet white fire, cleansing with spirit, and command the fire to consume all unwanted energies and forces from the object. Once the object is properly cleansed, you can consecrate it.

Consecrate the items with your intention. Hold each tool, individually, in your hands. Feel your pulse mingle with the object's pulse, and then clearly think of the intention for this item. What is its purpose? Hold the intention of its purpose. If it is a sacred vestment, ask yourself how does it unlock the magickal personality? Be clear in your thoughts, words, and visualizations when consecrating the tool. Only when you have infused the object with its stated intention is it truly ready for your working. All of the tools, vestments and the altar itself should be cleansed and consecrated.

Tools don't need to be purified and consecrated at every ritual, but are often re-consecrated after a period time. Some Witches renew their tools and altar monthly, every six months, or yearly. I tend to do it only once a year myself, unless I feel some tool has lost its charge or become contaminated by being handled by someone who does not respect its energy and intention.

These five essentials are important in most workings, though some traditions emphasize one or more of them over the others. Some folk traditions find purification and consecration less necessary then ritual or clear intention. Once you determine how to express the essentials of the working, you can determine how to integrate these twelve gateways to deepen your gnosis experience. Many of the practices lend so well to each other, they don't have to be formally combined, they simply encourage one another. If you are performing or attending ritual regularly, you have probably already used these techniques, alone or in combination. Let's look at some ritual structures to show how the gateway techniques can be used in combination. You ability to put these paths together is the key to unlocking their power.

Ecstatic Circle: An ecstatic circle is best when started with a central focus. For larger groups, a sacred fire, like a campfire made from sacred woods. In traditional Wicca sacred fires are started with nine woods in the cauldron or fire ring, though they are not always named. The most common are birch, oak, rowan, willow, hawthorn, hazel, apple, grape, and fir. Elder is never burned. Smaller groups without the space and resources for a large fire can make simple cauldron fires with rubbing alcohol and epsom salts. The rubbing alcohol can be infused with herbs for magickal intent, making what my friends at Otherworld Apothecary call "cauldron waters." The fire is used for a focus to gaze upon, calling upon the path of meditation, evokes the spirits of trees and plants, using the power of the herbal world, while dancing and/or singing. Traditions that don't use a fire often use a white stone in the center of the space, reflecting the sunlight or moonlight as a focus. A circle is cast around the space, usually with a group. Some members of the group have chosen to drum and/or chant, while the others dance. The dance can be a specific movement, such as the Mill or a grapevine step, or a free form ecstatic dance. For the creatively inclined group, masks can be worn as a part of the ritual. Members can also drink an infusion of ecstatic herbs just prior to the ritual, to aid in the raising of energy. As the dance continues, the light of the fire is the central focus, until it reaches its crescendo and the leader signals the drummers to stop. The dancers collapse, using the energy of the circle and fire to propel them into the otherworld on a shamanic journey.

Cauldron Water
Rubbing Alcohol
Mugwort
Wormwood
Scullcap
Patchouli
1 Pinch of Dragon's Blood
6 drops of Frankincense Essential Oil
3 drops of Myrrh Essential Oil
Epson Salts
Shake before using.

Ritual Bath: While we discussed a ritual bath as a purification rite as one of the five essentials, it can be a ritual in itself. If you light candles, incense, and use herbals, you are combining the path of meditation, giving a focus, and the path of intoxicants. Being alone and restricting yourself in the bath, and immersing yourself into very hot or cold water, you are using the paths of isolation and, if not pain, at least extreme sensation. You can have a profound meditative experience while in the bath.

Initiation Rituals: Traditional initiation rituals use many of these paths to induce the changes necessary for one to become a Witch or embrace the path of the priest/ess. Usually the initiate is told to fast before the initiation. It takes place in the covenstead or ideally, on land the coven had built a relationship with. The time chosen is usually on a dark or new Moon, or at a Sabbat, aligning it not only with the sacred land, but sacred time. Ritual bathing precedes all other work. Incense is used to both clear the space and set the tone for the initiation. The initiate is blindfolded, and often bound, skyclad. In British Traditional Wicca there is almost always scourging as a part of the initiation rite. In less well known initiation rites, sometimes there is a light blood letting, with the initiate being nicked or pricked by a sharp ritual tool. The Great Rite is enacted, in token or in body, and cakes and wine shared as a part of the celebration. Sometimes the new priest/ess will be urged to prove their skills by properly consecrating the wine and cakes. More tribal initiations might require the consumption of an herbal potion prior to the initiation, or at the beginning. Such powerful rituals combine almost all of the paths of power.

Dream Star: A simple ritual I learned to facilitate group dreaming involves participants lying on their backs, feet out towards the edge of the ritual space and heads together toward the middle. They should be arranged in a geometric star pattern for the number of practitioners, with nine being ideal. They are restricted to stay in their assigned space. In the center is a candle and some incense burning to facilitate dream work. Everyone drinks a sleep—and dream—inducing tea prior to the working consisting of Chamomile, Passion Flower, and Hops in equal parts. One person sits outside of the star, to act as guide, and to make sure no one knocks the candle or incense over. The guide leads the group in breathing exercises and a light hum upon exhale to link their energy together with the intention of dreaming as a group. Then they are allowed to drift asleep and dreams are compared to see who was able to "meet up" in the spirit world and to what ends. Those that grow proficient in dreaming as a group can then set a more specific intention for the journey to accomplish a magickal goal or make contact with a specific entity. Through this technique you can combine herbal magick, restricted movement, and breath control with dreaming.

Fig. 58: Dream Star

Sexual Journey: The Sexual Journey ritual combines herbal aphrodisiacs, music, breathwork and of course, sex to induce a consciousness expansion for a spiritual journey. I feel one of the best intentions behind this ritual is to commune with the gods and goddesses of love, to know their mysteries on a deeper level, in both spirit and flesh. It's best done with a partner. Prepare a cordial of damiana, coriander, and rose-hips (See **Chapter Six** for cordial instructions). During the ritual, burn the incense described below. Play some percussive music that builds in intensity, or any sensual music you feel will help induce the mood and build in intensity. Create your sacred space and preparations. Drink the cordial together. Gaze into each others eyes. Breath in unison. Invoke the gods and make love. Feel your consciousness expand to include each other, and then outward to the worlds around you, physical and non-physical. Upon climax, use the energy and altered awareness to enter a rapport with not only each other, but the deities of love and sensuality, and learn their mysteries.

Sexual Journey Incense

3 Parts Red Sandalwood

2 Parts Orris Root

1/2 part Basil Leaves

1/2 part Damiana Leaves

1/2 part Jasmine Flowers

1/2 part Rose Petals

1/4 part Belladonna Flowers

1/8 part Datura Seeds

1 Part Honey to Bind

Allow to dry and ideally wait a month before using.

Divination-Seership Ritual: While many Witches act as psychics and readers, few ritualize the process. It's often done in a more clinical setting, as a reader in a holistic center or psychic fair, imitating the protocol of a counselor, rather than a Witch. In days past, a reading can be just as much of a ritual as a sabbat, and require preparation to reach the appropriate state of consciousness to bring back useful information. Rituals for divination and oracular workings were major works in time pasts. A ritual to enhance psychic sight or the ability to read a divination tool such as tarot, runes, or crystal gazing can involve many paths. It is best done when the Moon is full, for psychic powers are at their peak. A properly prepared ritual space following the five essentials prevents unwanted energies from entering, biasing the information received. While most psychics today try to look fairly "normal," the use of ritual clothing is for both the psychic-Witch and client, to induce rapport between them to clear the lines of communication between them, and the spirit world. An herbal infusion to aid in psychic ability, even a tea of common mugwort, facilitates the process. For such intense rituals, I like to use a mantra or word of power, not only repeated by myself, but by the client, to attune us and induce trance in both of us. I like the Hebrew name of God for the Moon sphere Yesod – Shaddai El Chai. When the mood has been set and a sufficient ritual connection been made, I read the cards. It may seem far more elaborate than necessary for a simple card reading, but when I do, I find the information is deeper, more detailed, more intense and, ultimately, more helpful for me and my client. I don't use it for every reading I give, but for some special cases, I do find it worthwhile.

Oracular Invocation: Just as divination can benefit from a ritualized working, sometimes you seek information directly from the gods, and such invocations should always take place in a ritual format. Many of the paths can be combined to create not only a more powerful working, but make the process easier for the priest/ess invoking an entity for the benefit of the community. For such workings, I've found having a good relationship with the spirit of the land where the ritual is to take place is essential. Start by making offering to the genius loci and ask this spirit for support during the ritual. In various forms of oracular working, particularly Norse, the priest/ess is seated on a "high seat" apart from the rest of the group. In Greek oracular traditions, a tripod seat might be used. Also borrowing from the Greeks, I've found a simple incense of bay leaves, burning beneath the oracle's seat, to be quite effective. Those who find bay too strong on its own can mix it with other herbs, woods, and resins of a psychic or oracular nature, or herbs sacred to the deity called. A blindfold or veil can help the priest/ess focus on the spirit world, rather than the material world, and unite with the deity or spirit the community seeks to invoke. This can be combined with traditional Wiccan Drawing Down the Moon or Drawing Down the Sun rituals for the Moon and Sun deities, using the Great Rite in token and the five fold kiss. Having the community chant the deity's name, or a simple tonal, helps everyone attain a greater group consciousness, and attune to the chosen deity, rather than summoning another entity. If you are not already familiar with bodily invocation practices, you should learn the basics of such work before combing it with other techniques or attempting to perform it for a larger group.

Dream Healing: Though there are many forms of healing involving herbs, energy work, and spirits, and a wide range of creative applications, I have found this ritual quite successful in both healing, and getting to the potential root of an illness. It is an homage to the Dream Temples of ancient Egypt, Greece, and Rome, where priests put a patient into a hypnotic dream state through ritual. It can also be adapted as an initiatory death-rebirth ritual. I perform this ritual just before sunset, as the light descends into the darkness. If the person is not on any conflicting pharmaceutical prescriptions, we start with a tea made from equal parts passion flower, valerian, and lemon balm, mixed with honey. This helps relax and bring sleep. Though some people say they don't have restful dreams when taking Valerian, the purpose of this ritual is not to rest, but to heal. The tea simply aids in the trance state, though Valerian acts as a stimulant in about ten percent of the population. The client then strips down to whatever level of dress is comfortable, if not skyclad, and is wrapped in bandages soaked in an infusion of the herb known as heal all. Those lacking bandages can use a cotton sheet. They look something like a mummy from Egypt. The mouth is left open, and the two can discuss how tight or loose, or if there is anything not to be wrapped prior to the ritual. Obviously, this is not a technique for those who fear restriction, for it will be difficult to move, or get out of the wrappings without the aid of another. The "helper" for the ritual keeps watch, so if the person wrapped experiences extreme discomfort or panic, there will be someone to help them. Ambient trance music is played and an invocation is made to the Gods of Healing. The intention is for both healing and understanding the source of the illness, so the message can be integrated and the illness fully healed. The helper leads the practitioner into a trance state using hypnotic meditative techniques such as a countdown and imagery to conjure the feeling of a temple of the ancient past. The practitioner is then allowed to trance/journey/sleep, and at a predetermined time, gently woken by the helper, guided back through the imagery, unwrapped, and the dream/journey discussed in detail. Sometimes the practitioner experiences a conversation with the illness itself, or journeys back in time to the "karmic" roots of the illness, to understand the pattern where it first originated. Some receive specific instructions on what to do to heal, in terms of treatment both magickal and medical. Other simply awaken changed, with little conscious memory of the inner world experience. If an immediately healing does not occur, a change in consciousness usually does, that leads either to direct healing, or a new path that offers greater healing. The ritual space is released, and any advice given during the trance should be put into practice. This ritual requires an experienced "helper" and should not be undertaken by those just starting the path of the Witch.

ESBATS AND SABBATS

Magick circles taking place in celebration of the solar years or the phases of the Moon are the basic religious rites of Witchcraft. They are times of power not only for religious purposes, but to open the gates between worlds. Sabbats are rituals in celebration of the four solar holidays, the two solstices and two equinoxes when the sun changes from a mutable sign to a cardinal sign, initiating a new season, and the four Celtic fire festivals when the Sun is in the center of a fixed sign. Esbats are celebrations of the Full Moon or Dark/New Moon. Full Moons occur in the Zodiac sign opposite to the Sun's sign, while New Moons occur in the same sign the Sun occupies.

Because of the numeric correspondence between the original Paths of Power and the Wheel of the Year, there has been some effort to correspond the eight paths with the eight holidays. This effort matches up the most appropriate path to the holiday that resonates with it the most, and have that path emphasized in ritual. While I've seen several versions, this is the list that makes the most sense to me. Public versions of the Alexandrian Book of Shadows have a mandala of the seasons, traditionally listed eight paths and holidays.

Holiday	Path	Alexandrian Correspondence
Yule	Sound	Meditation
Imbolc	Meditation	Trance
Ostara	Breath	Drugs & Wine
Beltane	Sex	Dance
Litha	Movement	Great Rite
Lammas	Pain	Spells & Rites
Mabon	Intoxication	Scourge
Samhain	Isolation	Cords

With the addition of four more paths, they can be associated with the twelve signs of the Zodiac.

Zodiac Sign	Path	Alternate Version
Aries	Isolation	Pain
Taurus	Sex	Land
Gemini	Time	Time
Cancer	Dreams	Dreams
Leo	Ritual Clothing	Ritual Clothing
Virgo	Meditation	Meditation
Libra	Breath	Breath
Scorpio	Pain	Sex
Sagittarius	Movement	Movement
Capricorn	Land	Isolation
Aquarius	Sound	Sound
Pisces	Intoxication	Intoxication

In your next Sabbat or Esbat, try to make one of the paths your focus for the ritual. Obviously other techniques can be blended into the ritual based on the nature of the work, but if you focus one technique per sabbat or esbat, you might find yourself deepening your personal or group work with that technique.

All the paths of power lead to the center. They lead to that place that is not a place, that time that is not a time, the temple between the worlds. They awaken within us the state of consciousness beyond our body, beyond our limits, to the true meaning of the word ecstasy, beyond the flesh, but they also awaken us to the divine paradox of the flesh. They awaken the god within the flesh. These paths of power are coded deep within our being, within our soul, but also our flesh and blood, our very DNA. Our ancestors, of not only hundreds or even thousands of years, but since our race began, have been using these techniques to find the divine. Their divinity lives on within us. When we sing, drum, dance, scourge, ingest herbs, mate, sit in the darkness, or gather under the full Moon, we are reaching back through our blood and spirit to that ancient wisdom within. We are triggering memories buried deep within us. We are firing codes within our body systems, sending messages to wake up. We are awakening the god within, the Higher Self, the holy daimon, the watcher within. We are embracing the paradox of the divine within our flesh and within our spirit. We become the divine within our body, beyond our body and through our body, reaching to the center while simultaneously reaching out to the cosmos. When we walk the paths of power, we open the gates. We hold them open so we may enter the mysteries, the deep spiraling center, yet we hold them still so we may walk out, and bring that divine state of being to our everyday life, to our people and to the world.

BIBLIOGRAPHY

Abel. Ernest l. *Intoxication in Mythology: A Worldwide Dictionary of Gods, Rites, Intoxicants and Places.* McFarland & Company, Inc., Jefferson, NC: 2006.

Andrews, Ted. *Magickal Dance: Your Body as an Instrument of Power.* Llewellyn Publications, St. Paul, MN: 1993.

Belanger, Michelle. *Psychic Dreamwalking.* Weiser Books. Boston, MA: 2006.

Buckland, Raymond. *Buckland's Complete Book of Witchcraft.* Llewellyn Publications, St. Paul, MN: 1986.

Cabot, Laurie with Tom Cowan. *Power of the Witch: The Earth, the Moon and the Magical Path to Enlightenment.* Dell Publishing, New York, NY: 1989.

Cartledge, Paul. *Sparta and Lakonia. A Regional History 1300 to 362 BC.* Routledge, New York, NY: 2002 (2nd edn).

Chia, Mantak. *Awaken Healing Energy Through Tao.* Universal Tao Publishing, New York, NY: 1983.

Clark, A.J. *The Sacred Mushroom Church of Switzerland Flying Ointments. https://www.tupg.org/smcs/forum/index.php?showtopic=1061*: October 28, 2008.

Coyle, T. Thorn. *Evolutionary Witchcraft.* Tarcher. New York, NY: 2005.

Dawkins, R. M. The Sanctuary of Artemis Orthia at Sparta London : MacMillan and Co., Limited, 1929.The Society for the Promotion of Hellenic Studies; Supplementary Paper No.5 DF261.S68D3 - *http://efts.lib.uchicago.edu/cgi-bin/eos/eos_title.pl?callnum=DF261.S68D3*: April 15, 2008.

deVries, Eric. *Hedge Rider.* Pendraig Publishing, Sunland, CA: 2008.

Dominguez, Ivo. *Castings: The Creation of Sacred Space.* SapFire Productions, Inc. Georgetown, DE: 1996.

Dyer, Dr. Wayne W. *Real Magic: Creating Miracles in Everyday Life.* Audio Cass. Harper Audio/ HarperCollins Publishers, Inc. New York, NY: 1992.

Edson, Gary. *Mask and Masking: Faces of Tradition and Belief Worldwide.* McFarland & Company, Inc., Jefferson, NC: 2005.

Fortune, Dion. *The Goat Foot God.* Samuel Weiser, York Beach, ME: 1972.

Fortune, Dion. *The Sea Priestess.* Samuel Weiser, York Beach, ME: 1972.

Foxwood, Orion. *The Faery Teachings.* R.J. Steward Books. Dexter, OR: 2007.

Fries, Jan. *Seidways: Shaking, Swaying and Serpent Mysteries.* Mandrake of Oxford, Oxford, UK: 1996.

Frosts, Gavin and Yvonne. *The Magick Power of Witchcraft.* Parker Publishing. Mira Loma, CA: 1980.

Goodman, Felicitas D. *Where the Spirits Ride the Wind: Trance Journeys and Other Ecstatic Experiences.* Indiana University Press. Bloomington & Indianapolis, IN: 1990.

Gore, Belinda. *Ecstatic Body Postures: An Alternative Reality Workbook.* Bear & Company. Santa Fe, NM: 1995.

Graves, Robert. *The White Goddess. Farrar, Straus and Giroux.* New York, NY: 1966.

Gray, William G. *Western Inner Workings: Sagreal Sodality Series Volume I.* Samuel Weiser, York Beach, ME: 1983.

Guiley, Rosemary Ellen. *The Encyclopedia of Witches and Witchcraft.* Checkmark Books, New York, NY: 1999.

Grimassi, Raven. *Encyclopedia of Wicca & Witchcraft.* Llewellyn Publications, St. Paul, MN, 2000.

Grimassi, Raven. *Wiccan Mysteries.* Llewellyn Publications, St. Paul, MN, 2002.

Grimassi, Raven. *Witchcraft: A Mystery Tradition.* Llewellyn Publications, St. Paul, MN, 2004.

Grimassi, Raven. *The Witch's Craft.* Llewellyn Publications, St. Paul, MN, 2002.

Gwyn. *Light from the Shadows: A Mythos of Modern Traditional Witchcraft.* Capall Bann. Milverton, Somerset, UK: 1999.

Jastrow, Joseph. *Error and Eccentricity in Human Belief.* Dover Publications, New York, NY: 1962 .

Khalsa, Gurucharan Singh Khalsa, Ph.D. *Happiness is Your Birthright: The Complete Series. Book and Tape Set.* Khalsa Consultant, Inc. Wellesley, MA: 1997.

Knight, Gareth. *The Rose Cross and the Goddess.* Destiny Books, New York, NY: 1986.

Kraig, Donald Michael. *Modern Magick: Eleven Lessons in the High Magickal Arts.* Lewellyn Publications, St. Paul, MN, 1988.

The Kybalion: Hermetic Philosophy by Three Initiates, The Yogi Publication Society, Chicago, IL: 1912.

Madden, Kristen. *Magick, Mystery and Medicine: Advanced Shamanic Healing.* Willow Tree Press, 2008.

Merry, Eleanor C. *The Flaming Door.* Kessinger Publishing. Whitefish, MT: 2010.

Metzner, Ralph. *Sacred Vine of Spirits: Ayahuascha.* Park Street Press. Rochester, VT: 2005.

Miller, Richard Alan. *The Magical and Ritual Use of Herbs.* Destiny Books, Rochester, VT: 1983.

Morrison, Dorothy and Kristin Madden. *Dancing the Goddess Incarnate.* Llewellyn Publications, Woodbury, MN: 2006.

Oesterley, W.O.E. *Sacred Dance in the Ancient World.* Dover Publications, Mineola, NY: 2002.

Passion, Lady and Dievei. *The Goodly Spellbook: Olde Spells for Modern Problems*. Sterling Publishing Co., Inc, New York, NY: 2004.

Penczak, Christopher. *The Inner Temple of Witchcraft: Magick, Meditation and Psychic Development*. Llewellyn Worldwide. St Paul, MN. 2002.

Pendall, Dale. *Pharmakopoeia*. North Atlantic Books. Berkeley, CA: 2009.

Pendall, Dale. *Pharmakodynamis*. North Atlantic Books. Berkeley, CA: 2009.

Pendall, Dale. *Pharmakognosis*. North Atlantic Books. Berkeley, CA: 2009.

Rush, John A. *Spiritual Tattoo: A Cultural History of Tattooing, Piercing, Scarification, Branding and Implants*. Frog Ltd. Berkeley CA: 2005.

Sloss, Andy. *Celtic Tattoos: Learn the Traditional Art of Celtic Body Painting*. Carlton Books, London, UK: 2007.

Stewart, R.J. *The Spiritual Dimensions of Music*. Destiny Books. Rochester, VT: 1990.

Telynoru, Jhenah. *Avalon Within*. Ninth Wave, Seneca Falls, NY: 2004.

Tunneshende, Merlyn. *Don Juan and the Art of Sexual Energy*. Bear & Company. Rochester, VT: 2001.

Vayne, Julian. *Pharmakon: Drugs and the Imagination*. Mandrake of Oxford. Oxford, UK: 2006.

Valiente, Doreen. *An ABC of Witchcraft*. Phoenix Publishing, Custer, WA: 1988.

Valiente, Doreen. *Natural Magic*. Phoenix Publishing, Custer, WA: 1985.

Valiente, Doreen. *Witchcraft for Tomorrow*. Robert Hale Publishing, London, UK: 1993.

Villoldo, Alberto. *Mending the Past and Healing the Future with Soul Retrieval*. Hay House, Carlsbad, CA: 2005.

Watkins, Alfred. *The Old Straight Track*. Abacus Little Brown. London, UK: 1988.

Weed, Jason J. *Wisdom of the Mystic Masters*. Prentice Hall Art. NJ: 1971.

Wilde, Lyn Webster. *Becoming the Enchanter*. Tarcher. New York, NY: 2002.

Wilson, Steve. *Chaos Ritual*. Neptune Press, London, England, UK: 2004.

INDEX

ABOUT THE AUTHOR

Christopher Penczak is an award winning author, teacher and healing practitioner. As an advocate for the timeless perennial wisdom of the ages, he is rooted firmly in the traditions of modern Witchcraft and Earth-based religions, but draws from a wide range of spiritual traditions including shamanism, alchemy, herbalism, Theosophy and Hermetic Qabalah to forge his own magickal traditions. His many books include *Magick of Reiki, The Mystic Foundation, The Three Rays of Witchcraft,* and *The Inner Temple of Witchcraft.* He is the co-founder of the Temple of Witchcraft tradition, a non-profit religious organization to advance the spiritual traditions of Witchcraft, as well as the co-founder of Copper Cauldron Publishing, a company dedicated to producing books, recordings, and tools for magickal inspiration and evolution. He has been a faculty member of the North Eastern Institute of Whole Health and a founding member of The Gifts of Grace, an interfaith foundation dedicated to acts of community service, both based in New Hampshire. He maintains a teaching and healing practice in New England, but travels extensively lecturing. More information can be found at *www.christopherpenczak.com* and *www.templeofwitchcraft.org.*

The Temple of Witchcraft
MYSTERY SCHOOL AND SEMINARY

Witchcraft is a tradition of experience, and the best way to experience the path of the Witch is to actively train in its magickal and spiritual lessons. The Temple of Witchcraft provides a complete system of training and tradition, with four degrees found in the Mystery School for personal and magickal development and a fifth degree in the Seminary for the training of High Priestesses and High Priests interested in serving the gods, spirits, and community as ministers. Teachings are divided by degree into the Oracular, Fertility, Ecstatic, Gnostic, and Resurrection Mysteries. Training emphasizes the ability to look within, awaken your own gifts and abilities, and perform both lesser and greater magicks for your own evolution and the betterment of the world around you. The Temple of Witchcraft offers both in-person and online courses with direct teaching and mentorship. Classes use the *Temple of Witchcraft* series of books and CD Companions as primary texts, supplemented monthly with information from the Temple's Book of Shadows, MP3 recordings of lectures and meditations from our founders, social support through group discussion with classmates, and direct individual feedback from a mentor.

For more information and current schedules, please visit the Temple of Witchcraft website: *www.templeofwitchcraft.org*.

CPSIA information can be obtained at www.ICGtesting.com
Printed in the USA
LVOW111157030912

297147LV00001B/3/P